STATE AND ECONOMY
IN CONTEMPORARY CAPITALISM

STATE AND ECONOMY IN CONTEMPORARY CAPITALISM

Edited by Colin Crouch

ST.MARTIN'S PRESS NEW YORK

Library of Congress Cataloging in Publication Data

Main entry under title:
State and economy in contemporary capitalism.
Bibliography: p.
Includes index.
1. State, The — Addresses, essays, lectures.
2. Communist state — Addresses, essays, lectures.
3. Capitalism — Addresses, essays, lectures.
4. Economic policy — Addresses, essays, lectures.
I. Crouch, Colin.
JC325.S735 1979   320.1   78-26539
ISBN 0-312-75601-1

320.1
S797

CONTENTS

STATE AND ECONOMY
IN CONTEMPORARY CAPITALISM

INTRODUCTION

The recent rapid growth of interest in theories of the state can be readily explained by the rise in the importance of and controversies surrounding the institution in question in most advanced capitalist societies. It ought therefore to represent a rare and happy example of political sociology responding to a widespread concern in the society at large and in turn enlightening public debate. In fact it is doubtful if anything of the kind has occurred, beyond a rather distorted political debate over corporatism and fears of overloaded government. For a start, those involved in public affairs usually have too many axes of their own to grind to welcome the frequently very different analyses of academic outsiders. But also, much of the academic literature has been highly abstract, virtually metaphysical, especially that from the various Marxist schools which in fact constitutes the bulk of the writing in question.

Hopefully the present volume will do a little to bridge the gulf between issues of general social interest and academic theory. The authors all come to terms with the questions raised in the recent revival of literature on the theory of the state, but all are also concerned to fashion those themes in the service of making sense of developments taking place in the 'real world'. The contributors represent a wide range of different intellectual traditions and ideological standpoints, reflecting the variety of approaches possible to the subject in hand. Important disagreements therefore exist among them and no one is responsible for the ideas expressed in any paper other than his own — certainly, my own essay should not be read as any kind of consensual editorial paper. However, we are all united in trying to understand the combination of political, economic and social forces which together have recently made the position of the state in advanced capitalist societies problematic: problems of state intervention in economic policy, industrial relations and planning of the corporate state; and of public spending, collective consumption and the Keynesian strategies which until recently represented the main intersection between economic, social and political forces.

Colin Crouch

1 THE STATE, CAPITAL AND LIBERAL DEMOCRACY

Colin Crouch

It is remarkable to what extent the recent spread of interest in the state
has led to the elaboration of social theory solely within the Marxist
tradition. There have been *writings* on the subject from a range of other
positions, some of which are discussed below, but little attempt at
systematic theory. It is particularly strange that so little has emerged
from the American pluralist tradition of political science, which has for
so long dominated the subject and prided itself on the superiority over
Marxism of its ability to conceptualise the political. True, much of its
empirical work has been in the area of 'community power' rather than
of the nation state (Dahl, 1961; Polsby, 1963), but then the Marxist
literature has also contributed at the former level through the studies of
urban political economy of the French school (see the paper by Harloe
in this volume). The reason may be that only Marxism has a theoretical
apparatus capable of tackling the relationship between the political and
the economic, which is particularly important in any study of the state
in contemporary Western society.

The Marxist tradition therefore provides the best starting point for
work in this field. There remain however several highly unsatisfactory
aspects in most of this literature as it has so far developed. In particular,
and rather surprisingly, there is no acceptable answer to the fundamental
question: why must the state in a capitalist society serve the interests
of capitalism? Further, the reluctance of most Marxist theory to admit
any element of genuine pluralism within the polities of the liberal
democracies leads to a convoluted process of redefinition and circum-
locution. Much of the present paper will be taken up with an elaboration
of these and other criticisms and an attempt to reformulate parts of
state theory to meet them.

But it is in the interests of neither Marxist sociology nor the subject
as a whole for Marxist literature to be regarded as isolated and self-
contained; it is part of a more general corpus. Where current writing on
the state is concerned this involves two main strands: the thesis of
'overloaded government' and (a field that includes several Marxist
writers) theories of the corporate state. These will first be discussed in
order to trace ideas overlapping with the Marxist literature and points

to which the latter might pay more attention.

Overloaded Government

While pluralist theory as such has been recently dormant, there is a discernible response among writers associated with the pluralist school to travails of Western political systems which had until recent years been regarded as mature and well balanced. This is the thesis that liberal democratic governments have become 'overloaded' by excessive demands from their citizenry.[1] It is political science's corollary to the monetarist doctrine among economists. The latter holds, *inter alia,* that inflation would be ended if only governments would stop printing money, and the solution to the problem is seen as resting in the hands of governments alone. The overloaded government thesis represents an advance on the naivety of the political analysis of monetarism, without necessarily dissenting from the overall argument. Government policies leading to inflation, excessive taxation, inadequate industrial investment and other disorders are seen not as simple matters of inadequate political will, but as the result of forces within the society imposing too many demands on the popularly responsive apparatus of the liberal democratic state.

The causes of these increased demands are various, though prominent among them is the idea of increased expectations: generations accustomed to two decades of affluence expect constant improvements both in their private consumption and in public services. Very similar are agruments which point to the decline of deference (people no longer know their place and, encouraged perhaps by television advertisements, demand the same standard of life as the society's elites). At the same time, the experience of near-full employment has relaxed several of the constraints which previously limited the pursuit of material progress. A more cynical version of the argument refers to governments offering 'bribes' in the form of increasing public expenditures, unmatched by higher taxes, to win the allegiance of sections of the electorate, particularly near election time — giving rise to the theory of the political trade cycle (Buchanan and Wagner, 1977; Nordhaus, 1975; MacRae, 1977; Wagner, 1977).

How these arguments flow from the assumptions of pluralist theory is not always obvious, but it emerges clearly from the contribution by Huntingdon (1974), in which he speaks of a wide range of social groups becoming organised and active so that the relationship between governments and interest groups becomes taut and strained. This follows from the important postulate of pluralist theory that for pluralism to 'work'

there has to be a large amount of political apathy, an 'excessive' degree
of participation both placing too many demands on political authorities
and leaving no 'slack' for organisation by new interests (Dahl, 1961;
Kornhauser, 1960).

Taken together these arguments suggest strongly that the pluralist
political formula was always heavily dependent on economic conditions
of growth and rising mass prosperity. By the 1950s the countries of the
advanced capitalist world had produced a combination of individual
liberties and universal political citizenship probably unparalleled in the
history of large-scale societies, and it had all been achieved within the
framework of a capitalist mode of production and its concomitant
inequalities. The achievement mocked both the predictions of Marxist
theory and the practice of the countries of the Soviet bloc, and all this
was duly and understandably celebrated in pluralist literature. But, as
some observers noted at the time, the phenomenon could not be explained solely in terms of political variables (Dahrendorf, 1964): the
period was one of economic progress following hard on the deprivations
of two world wars and the inter-war depression. Many popular demands
could be satisfied through economic means, with an extensive degree
of democracy therefore imposing little pressure on the polity. In terms
of the satisfaction of demands this was an episode of economism *par
excellence.* Since the late 1960s Western economies have experienced
much greater difficulty in securing economic advance. The state has
been brought more to the centre of the stage: because it has become
deeply involved in attempts at economic revival; because more demands
fall on its shoulders with the failure of the economy, while it has itself
increasing difficulty in meeting demands as a result of the economic
downturn; and finally because it has to play an important part in trying
to reduce popular demands in line with reduced economic capacity (by
means of restrictive economic policies, attempts at understandings on
restraint with the leaders of organised groups, and, occasionally, straightforward repression).

While there is widespread agreement among broadly pluralist writers
that overloaded government is a problem, it cannot yet be claimed that
there is any major consensus on a solution. Complaint about excessive
expectations is one thing; discovery of means to reduce them is another.
Some contributors to the debate have however formulated some
distinctive ideas. If there is a crisis because of excessive vulnerability of
government to popular demands, then means must be found of insulating
governments, of putting a whole range of issues beyond the reach of
democratic politics (Brittan, 1978; Parkin, M. 1975. Rees-Mogg, 1975).

For example, it was once believed that the gold base of the currency
was an issue which had to be kept beyond politics, because to tamper
with it meant rapid doom. The collapse of this still left intact for a
while the belief that the level of unemployment was something about
which governments could do little. The full acceptance by most Western
governments of Keynesian economic policy ended this illusion and
threw most economic variables open to political manipulation — democratic demands being checked by no equivalent responsibility on those
making them to respect the laws of economic scarcity. True, Keynes's
own prescriptions provided for deflationary as much as expansionary
policies, depending on the economic conjuncture. But, it is argued,
within a democratic polity a ratchet effect operates to ensure that
deflation is always inadequate and expansion excessive: public pressure
keeps public spending too high but unemployment and taxation too low.
Rigid control of the money supply and the insulation of central banks from
democratic influence are seen as the new barriers which will limit the
ability of popular demands to sway public policy. The only alternative,
apart from chaos, is more state control of the economy so that governments can manipulate the variables left free by Keynesian policy. This
is seen as automatically leading to a diminution of liberties. Thus, in the
eyes of the most candid commentators, democracy has to be limited in
order to preserve liberty (Brittan, 1978).

It is as might have been anticipated: if the combination of liberty
and democracy within capitalism which constitutes Western pluralism
was dependent on an advancing economy, the eclipse of that economy
must lead to a re-examination of the political ablance.[2] Themes of
debate which seemed in the first two postwar decades to have
disappeared from the political landscape return with all their nineteenth-
century vigour: can individual liberty survive universal suffrage? Can the
capitalist economy accommodate organised labour? How can the
economy be put beyond politics? It would be premature to claim that
these arguments have secured dominance as the school of political
thought having most influence on public policy, though its economic
counterpart, monetarism, is very near to having done so. It would also
be quite wrong to claim that it represents the stream into which
pluralist theory has finally flowed. But it is notable that arguments of
this kind represent one of the few innovative contributions to political
debate among political scientists outside the Marxist camp in the 1970s.

The Corporate State

The revival of interest in the corporate state reinforces the impression

that with the apparent passing of the Keynesian period of postwar
economic development the capitalist world is returning to some of the
political preoccupations of earlier decades — broadly those from 1870
to 1940. It was from the 1870s onwards that the industrialising countries of Western Europe began to come to terms with two developments
which had not been part of the canon of early capitalism: the inevitability of the organisation of labour; and the need to be able to ensure the
viability and progress of a particular national economy within the
potentially destabilising context of international trade, particularly
during periods of recession. The capacity and willingness of industrial
polities to respond to these issues varied with the extent of the commitment of their institutions to classical *laissez-faire* capitalism.[3] The
question cannot be argued in full detail here, but a good contrast is
provided by the cases of Britain and Germany. In the former country a
lengthy development of industrialisation in a context of individualism
and restricted state involvement imparted a deep liberalism to political,
legal and economic institutions to which neither corporatist industrial
relations nor state-regulated capitalism could be easily wedded. In
Germany industrialism was from the outset led from above by a strong
state which was building at the same time a modern economy and a new
nation on the basis of institutions and legal codes which had changed
little since medieval times. As a result the liberal phase of German capitalism was brief, possibly non-existent, and the country was well equipped
for a corporatist integration of labour and state-aided, state-protected
industry (Schmitter, 1977; Crouch, 1978).

In the period before World War I the main result of these new
orientations was the policy of imperialism. Although this was associated
with policies of trying to produce a nationalistically integrated and hierarchically ordered society at home, corporatist labour relations remained
largely an ideological aspiration, primarily of Roman Catholic social
thought trying to find a way between the conflictual individualism of
capitalism and the disruptive, anti-hierarchical (not to mention
atheistic) aspirations of the growing socialist movement of organised
labour.

If the Great War ended the age of imperialism (though not the fact of
empires) it also provided the basis for a new integration of state, capital
and labour. In modern wars of total mobilisation, all capitalist societies
are corporatist: the need to win the war creates an overwhelming moral
unity and defines an external enemy so clearly that internal conflicts
pale into insignificance; the state engages in a degree of propaganda and
popular activation not normally seen in capitalist societies — politics

ceases to be a mere 'sideshow in the circus of life' (Dahl, 1961:100) and becomes literally a matter of life and death; the degree of economic regulation in which the state engages increases massively since it has to ensure the needs of the single overriding extra-economic priority of fighting the war; and the working class is taken into a highly corporatist relationship, with civil liberties restricted because of war needs, but concern for its physical and moral welfare considerably increased.

During the extreme crises of the 1920s and 1930s these models of state action to incorporate organised labour and to protect industry remained relevant to economic and social policy, though with very different emphasis in different countries. For example, in Italy it was under the fascist regime, with its self-conscious adoption of corporatist rhetoric, that a system of organised industrial interests responsive to state direction was established, after the crushing by force of the oppositional labour movement. In Germany corporatist organisations involving the autonomous labour movement, together with protective measures for private industry, were developed by the centre-left governments of the Weimar republic, and it was largely the *petit-bourgeois* forces left *outside* that system who gave support to the Nazi movement. This was thus in certain important respects hostile to corporatism in the name of a more inclusive state unimpeded by interest groups — an important and often overlooked difference between the Italian and German fascist movements (Maier, 1974). In contrast again, in Britain a policy of industrial protection, cartelisation and restriction was adopted only with extreme reluctance by governments and industrialists still preferring a liberal economic system, while a corporatist strategy towards labour was pursued only fitfully — for much of the period the high level of unemployment and the demoralisation of labour after the General Strike of 1926 seemed to make political recognition of organised labour unnecessary.

During World War II the fascist countries were already under a form of corporatism; in Britain the war effort had the implications for domestic organisation discussed above; while in the occupied countries the labour movement and those sections of capital which did not collaborate forged a unity in the Resistance that facilitated corporatist developments in the early postwar years. However, as I have discussed elsewhere (Crouch, 1978), the wartime build-up of corporatist potentialities petered out during the 1950s as the years of unprecedented economic growth and mass prosperity provided an original and apparently secure basis of social integration for advanced capitalist societies. Apart from a motley collection of countries including Spain and

Portugal, the Netherlands, Peronist Argentina and possibly Sweden and Norway (Schmitter, 1977) the concept of corporatism became of declining relevance as an element in the analysis of contemporary politics.

During the past decade all that has changed. The decline in economic fortunes and associated rise of detailed state economic activity, together with the resurgence of industrial conflict and government attempts to regulate it, have revived the concept of the corporate state. Although the various authors who have contributed to the theme differ among themselves, and everyone has contributed his own classification of types of corporatism, there is a reasonably wide and fruitful area of agreement, which may be summarised in the following terms.[4]

1. Corporatism is best regarded as a strategy pursued by capitalism when it cannot adequately subordinate labour by preventing its combination and allowing market processes to work. If liberal capitalism operates through individualism and the rigorous separation of the economic, political and ideological (or normative) spheres, corporatism entails the opposite. Subordinates and other economic actors are organised, and order is secured by the hierarchical control of organisation. Regulation through organisation almost necessarily involves the state as the only institution capable of securing centralised order (the merging of the political and the economic); while a high degree of normative integration is also necessary to ensure consensus over hierarchy. It is this *reversal* of some of the achievements of the liberal phase of capitalism that imparts the element of medievalism so important to corporatist ideology.

2. It follows from the above that corporatism is a *class* concept and belongs to the analysis of capitalist society. It has to do with ensuring the subordination of labour and represents an alternative strategy for capital when the classic pattern of control through markets is unavailable (or is for other reasons not pursued). Most analyses of corporatism have adopted this approach, but an important exception is J.T. Winkler (1976a).[5] His primary focus is on industrial rather than industrial relations policy. This is in itself not objectionable (see 3. below), but he detaches the concept entirely from class relations, regarding it as essentially a relationship of tension between the state and private industry; industry remains in private *ownership* but subject to *control* by the state — a new formulation of the division between ownership and control. There are two problems with such an analysis. First, it ignores the fact that the regulation of labour in the interests of capital has been an important aspect of most corporatist policies. Second, it leaves implicit and poorly theoretised the relationship between capital

and the state. Whose interests does the state serve and why? If, as will
be further discussed in a later section, there are good reasons for
believing that most actions of the state are taken in the interests of at
least certain sections of capital, then the idea of corporatism being a
matter of the state, as a separate entity, imposing constraints on industry
becomes highly suspect. On the other hand, to anticipate subsequent
arguments, Winkler's arguments are not to be as easily disposed of as
current versions of Marxist theory assume, and it is the problematic
status of corporatist strategies within liberal democratic capitalist
societies which leads us to raise certain queries of the Marxist account.

3. While corporatism certainly has to do with industrial relations, it
would be wrong to regard it as a concept which can be analysed within
the variables of industrial relations in isolation. Some of the conditions
of corporatism may reflect developments in other areas of the economy, such as: defensive rationalisation and cartelisation; an increasing
degree of concentration in industry to take advantage of modern technology and the economies of scale; state participation in economic
planning; and other processes which at least partially suspend the full
force of market competition. The reason for this is as follows. One does
not need to accept the Marxist labour theory of value to recognise that
ultimately every price reflects the cost of the labour input of the good
in question. Any policy which partially suspends market forces needs
to find alternative means of restraining prices — ultimately the price of
labour. Where imported goods are concerned this is achieved through
tariffs and other protectionist measures. Within the domestic market in
an economy with an organised labour movement similar control
can be secured only by incorporating labour's organisations within the
structure of economic regulation. Where labour is weak and non-disrupt-
ive the general economic policies associated with corporatism may be
able to dispense with a labour relations policy — as was perhaps the case
in Britain for much of the 1920s — but this is likely to be temporary;
if the corporatist policies are at all successful in stabilising the economy
in conditions of suspended competition, labour will become powerful.

It will be noted that not all the developments associated with
corporatism immediately involve the state — indeed some of the more
idealistic versions of corporatist theory virtually ignored the state and
envisaged a corporatist system emerging out of a chain of autonomous
agreements between employers and workers. This is as naive as
syndicalist theory, to which it is not unrelated, but it is important to
regard the state's activity as *part* of a wider pattern of developments
which reduce the fragmentation, atomisation and competition among

economic units which characterised classical capitalism. Particularly useful here is a concept closely related to that of the corporate state which
is also enjoying a revival of interest — that of 'organised capitalism'
developed in Weimar Germany by Hilferding, Naphtali and others.[6]
Hilferding discerned a series of related processes taking place within
modern capitalism, some involving the state, others not. Included were
concentration in industry, trade and banking; the bureaucratisation of
and introduction of planning into the firm consequent on the emergence
of professional management; the increasing organisation and extension
to a national basis of industrial conflicts; growing state intervention to
restore the economic equilibrium constantly disrupted by the chaos of
capitalist markets; state intervention in social policy to reduce insecurity;
imperialism; the growing importance of political parties and an
expansion of the role of the state to embrace general guidance *(Leistung)*
of the whole society rather than simply the maintenance of order
(Ordnung); the development of ideologies of scientific efficiency.

Hilferding considered that these processes would mean increasing
economic stability and a societisation of processes formerly left to the
autonomous regulation of the market. As a reformist Marxist he believed
that this marked the start of the transformation of capitalism into a
planned, rational socialist economy, especially as increasing participation by the labour movement was necessary in the institutions established to secure stability. Concomitantly he saw a need for workers to
share control in running industry at the level of the firm — a contribution of his thought which has survived in the German labour movement's advocacy of *Mitbestimmung*.

Clearly, Hilferding is discussing the same processes as those usually
labelled as corporatism: the establishment of a capitalist order secured
through organised co-ordination rather than through markets, with
labour's organisations integrated into the process of control. However,
where most concepts of corporatism see this process as one in which
labour is subordinated, Hilferding considered that through such
mechanisms labour *might* succeed in transforming capitalism and gaining dominance. His optimism and, as a result, his overall theory are
generally considered to have been discredited by the eventual fate of
Weimar — though certainly no more discredited than the official international Communist policy at that time of, first, conniving at any crisis
in the fragile structure of German liberal democracy and then temporarily co-operating with the Nazi regime. It has also been observed that
the defensive measures of European capitalism in the 1920s did not have
the stabilising and progressive, let alone transformative, potentialities
that Hilferding believed; however, the same critics point out that the

Keynesian economic policies which became dominant by the 1940s
did provide the kind of politicised stabilisation of capitalist economies
for which he had been looking (Winkler, H.A., 1974).

4. Hilferding's arguments that an organised capitalism presents
opportunities to organised labour has interesting implications for
corporatist theory — implications which are echoed in much recent
literature. Because of its origins in nineteenth-century anti-liberal
Conservatism, and even more because of its use by fascist regimes in
Italy, Spain and Portugal, the corporatist state is often regarded as highly
hierarchical with few elements of pluralism. This assumes that a corporatist strategy employed by dominant elites is actually successful. There
is one major condition for this success: the organisations which
simultaneously represent and discipline the working class have to
operate primarily downwards, ordering and controlling their members.
If in fact they instead (or even also) work upwards, conveying demands
to the state and to organised capital, not only do they impart a strong
element of pluralism, but it is a pluralism which is less constrained by
the market and by the institutional segregation of polity and economy
characteristic of liberal capitalism.

In classic corporatist ideology this problem was overcome by envis-
aging that all classes of society would be united morally and normatively,
usually through the agency of the Catholic Church, in a manner that was
considered to have been characteristic of medieval, feudal society before
the disruptive impact of liberal, individualistic capitalism. The ambition
was always improbable; the construction of a positive ideological unity
in a capitalist society has proved to be a difficult task (Hirsch, F., 1977).
Some success was achieved with the creation of a Catholic labour movement in opposition to the existing socialist one throughout continental
western Europe, though even this never saw its role in entirely
collaborationist terms.

The fascist countries had greater scope for creating ideological unity
than those with essentially liberal political systems, through their
intensive use of state propaganda and popular mobilisation under
nationalist slogans. However, this was heavily buttressed by the use of
massive coercion which in principle has no place in corporatism. To a
certain extent the widespread repression of dissidence was a condition
for the success of ideological mobilisation. In a society where autonomous groups are allowed to organise themselves, attempts at mobilisation by the right will be countered by similar attempts by the left, leading to a raising of political tension and a threat to social stability: hence
the tendency for mass mobilisation to be inversely related to the degree

of liberal freedoms present in a society.

These considerations lead us to predict two different destinies for corporatist strategies, depending on whether the social context in which they are launched is liberal or authoritarian (Schmitter, 1974). By liberal I here mean a society in which organisations (of capital, labour and other groups) develop autonomously within civil society, deriving their self-definitions and their power from their constituent parts — ultimately from individuals. By authoritarian is meant a system in which organisations are defined, allocated power and probably even created by the state, their base in civil society being weak. Clearly a scale of that kind is a continuum rather than a two-fold classification: for example while the Federal Republic of Germany and the United Kingdom would both be classified as liberal, the latter would rest more unambiguously near the liberal pole. Further, of course, the positions of individual countries change over time. However, for the purpose of the present discussions we shall speak in terms of the two extreme cases: liberalism and authoritarianism.

If the ruling classes of an authoritarian society make use of corporatist strategies they will do so through the creation of more or less artificial organisations — at least on the side of labour — whose scope and power will be subject to the whim of the state for as long as the state can remain effectively authoritarian. Repression can be easily mobilised to deal with dissidents. The corporatism will be hierarchical and relatively untroubled, though it will not really correspond to the ambitions of classical corporatist ideology which saw the necessary unity of such a system emerging spontaneously from the organism of civil society.

Against this, corporatism in a liberal society means coming to terms with autonomous organisations which will never be entirely successfully subjected to ideological hegemony and which must always do something to represent their members. Relations between the state and these organised interests are therefore always likely to be characterised by bargaining: something has to be exchanged for the social peace which the organisations are expected to deliver. This has at least two important implications. First, this kind of shifting, bargained relationship is very different from both the moral order of pure corporatism and the rigid control of fascism. Second, the fact that the bargaining takes place between organised labour and the state, and between peak organisations of capital and labour, opens up a range of issues to working-class demands which go way beyond the limited, institutionally segregated economistic demands of collective bargaining under liberal capitalism —

Hilferding's argument. It is for this reason that capitalist interests within liberal societies enter corporatist arrangements with great reluctance — they are corporatists *malgre eux*. They may be driven to corporatist strategies because these offer the only hope of coming to terms with a militant labour movement, or (as outlined under 3. above) economic problems not immediately connected with labour relations may lead them into that pattern of state intervention, organisation as interest groups and suspension of competition which entails corporatism.

This ambiguity in corporatism within liberal societies, and the different patterns produced by corporatist strategies within liberal and authoritarian contexts has been captured by several recent commentators, most notably by Schmitter (1974 and 1977), but also by Lehmbruch (1977), Harris (1972) and Crouch (1977). The theory of the corporate state is thus able to contribute much to an understanding of contemporary developments, placing them in historical context and relating changes in the role of the state to wider economic changes. However, by themselves accounts of corporatism do not explain why the state responds to capital's needs — especially since these needs are so reluctantly expressed. At this point one needs to turn to Marxist theory — bearing in mind that the distinction between liberal democracy and authoritarianism identified in the corporatist literature will create problems.

Marxist Theories

It has been mentioned that there is some overlap between the writers on corporatism and the Marxist school; perhaps more surprising there is considerable *rapport* between Marxists and proponents of the overloaded government thesis. Reactionaries and radicals alike celebrate the same evidence of discomfiture in the political compromise which has kept them both at bay for so long, even if at the end of the celebration they retire to opposite corners. For writers like O'Connor (1973) and, to a lesser extent, Offe (1972a, 1975a), it is the attempt at meeting welfare demands while also trying to advance the capitalist economy which creates the fiscal and general political crisis of the modern state — the same process described by conservative critics. Similarly, Poulantzas (1975:p.172) points to the way that an increasing number of issues becomes politicised, shifting struggle to the polity, which cannot cope with it. And Jessop (1978), in arguing that liberal democracy is associated with economic liberalism, consciously echoes the case of advocates of the free-markets economy. More generally, the notion of 'overload' appears as a Marxist 'contradiction': the state is called upon to perform functions which conflict fundamentally with its need, as a capitalist state, to secure the private accumulation of the surplus value arising from economic activity. A principal difference between the two traditions is that for Marxists the state's new functions are determined by the needs of the capitalist economy itself, rather than by popular pressure on politicians.

Alone among the various schools of thought involved in current discussions of the state, the Marxists can root their thesis in a general theory of society — a theory which gives an account: of the relative significance of different elements of social structure (giving, for example, priority to the economic and to relations rooted in the economy); of the way in which different aspects of structure are interrelated; of the motivations of human action which mobilise those structures and relations; and of the constraints which the latter in turn impose on human action. The only comparable edifice within modern sociology is the structural-functionalist theory of Talcott Parsons, which has had little to contribute to current discussion of the state.

One problem with Marxism is the large number of rival factions that exist within the corpus — extending indeed to writers' refutations of their own only slightly earlier work. Given that most Marxist writers are tied to a particular political cause, academic disagreements can imply a ferocious enmity. Little attempt will be made here to go into the fine details of these factional disputes, since the main intention is to elucidate the fundamental strengths and weaknesses of the overall Marxist contribution. Attention will be limited to those authors who are prepared in some way to acknowledge the 'relative autonomy' of the state. This rules out advocates of the original Soviet Marxist formulation of state monopoly capitalism, with its complete failure to distinguish between liberal democracy and fascism, and other theories which maintain a naive conception of the relation between ruling classes and the state.

The central insight of the French structuralist school, which has made most of the running in the development of Marxist state theory, is that capital is composed of several distinct 'fractions', whose interests may often conflict (Poulantzas, 1973; 1975). In the overall interests of the capitalist system it is therefore necessary that the state not be a mere tool of capitalism — the fractions cannot unite in order to wield such a tool effectively, and the only other alternative would be for the state to be wedded to one particular fraction which would not serve the interests of capital as a whole. The state's relative autonomy is therefore necessary so that it can establish what are the general interests of capital and pursue them, if necessary, against the interests of individual fractions.

The argument of most of the German 'capital-logic' school is, despite certain differences of approach, basically the same on this question (Holloway and Picciotto, 1978).

This formulation is useful in the empirical analysis of state policy and the political strategies of different capitalist fractions (an example of such use, though much modified, is the paper by Strinati in the present volume). There are however two major problems with it: the account it gives of why the state in a capitalist economy is necessarily a capitalist state, and the relationship of working-class organisations to the state's relative autonomy. The first point is important because, by correctly abandoning naive notions of the state being under the direct control of capitalists, structuralist theory has deprived itself of the most obvious if wrong answer to the question. Instead the account it gives is a straightforward functionalist one: the state is capitalist because that is the character of the society in which the state finds itself. The state can, therefore, only cease to be capitalist if capitalism is itself destroyed. Apart from the general problem of whether a functionalist account can be held to *explain* anything, this is couched at a very high level of abstraction. As it stands it is of little help in explaining why, in any given situation, political actors are forced to act in a way compatible with the general interests of capitalism. The German school, by relating the process more overtly to problems of capital accumulation add considerably to precision on this point; and the more historical approach of some representatives of that school gives a certain answer to the question why, but the attempt at deriving logical necessities from such broad categories as capital and accumulation needs is unsatisfactory. Both theories are notorious for their inability to cope with action, and the dismissive way in which Poulantzas and others claim to reject the force of that criticism (e.g. Poulantzas, 1976) does not dispose of the fact that if sociology is to serve any purpose it must be because it explains and interprets concrete human behaviour.

For French structuralism all questions are resolved at the level of general theory; little remains for short-range theories of action or for empirical justification (Poulantzas, 1975: 158, 161 fn). Thus, the state is assumed automatically to care for the general interests of capital, because that is the role assigned to the state in the logic of structures. There is little place for possibilities such as that discussed by Longstreth in the present volume, where, not through abstract structural logic but through specific institutions, a particular fraction of British capital — the financial sector — has been able to dominate state policy to the possible *detriment* of the long-term interests of capital as a whole (not to mention the whole society).

If the theory cannot deal with wayward behaviour within capital, even less can it cope with labour.[7] Given the account of why the state is capitalist outlined above, it is clear that the state's relative autonomy does not encompass any capacity to respond positively to working-class demands and pressures. For the theory to admit this would involve either (1) acknowledgement that the state within a capitalist society can nevertheless be responsive to interests other than those of capital, thereby undermining the entire functional nature of the analysis or (2) arguing that capitalism is a social system of such inbuilt pluralism and liberty that its own logic can serve the interests of labour as well as capital. This latter is of course the position of the ideological defenders of capitalism, and it is in some respects a powerful argument, but it is hardly Marxist — though Offe and Ronge (1976) come very close to a sophisticated formulation of it when they argue that capitalism reflects the interests of *all* members of a society to the extent that those interests can be expressed through the workings of capitalism.

Now, two of the most remarkable facts about the liberal democratic capitalist societies are, first, the extent to which their ruling classes mistrust the state and try to limit its activities, and second, the relative responsiveness of the polity (in contrast with the situation in virtually all other known large-scale societies) to working-class demands. This latter point may be only a matter of degree, but relativities and comparisons are highly important. There must be something radically wrong with a theory which not only ignores these important facts, but also necessarily denies them.

The facts are of course related. The *central* reason why capitalist interests mistrust the state is not the fear that it will be other fractions of capital which gain its favour (though this may sometimes be the case) but that it will be responsive to class interests other than those of capital.[8] The attempts of Marxist analysis to get round this problem are not convincing. An example may be taken from a recent study (overall a sensitive and subtle one) of the nationalisation, denationalisation and renationalisation of the British steel industry (McEachern, 1977). For present purposes the author's central problem is how to account for capital's eventual acquiescence in public ownership of the industry, while its opposition in the 1950s had been extremely strong. The author is able to adduce several good arguments. By the time of the 1964 Labour Government private capital had learned that nationalisation as practised in Britain did not threaten its interests as had once been feared; and the industry was in such a poor condition that it could not provide

large profits but needed large-scale reorganisation which would require
state help. This certainly explains why opposition became much less
intense and why organised capital as a whole did not take up the
clamour of the steel owners themselves. But McEachern wants to go
further than this; it is not just that capital was able to take advantage
of nationalisation once it occurred, or to ensure that the nationalised
industry behaved in ways acceptable to it, in the sense of making the
best of a fairly bad job. He has to assert (p.278) that public ownership
was *the* solution that *best suited* capital and that capital was the interest
on whose behalf the nationalisation was finally carried out.

It is very difficult to square such an account with the actual positions
adopted by capitalist interests. An alternative formulation which does not
incur such difficulties but which also retains McEachern's overall conclusions about the significance of nationalisation runs as follows: the
drive for the public ownership of steel originated from and remained
with the left wing of the Labour Party. Its presence in the party's
programme and eventual implementation owe much to the need of the
party leadership to offer the left something, while the fact that the
industry was becoming a problem requiring some sort of action, together with the relative diminution of the opposition from capital, made
it a concession that was reasonable and uncostly to make. Given the
overwhelming importance of capitalist mechanisms in the British economy, the nationalised industry then took its place as just another large
employing organisation offering little challenge to capital. However,
since every accretion of state power is seen by capital as *potentially*
encroaching on the prerogatives of private control of the economy,
capitalist interests would always have preferred an arrangement that
retained private ownership. Some of the underlying assumptions of such
an account are spelt out in more detail later in this paper (pp.36ff.) For
the present we need merely to ask why most Marxist accounts find it
necessary to go beyond such an interpretation in order to tie policies of
this kind more tightly to the interests of capital as a whole, despite the
loss in plausibility which this involves.

The reason is that to argue that capitalism 'made the best of a bad
job' is to imply that non-capitalist interests were at least able to initiate
a policy, even if in the subsequent implementation they lost control of
it. To concede that is too much for a theory which locates the state
solely within a role functional to the maintenance of capitalism and
representative of capitalist interests — general or particular. It is almost
as though, having admitted the idea of the relative autonomy of the
state, a structuralist theory has to move quickly to close the loophole

to elements of pluralism which this might imply by pitching the theory
at such an abstract, rigid level that all questions of the respective
positions of labour and capital are resolved in the initial formulation
and not left open to any modification by actual behaviour.

Rather different is the approach of Miliband (1977), whose account
of politics in capitalist society is far more flexible and allows for the
albeit limited political power of the working class (e.g. pp. 75,97).
Unfortunately, however, this mainly emerges in Miliband's empirical
accounts. At the level of theory he is silent. His theoretical answer to the
question — why is the state in capitalist society a capitalist state? — has
three parts: the role of interrelated elites from common social back-
grounds in policy-making, the activities of pressure groups representing
powerful interests, and structural analysis *à la* Althusser and Poulantzas
(pp. 68-73). The first two are the themes which figured so prominently
in his earlier work on the capitalist state and which occasioned the protracted debate with Poulantzas *(New Left Review,* 1969). The addition
of the third item represents a kind of concession to the structuralists
and is rather surprising. Miliband's use of the idea of structural constraint in his empirical accounts is by no means as abstract and rigid as
theirs is; he concedes too much to them in giving them title to his
concept of it. In discussion, he does distinguish between authoritarian and
liberal-democratic forms (1977:p.75). However, the fact remains that
up to now, he has not done so at the level of theory.

But if this remains the position of most Marxist writers, there have
recently been interesting exceptions who are able to remain within the
Marxist camp by making use of the formula that the class struggle is
reflected in the policies of the state, by which is meant that the state, in
order to maintain the social peace necessary for capitalism, has to make
concessions to working-class interests; some state policies will therefore
work to the advantage of workers, possibly even against the immediate
interests of capital. The state's relative autonomy from specific capitals
in order to safeguard the long-term conditions for capital as a whole
here involves it making real concessions. The argument can, for example,
be deployed to account for certain aspects of the welfare state —
especially now that edifice is being threatened, and that to regard it
as merely a device for incorporation, as was common in the 1960s,
therefore becomes difficult to maintain. Different writers evaluate these
'concessions' differently. For some, since a concession is something
which has to be offered to secure capitalism's own peaceful future, it
may therefore be regarded as something in capitalism's own interests,
and virtually written off as a working-class gain or as evidence of

countervailing working-class power (McEachern, 1977; Warren, 1973). But this ignores the elementary point that much as capital might benefit from offering concessions, it gains much more if it does not have to make them, and that situations in which it does have to make them must be evidence of countervailing power.

Other writers are less grudging; for example, for Gough (1975), certain social policies constitute straightforward working-class gains which capitalism can only with great difficulty roll back. In ascertaining which policies come in this category he develops an analysis of state expenditure that is very useful indeed, though it does include one argument which has surprising implications. In common with other Marxists he points out (p. 21) that much spending on such matters as education, health, transport are made necessary by the needs of capitalism itself. This is so, but if it is also true that such expenditures are actually valuable to the working class, it is in effect being argued that over important areas of life capital and labour do have certain interests in common, and that the latter can benefit from the needs of the former. This goes beyond Offe and Ronge's argument that capitalism serves the interests of everyone to the extent that they are members of capitalist society; capitalism can also generate actions by the state which compensate for certain disadvantages in market transactions. Are Marxist theories really ready to concede that much?

The concept of class struggle being reflected in the state's policies is also developed by Esping-Andersen *et al.* (1976). On this basis they draw up an elaborate typology of working-class demands, distinguishing between those in the areas of production and circulation, commodity and non-commodity form, and those which are reproductive and those which are unreproductive of capitalist relations. They are then able to classify different demands in terms of the kind of state response which meets them and the chances or not of their being satisfactorily met within the framework of a capitalist society. This constitutes real progress on the typical implicit Marxist typology which tends to label any demand which is met as a concession by definition not worth having and any which is not as a likely cause of the imminent collapse of capitalism. What they are unable to do is to distinguish those demands which are unlikely to be easily met but which, if pressed, can be expected to lead, not just to breakdown and disorder, but to the emergence of progressive changes. This is an important question to which we shall later return.

Analyses of the kind discussed go a long way towards bridging the gap between a Marxist theory of the state and the queries of those who

either suspect a functionalist analysis of why the state has to be capitalist or who consider that state theory should reflect in a more straightforward way the realities of liberal democracy. On the evidence in the
literature at hand, the gap may actually be closed in the account of
Esping-Andersen *et al.*, but Gough's position is more typical in that he
wants to insist that the state *represents* the interests of capital alone;
the institutions of liberal democracy are essentially mere legitimation
and ideology (p.81); and policies which meet working-class demands are
concessions made to a class which itself stands quite outside and
beneath the state — indeed, his account would hardly distinguish between
Bismarck's Germany and contemporary Western Europe. Despite the
great advance which his analysis presents he shares in the general failing
of the Marxist tradition to theoretise the liberal democratic state. Why
should this weakness be so persistent?

   The answer lies in two very important elements of Marxism: the
tendency to excessive rigidity in the concept of capitalism and an
unhelpful formulation of what constitutes class interests. Both relate to
the same underlying paradox: the unwillingness of most Marxists
seriously to discuss social change. Too much has been invested in the
dramatic idea of the revolution, which is regarded as a culmination of all
history (strictly, pre-history), after which all is utterly changed. Marx
himself seems to have shared this view, and in many of his writings he
looks forward to an imminent short, sharp struggle after which the
construction of something new would begin. However, he did at times
recognise the possibility of peaceful transitions (in the liberal democracies, in fact); more important, he did develop the idea that in the
period before the revolution social changes would appear within the
womb of capitalist society that prefigured, albeit in distorted form,
post-revolutionary developments. Difficult though this instance of a
policy of 'picking the winners' might be, it is essential that some attempt
be made to identify such changes if Marxist theory is to be framed in
terms of actual social relations. One important aspect, which will be
discussed later in this paper, is that without such an approach one can
never distinguish, before the event, actions which are likely to be
'progressive' from those which are merely destructive. It is true that
some recent social occurrences, such as the growth of workers' co-
operatives, have led some Marxist writers to show more interest in
developments 'within the womb of capitalism', but the overwhelming
stress of theory (particularly state theory) is on demonstrating (1) how
thoroughly capitalist present society is, (2) how it is nevertheless riven
with contradictions which must destroy it and (3) how these will issue

into a relatively short, violent revolutionary struggle. Analysis is over-whelmingly concentrated on (1) and (2) — (3) is just asserted. Very little is written on the kinds of social forms that are expected to develop within the transition or on the relationship which social organ-isation after the revolution will have to that before. All that is, as it were, beyond the wall of time.

Thus, Poulantzas (1977: pp. 82 and 106), having argued well and convincingly that the Communist parties of the West are naive in believ-ing that their capture of the state through an election suddenly converts a capitalist state into an instrument for socialism, goes on to conclude that the labour movement has to 'smash' the state. This concept is left as crude as the language which embodies it. As Miliband asks (1977: pp. 178 ff), with what instrument is the state to be smashed? What organisation emerges from the task of smashing the state? And what relationship does it have to subsequent social arrangements? Similarly, Warren (1973: pp. 96, 97), after a careful and detailed account of economic planning in Western Europe, contrasts the scope for peaceful and 'short, violent' transitions to socialism; after an analysis of the former, which finds it wanting, the latter is just asserted, without analysis.

It is because the process of social change is put beyond time and cast in this unexamined and static mould that the concept of capitalist society is left so rigid. It is not possible for most Marxists to envisage significant shifts in power relations between the classes within capitalism, because changes of that kind are reserved for the period the other side of the revolution and hence beyond intellectual analysis. Of course, that does not mean that Marxism regards the operation of capitalist society as a matter of effortless smooth functioning; rather, the society is seen as torn by major contradictions, and it is from the incapacity of the society to cope with these contradictions that the revolution emerges. However, it should be noted that this concept of social change is singularly rigid: a contradiction develops, capitalism is unable to cope with it, and the result is a fundamental crisis from which emerges a socialist transformation. The trouble is that many of the conflicts and crises that Marxists have confidently labelled contradictions of this type have subsequently proved to be resolvable within the framework of capitalism, though perhaps with major shifts in the alignment of class forces within it. As Daniel Bell has noted (1976: p. 235), the first generations of Marxists predicted the collapse of capitalism because the unplanned and anarchic nature of the market would lead to an excessive concentration of industry, resulting in a declining rate of profit. After the 1930s, when capitalist states began to use public spending to resolve such crises, Marxists argued that this could only be done through spending on armaments and defence, not on social policies. Now, with such writers as O'Connor, the fundamental flaw is seen as a fiscal crisis resulting primarily from high state *social* expenditure necessary to the maintenance of capitalism. Bell (1976: p. 236) comments:

> Each of the three versions held the dismal fate of capitalism to be inevitable. And at some point, since all social systems change, capitalism may expire and Marxist 'theory' will claim the victory. But if the reason for capitalism's demise is the expansion of social expenditures, the labeling is a conceit. To call the heart of this argument 'Marxism' is part of that incorrigible radical myth making which seeks to convert every crisis into proof of the validity of a (constantly redefined) ideology.

There is clearly something fundamentally wrong with a theoretical position which is repeatedly taken by surprise in this way, and which after each instance simply redefines the existing postulates of the theory until the next historical refutation.

The Marxist conception of class interests encounters different problems, but resulting from the same cause. In some ways its concept of interests is among Marxism's strongest points. Marx stressed the importance of the pursuit of class domination (and its concomitant material advantages) as the goal of class interest and showed how to interpret class actions in terms of their contribution to that goal; this provides a unifying concept of goal maximisation that is potentially of as much value to sociology as that of profit maximisation is to classical economics — indeed, both have a common origin in Ricardo.

Marxist theory is particularly good at deriving the interests of capitalist classes, because capitalism is the structure in dominance and capitalism's interests are expressed in a continuous series of incremental decisions aimed at maintaining that dominance in changing circumstances. For working-class interests however there is a problem. For Marxists, the working class will only realise its interests the other side of the revolution; in the meantime therefore its interest consists in pursuing those strategies which will make the revolution. The possibility of immediate material gains through, for example, successful wage demands, is recognised, but these only correspond to long-term class interests in so far as their pursuit results in crises for capitalism. The 'capital-logic' school solves this problem most unsatisfactorily by regarding proletarian material interests as 'commodity fetishism'. To generalise this to refer to virtually any pursuit of material interests is both utterly unrealistic in its perspective on human life and takes the edge off the real, if limited, application of the idea of fetishism (Holloway and Picciotto, 1978: p.24). An example of how this conception of interests operates may again be taken from the policy adopted by German Communists under the Weimar Republic. A revisionist like Hilferding advocated support for the infant German liberal democracy, because in terms of his conception of socialism emerging gradually from a series of changes within the structure of capitalism, the establishment of parliamentary democracy constituted one such change (Kocka, 1974). For the Communists, on the other hand, the Weimar Republic was a development entirely contained within, and probably contributing towards the stability of, capitalism. Therefore any action which threatened the viability of the republic threatened the stability of capitalism, which would hasten the revolution and thus the real interests of the working class. The two arguments therefore produced directly opposite analyses of wherein lay the interests of the working class.

Grasping this central Marxist meaning of interests enables us to give a more satisfactory account of the idea of 'concessions' discussed above (p. 28). In an orthodox Marxist analysis an accretion of working-class power occurs within capitalist society only to the extent that the class is able by its actions to intensify the contradictions of capitalism and prepare the conditions for revolution. Apparent increases in power which lead to the class securing a better return *within* a more or less stable framework of capitalism do not hasten the realisation of its long-term ends, may indeed hinder them by 'buying time' for capitalism, and therefore should be added to capital's side of the balance, not labour's. But the increase in the coherence of the theory rests on the very shaky foundations that constitute this approach to interests.

The problem is that the claim that working-class interests will be properly met after a revolution is not a statement which can be made by social science; it lies beyond the scope of any general predictive laws which it is in our power to construct. Marx's belief that long-term historical laws of that kind could fall within the purview of science was shared by many nineteenth-century thinkers, but it is not possible to retain that view in the face of modern knowledge of the scope of science. There is therefore a complete asymmetry in Marxist literature between the treatment of capital's interests and those of labour. The

former are derived from everyday practice within existing, more or less
known societies; the latter are posited on the basis of a social structure
which is not and cannot be known. This constitutes a colossal double
standard within Marxist analyses.

Does this mean, then, that working-class interests can only be established in terms of the opportunities presented to labour within capitalist
society? Not quite. It is perfectly reasonable to argue as follows: within
capitalism labour is subject to constant subordination; labour therefore
has an interest in the development of any mode of production that will
reduce or eliminate that subordination; it is therefore in labour's
interest to support revolutionary (that is, system-transforming) strategies
provided (1) that there is a reasonable expectation that the result of the
change will be a system that does in fact reduce or eliminate domination
and (2) that the material advantages already gained by the class within
capitalism are not put in jeopardy. Clearly, these are tough criteria to
meet in practice; can there ever be a reasonable expectation that a major
social change will work to the advantage of a particular class? The idea
of developments taking place within the womb of the old society
provides the only means of meeting that criterion; if a particular form
of social organisation is seen to work in a certain way, it is rational for
the interests associated with it to work for the elimination of all barriers
to its extension, and since their interests are already defined in its terms
there is good reason to expect that they will remain with it. It was in
some such manner that the capitalist mode of production emerged out
of feudalism; the matter was never really resolved by short, sharp,
clear-cut class confrontations, even in France.

But to argue that a class's interests in extensive change can only be
established if elements of the predicted new situation have already
started to occur, and in a sufficiently substantial way to constitute a
true interest, would seem to suggest that extensive social change
favourable to the working class can only occur in relatively liberal
societies which are able to tolerate a certain degree of countervailing
innovation; in more rigid societies there would be no prospect of such
changes. Yes, this is the case; one important contribution of Marx was
to draw attention to the constraints imposed on human choice by the
determinism of social structure. If the only structure which a working-
class movement can create within a particular society is its own
clandestine party, which becomes an armed party, then all it has
created is a coercive force counter to the state's coercive force, which
after success in conflict will remain a coercive force, responding to the
interests of those who control it rather than to those who might have

been seeking a new mode of production. This essentially anti-Leninist point has here been derived in an abstract and theoretical way, but the present century has provided many historical examples to illustrate it.

Of course, Marxism, indeed Leninism, has always recognised and condemned 'adventurism' — the act of making challenges to capitalist power before the time is ripe. But given the absence of any clear theory on when the moment for change has occurred, the task of assessing the ripeness of time has in practice become little more than a political football kicked between leaderships and dissident groups. A prime case is the French Communist Party, where responsibility for defining the right historical movement became a device whereby the central bureaucracy maintained its hold on the unity of the movement; and much of the energy of the *mouvement de mai* in France in 1968 was devoted to attacking the doctrine of 'possibilism', as this became known, and elevating 'adventurism' into a virtue (Cohn-Bendit, 1968). Given the weaknesses of theory discussed here, Marxist movements which escape the problem of bureaucratism are always prone to the temptations of adventurism, partly because of the natural impatience of those desiring radical change and partly because of the argument, criticised here, that since liberal democracy offers 'concessions' which divert the working class from its long-term interests, it makes sense to take actions which force capitalism to discard its liberal mask and thus get rid of the diversion. This is of course the doctrine being pursued by the Baader-Meinhoff group in Germany and the *Brigate Rosse* in Italy — both logical if desperate developments from the movements of the late 1960s, and both further examples of neglect of the crucial question: have pre-revolutionary changes provided such a base that one can confidently predict that socialism rather than barbarism will ensue from any major social breakdown?

Despite its important contributions and despite the great progress which has recently been made in the sophistication of its theories, the Marxist account of the state retains these major flaws which restrict its value to social science. Most important, these deficiences still prevent it from giving an adequate answer to the question of why and to what extent the state in a capitalist society necessarily acts in the interests of capital.

A Reformulation

Ironically, an answer to that question which is compatible with many of the positive findings of Marxist writing may be derived from a recent contribution by C. Lindblom (1977), a leading figure in the American pluralist school. While his new book puts him somewhat outside the mainstream of pluralism, and while he pays considerable tribute to Marx, Lindblom can hardly be counted as a Marxist; however, his contribution to the theory of capitalist (or, in his terms, business) domination of the state is more cogent than virtually all the straightforward Marxist contributions, while it at the same time fulfils the important requirement of any theory of the state in liberal democracy of providing a place for the power of non-capitalist interests[9].

Lindblom (1977, chs. 13,14) regards governments in the liberal democracies as being subject to two major pressures: polyarchy and the privileged position of business. The former refers to the familiar institutions, unique to advanced capitalist societies, of free elections, a wide range of autonomous interest groups, freedom of political debate etc.[10] These are the pressures which ensure that these states, unlike virtually any other, are not responsive to dominant elites alone. The latter recognises the fact that governments in such societies *must* pay attention to the demands of business interests because the production of the goods and services needed by everyone rests in the control of these interests, and governments dare not take actions which might restrict this production. In other words, capitalists do *not* just produce their own profits or, in Poulantzas's phrase, simply reproduce capitalism; they have control of a productive power on which everybody is dependent for basic material needs — recognition of this fact being without prejudice to the question of whether production *could* in principle be organised differently. Offe (1975: p.126) makes a similar point: the state is dependent on accumulation and has to *maintain* it, but it cannot itself *do* it. In Lindblom's words (pp. 122-3):

> Because public functions in the market system rest in the hands of businessmen, it follows that jobs, prices, production, growth, the standard of living, and the economic security of everyone all rest in their hands. Consequently government officials cannot be indifferent to how well business performs its functions. Depression, inflation, or other economic disasters can bring down a government. A major function of government, therefore, is to see to it that businessmen perform their tasks.

So long as this remains true, capital retains something of the function of being, in Marx's terms, the class whose interests embody the interests of society as a whole — albeit in distorted form — and the state as care-taker of the general interest will be tied to it. Further, as Lindblom

points out (pp. 152-7), in the imperfect competition of the modern
economy businessmen have considerable discretion in deciding what they
will do and what they will need as incentives to do it. One cannot therefore be sure that the claimed 'needs' of business are strictly needs;
but governments challenge the claim that they are at their own peril,
because ultimately only business can tell what its own needs are.
Lindblom continues (p.173):

> One of the great misconceptions of conventional economic theory
> is that businessmen are induced to perform their functions by
> purchases of their goods and services, as though the vast productive
> tasks performed in market-oriented systems could be motivated
> solely by exchange relations between buyers and sellers. On so
> slender a foundation no great productive system can be established.
> What is required in addition is a set of governmentally provided
> inducements in the form of market and political benefits. And
> because market demands themselves do not spontaneously spring
> up, they too have to be nurtured by government. Governments in
> market-oriented systems have always been busy with these
> necessary activities.

Having established these crucial points Lindblom goes on to argue,
similarly to Miliband, that in addition to this structurally privileged
position, business is able to wield its massive resources to secure dis-
proportionate influence within the ostensibly rival sphere of polyarchy
itself — interest groups, parties and electoral politics. Finally (ch.16)
business is also able to mould public opinion so that 'citizens' volitions
serve not their own interests but the interests of businessmen'(p.202).
But it is the account of structural privilege which is most interesting,
because it is so much more convincing and powerful than the abstract
functionalism that contemporary Marxism has chosen. It is a formulation that some of the more flexible Marxist accounts, such as those of
Miliband, Gough and Esping-Andersen *et al.* might be capable of
incorporating, but the more elaborated versions would have difficulty.
It rests, first, on the assumption that governments in liberal democracies
are responsible to the people as a whole as well as just to capital, which
we have seen causes problems for Marxism's rigid conceptualisation
of what comprises capitalism. Second, general popular demands for
increasing material prosperity, employment, stable prices, stability are
seen as requiring governments to depend on the institutions capable
of providing these goods; this involves an encounter with the question

of what constitutes working-class interests, the sticky point in Marxist theory discussed above.

However, once these points are accepted, Lindblom's account produces similar conclusions to certain Marxist positions. For example, it would support Poulantzas's argument on the folly of Communist (or, for that matter, Social Democratic) parties trying to secure 'socialism' simply by taking control of the state. At the same time, since scope for autonomous working-class pressure (an aspect of polyarchy) is built in at the level of theory, such facts as the constant suspicion of the state expressed by capital (or businessmen) become explicable in a way that Marxists find difficult.

The next task is, starting from Lindblom's account but extending it, to construct a general theory of the role of the state within a liberal capitalist society. In doing so I shall not follow Poulantzas in regarding the state as merely a class relation (1975:pp.26,98), nor can I agree with his statement that 'The state is not an instrumental entity existing for itself, it is not a thing, but the condensation of a balance of forces', or with the assertion (Müller and Neusüss, 1978) that all political relations can be reduced to those of class. This implies that the state has no role other than that determined by class relations nor resources other than those concerned with the positions of classes. But the 'monopoly of the legitimate use of the means of violence' in Weber's (1968 edition) phrase, or the 'method of organising the public power of coercion' in Laski's (1935:ch.1) is not entirely reducible to questions of class relations. The ultimate political question, the Hobbesian problem of order, is admittedly shot through with class implications in any society divided into classes: so much of social order is concerned with the maintenance of a particular mode of production. But it is only by the most convoluted reasoning — sometimes indeed found in Marxist accounts — that *all* such questions can be interpreted as class questions.[11] The issues concerning men's access to means of violence, the attempt to concentrate this in a central power and the institutions which are then established to limit and channel that usage are questions *in themselves*. To assume them to be class questions *ab initio* involves either definitional tricks or metaphysics; in contrast to assume them to have their own social place and *then* to demonstrate that many of them become enmeshed in account of the class role of the state which is amenable to rational test.

In practice the state consists of a web of institutions which find their ultimate sanction in the monopoly of coercion, but which depend for their smooth functioning on that coercion not being wielded — hence, despite the military sound of many definitions of the state, such as those of Weber and Laski quoted above, the frequent *contrast* made between political and military forces, as, for example, in the usage of both the British government and the Republican groups in Northern Ireland. The state's personnel ordinarily have a strong interest in maintaining the stability of institutions which stand between the society and the collapse into civil war; the ease of their own jobs, the prestige of the institutions with which they are identified, ultimately perhaps their own physical safety and (in the case of elected politicians and those about them) their survival in office all depend on continuing social stability. It is that pursuit of stability which provides the clue to the ultimate motivation of state action. Most of the time this is best served by securing the interests of the existing mode of production, because it is on that that prosperity seems to rest, and in a liberal democracy prosperity is usually crucial to social stability. But all this is true, not by definition (as Poulantzas would seem to have us believe), but because it can be demonstrated by inspection of the logic of interests of those involved; and of course the latter approach does leave open the logical possibility of exceptions which attempts at establishing the case by definition automatically exclude.

The location of such a state within society is represented diagrammatically in Figure 1.1: The Responsiveness of the State to Different Class Interestsof state action (for which there may be little or no behavioural evidence) and the practices of interest groups, thereby accommodating both the two main contending schools of thought on the analysis of power.[12] Structural power is thus made manifest when the state has to favour the particular interests of a class in order to pursue certain general interests. The arrow moving from bottom right to top left reflects the fact that in order to respond to popular demands for material progress the state has to guarantee economic success, entailing dependence on capitalist interests. It is in this way that capital's interests may often be more readily served by a liberal democratic rather than an authoritarian regime; a non-democratic government will have fewer constraints preventing it from pursuing non-economic priorities, such as foreign military adventures.

One difficulty with the two right-hand boxes (indicating the strengths of the classes within polyarchy) is that the model does not assign relative weights to them. It solves the old conundrum about how it is that the essentially minoritarian interests of capital are so often able to triumph in majoritarian democracy, but how often, and under what circumstances? The question cannot be resolved at the level of general theory embarked on here, but neither should it be abdicated to

Figure 1.1: The Responsiveness of the State to Different Class Interests

Means of influence

	Structural	Elite	Polyarchic
Capital	Dependence of social stability on economic success makes necessary dependence of state on class which provides investment and manages economy	State responsive to business advice because of dependence on economic success; only capital can interpret its own needs to state Capital's superior power to organise interest groups also enables it to provide organisations taken into state's confidence	Capital's superior economic resources enable it to organise interest groups and lobbies, to control information via ownership of media, and to finance political causes favourable to its interests
Labour	Need for healthy, etc. workforce if economy is to progress makes it necessary to provide certain basic needs; similarly need for high level of mass consumption	Some minimal working-class representation on bodies administering welfare state, but cut off from any real representative role Some representation in decision-making by labour organisations, but weakened by problems of leader-member relations in mass organisations	Labour's sheer weight of numbers makes elected governments dependent on meeting some of its needs; capacity for organising parties and other representative organisations

successful use of propaganda may turn mass opinion in capital's favour

popular demands for economic prosperity strengthen politicians' dependence on capital

Class interest favoured

empirical test alone. Rather, hypotheses need to be developed about both the conjunctural and the longer-term tendencies likely to advance particular interests — such as the level of unemployment or the capacity of various groups to form coalitions at certain moments.[13]

There is less eclecticism with respect to the left-hand structural boxes. The central assumption here is that, following Lindblom, since the economy is in primarily private ownership the state is fundamentally dependent on capital for economic success. But is it possible for modifications to take place within capitalist society such that capital can only achieve *its* goals if the state also meets certain working-class interests? Or, more directly, are there cases where working-class interests have to be met if certain aims in the general interest of the society are to be successfully pursued?[14] This of course relates to two major preoccupations of this paper: the need to avoid an over-rigid conceptualisation of capitalism, recognising the possibility that varying class interests might be met within capitalism under varying conditions; and the attempt at identifying changes in class relations which might presage wide-ranging social changes that are not introduced by the *deus ex machina* of revolution.

One can envisage such historical possibilities. First, in wartime a state may be forced to pay exceptional attention to the physical welfare of the working class, going beyond the concern that it might have during normal periods of peaceful capitalist activity. This is because it is in the general interest of the war effort that particular concern be given to the class on whose backs it will be won or lost; the general interest depends on the class interest. Such cases are only temporary. More permanent and of greater consequence are all those instances, some of which were discussed above in connection with the work of Gough and O'Connor, whereby the interests of capital, or of economic development, cannot be met unless certain working-class needs which are not fulfilled by the operation of the capitalist market and which are not *per se* in the interests of capital, are met by the state: health, education, full employment, etc. Similar arguments apply to the closely associated adoption of Keynesian policies, especially in so far as these developed out of concern over underconsumption and the need to redistribute spending power away from those classes with the lowest marginal propensity to consume.

The ordinary operation of trade union strength does *not* constitute an example of the advance of working-class interests serving to advance the interests of the society as a whole — with the major exception of union wage pressure which forces companies to improve productivity in order to meet workers' demands. This is so for two reasons. First, very few wage demands serve the interests of the whole of labour; they are highly sectional and the nearer they approach the level of maximum solidarity (the shop floor) the more fragmented they become, as likely as not being financed at the expense of other fractions of the working class. Second, with the important exception mentioned, concessions to union demands do not produce any increase in the society's productive capacity; all a union or work group can offer is to cease the disruption of productive labour, a disruption which is in any case possible only because of the existence of the union or informal organisation.

A model of the relations of different classes to the state which concentrates on the structural base of class power and polyarchy alone ignores the important question of elites: the well-attested thesis that the capacity of a class to have its interests represented in the state depends on its ability to have personnel responsive to it within the relevant decision-making organs. By this 'responsiveness' one means something going beyond the automatic responsiveness guaranteed by structural factors. The state in a capitalist society will always respond to the interests of capital, but it may do so with differing degrees of precision and may vary in its responsiveness to capital's interpretation of its own needs. For example, it may always be the case that governments must acknowledge capital's concern about the impact of taxation levels on the incentive to invest, but given the difficulties of acquiring firm knowledge of the precise relationships involved, there is an area of discretion in the extent to which governments take seriously industry's complaints. It is at these points where the interpretation of interests becomes a matter of fine tuning, in areas where knowledge is imperfect, that elites become significant.

Unlike structural and polyarchic bases of power, the position of elites is derived, secondary. The fact that an interest is able to provide an elite gives it power, but that does not itself account for the power to generate the elite in the first place. This derives from positions within the two areas of political influence already identified; what an elite does is to represent the social interests made manifest through structure or polyarchy *within* the political apparatus.[15] The state responds to structural or electoral constraints impersonally and externally; the emergence of an elite representing an interest renders this personal and internal. The tendency towards 'organised capitalism' can therefore be seen as a force increasing the significance of elites. As markets become more organised there is room for more discretion in the way in which the stark necessities of an established interest are presented, while the growing intervention of the state creates a mass of organised, personal platforms for advancing the interest.

The pattern of elite operations to be expected in a liberal democratic, capitalist society are shown in the central columns of Figure 1.1. To the extent that the state intervenes actively in an area of policy it will tend to fashion, or facilitate, the formation of elites out of existing interest groups within the polyarchy. The process will tend to favour the interests of capital because of (1) the existing imbalance in the operation of polyarchy, (2) the greater difficulty of organising mass interests, including the need to develop organisations which then have their own problems of representativeness (Crouch 1977b) and (3) the fact that there will be areas where polyarchy has not extended to mass organisation, leaving elites as the normal available mode of operation of political interests. Where structural factors are concerned, the overwhelming predominance of capitalist interests has already been noted, and the significance of elites as representatives of these interests increases as capital becomes more organised. The weakness of any similar function for working-class interests is weakened further by the particular form which has been adopted in most societies for the regulation of welfare-state agencies. Typically, the rights which have been granted here are *passive* recipient rights, control resting entirely in the hands of government officials and professionals, with a very limited role given to consumer representation on purely advisory bodies in a few cases. To the very minor extent that there is some reflection of working-class interests in bodies of this kind, the problem of the difficulties of mass representation already referred to continue to apply. Overall therefore the result of elite activity is at least to reflect and probably to reinforce the responsiveness of the state to capitalist interests. To what extent it does so and in what cases it will not do so must be a matter for short-range and conjunctural theories. An important example of conditions under which capital may at least temporarily lose out in such situations would be the circumstances which led to the political predominance of British trade unions in the years 1973-6.

It is therefore possible, at the level of general theory, to construct a model of the forces represented in the state within a capitalist society which (1) accommodates the contributions of class, elite and interest group theories;[16] (2) reflects the extensive findings of Marxist literature concerning the fundamental biases in the operation of such a state; (3) provides an account of the structural determination of state policy which is not liable to the general weaknesses of functionalism; (4) enables differentiation between liberal democracy and authoritarianism;

and (5) provides for the theoretical possibility of major social change. This last point refers to the recognition within the theory of the possibility that changes can occur within the framework of a capitalist society which increase the structural power of labour. This in no way implies a theory of inevitability (whether of gradualness or of revolution); at the level of general theory it is not possible to make predictions concerning concrete historical developments. One can simply state the conditions for and implications of such changes occurring. To conclude the paper some brief consideration will be given to some *possible* developments of this kind.

The Capitalist Future; Some Brief Speculations

The liberal state exists outside civil society, acting on the latter by means of interventions and receiving inputs and reactions from the latter through representations. The recent enlargement of the role of the state has rendered its relations with civil society more close and complex than was ever provided for by these mechanisms, and many of the symptoms of 'overloaded government' reflect the strains under which they are placed. In particular, the fiscal system undertakes a vast burden of frequently contradictory tasks which hardly anybody can understand, provoking considerable popular resentment; and the network of relations between governments and interest groups becomes enormous, close and complex, overshadowing parliamentary institutions and reviving fears of the corporate state. The political right views all this as the consequence of socialism, a nightmare combination of Stalin and Mussolini. The left sees it as a symptom of the crisis of capitalism, the final removal of the liberal mask as it is forced to call on an increasingly repressive state apparatus — again reminiscences of Mussolini. This leaves what one has to call the centre, the established representatives of major interests and political office, in the curious position of maintaining a system virtually dubbed fascist by the 'extremes' on both sides. Clearly, not only is terminology confused but the actual direction being taken by events is unclear and probably varying over time. In suggesting that the situation provides some possibilities for an overall increase in the power of labour within capitalist society I am in no way attempting to predict the more likely outcome of this state of flux, but simply indicating what might occur given certain conditions, in illustration of arguments developed in earlier parts of this paper. More generally, I would certainly agree with Jessop (1978) that the period when capitalism was closely associated with liberal democracy has now closed, and that corporatist arrangements now seem most suited to its interests. The question remains, how successful can capital be in retaining control of corporatism?

The argument in outline is as follows. In liberal democracies working-class power has been kept at a largely passive level. Civil liberties, the right to organise and universal suffrage enable labour to disrupt but not to produce alternatives. So long as the disruption can be contained this suits dominant interests very well — though not as well as in a society where such concessions were unnecessary. The limitation of trade unions to oppositional bargaining might have its price in strikes and 'excessive' wage increases, but these do not challenge the essential control of industry. Financing the welfare state (and, of course, other items of public spending) through constant budget deficits might lead to inflation, but the state is thereby able to continue operating with traditional, only mildly interventionist, fiscal instruments.[17] But with the deteriorating international economic situation of recent years these costs have become increasingly burdensome. Some of course quite logically look for a solution in a roll-back of the degree of working-class power which has been gained and in at least several countries this may be what happens. However, if this proves impossible or unacceptable, there may well be moves in an opposite direction; indeed, the past few years have seen various examples. This means working-class interests gaining a far more direct role in decision-making, the concession of power being exchanged for the greater restraint in pressing demands that can be expected from interests that have a full share in making decisions.

A suitable slogan for this development would be 'no moderation without participation'. Of course, how radical this would prove to be would depend on the structure of the working-class movement and of the society concerned. For example, the West German labour movement seems to have been prepared for many years to offer considerable moderation in exchange for not very radical levels of participation; while the participation being demanded by Swedish unions, as described in this volume by Martin, is potentially very radical indeed.

Some of the ways in which the demand for participation as the price of future stability emerges can now be examined in more detail. Since the (largely half-hearted) responses of modern governments to labour's challenge primarily take the form of an albeit heavily bargained corporatsim, it is in that direction that we must first turn in order to examine possibilities.

A central problem of corporatist organisation is the arbitrariness and partiality of its representation and the unresponsiveness to popular control of its elites. In this it is often contrasted with the ostensibly fair

and universal system of representation embodied in parliament: every
adult has a vote, each vote is counted on the same system, and the
elected members work publicly through a known process of decision-
making (Moran, 1977). Of course, parliament's superiority of representativeness is largely formal. Not only does it falsely assume that the
electoral process alone determines the personnel who decide public
policy, but its claims that each vote counts equally, that members are
in some ways held to account as individuals for their behaviour at the
next election, and that the decisions of parliamentary government are
open are all invalid. Nevertheless, the system has deep legitimacy as one
providing genuine representation. It thus serves as a model against which
quasi-corporatist forms will be judged. There may therefore be pressure
for an increased participation by members of organisations involved in
corporate arrangements in the policy-making activity of those organisations, together with attempts at the extension of organisation and
participation to those outside the prevailing system of institutions. This
becomes even more important as an increasing number of social
processes are determined by organisations rather than by individual
market exchanges. In Hirschman's (1970) terms, if the chances of 'exit'
decline, it is important that opportunities for 'voice' increase. But 'voice',
active participation, is notoriously far more difficult to activate than
'exit' — it requires more effort while the outcome is less sure. A society
in which organised interests play an important role is therefore one in
which a far stronger degree of mobilisation is necessary than is usual in
capitalist societies in peacetime.

This kind of development can be highly ambiguous. Part of the
initial ambiguity of capitalist liberalism is that it offers freedom from
molestation by politics in exchange for isolation and atomisation. A
move towards a more participative society reverses this process; does
this mean the regimented mobilisation of a totalitarian society, or does
it mean the cohesive, articulated autonomy associated with community?
Partly this depends, once again, on the extent of polyarchy and the
strength of its institutions within an individual society; partly it depends
on the extent to which viable authentic communities (usually, that is,
residential, occupational and professional) form the units at the base of
the organisations. It also depends on how 'real' is the participation
being offered; if it is just a token, a means of securing loyalty through
manipulative involvements, then participation again appears in its
associations with totalitarianism. If on the other hand it marks a genuine
admission to power, to a share in the disposition of resources, it
strengthens true pluralism.

At many points throughout the advanced capitalist world initiatives of this kind have acquired political significance over the past decade: within industry, local government, educational institutions and parts of the welfare state. How significant they will prove to be it is not yet safe to predict; and whether developments in any particular case tend towards a totalitarian or polyarchic form will depend on various configurations of historical legacy, conjunctural power patterns and opportunities. However, it can be asserted that, *to the extent that* these changes do lead to a genuine increase in decision-sharing they will constitute an increase in the responsiveness of the state to working-class interests.

A different problem of quasi-corporatist organisation concerns the policy exchanges which the representatives of labour are able to secure as the price of their co-operation in the maintenance of order. The question is a large and difficult one, and attention here will be focused on one small aspect: the demand by unions for a share in industrial investment policy. The issue has been raised in several countries. Esping-Andersen *et al.*, in the paper already discussed, use it as an example of 'unreproductive-commodified-production' politics, relating it specifically to the case of Sweden, where the issue has been raised most convincingly. In so doing they lean heavily on the work of Martin (1975, 1977), whose paper in the present collection extends his analysis of the same question, relating it to the development of Keynesian policy. Investment control is clearly a crucial process in affecting the balance of class relations. As has been argued by Lindblom and discussed above, it is the state's dependence on capital's assessments of its own needs for future growth which constitutes the main basis of the overriding predominance of capitalist interests. Erosion of capital's sovereignty over investment would change this considerably; though it remains to be seen whether this can be done without an unacceptably large drop in economic efficiency.

An explicit use of Swedish experience to argue for a more flexible approach within Marxism to questions of the state and the nature of social change has been made by the Swedish sociologist Himmelstrand (1977). Adopting an approach explicitly sympathetic to that of Esping-Andersen *et al.* he concentrates on the essentially Marxist idea of the industrial forces of production becoming increasingly societal while its ownership and decision-making remain private. This is in fact rather similar to Lindblom's identification of business as a public area over which control is privately exercised. Rejecting the approaches of 'instrumentalist' and 'structuralist' Marxists as having nothing to offer in terms of a transition to socialism apart from ill-conceived attempts at maximising crisis, he defines socialism in terms of attempts at solving capitalism's problem with the societisation of productive forces. The way in which this occurs is seen as varying from society to society, and he goes on to give an account of Swedish developments essentially similar to that of Martin.

Finally, it is possible to find aspects of the fiscal crisis which lead to similar conclusions on the issue of participation to those discussed above. It is part of the compromised (or stalemated) position of the state in contemporary capitalism that it assumes a whole series of humanitarian, even compassionate, responsibilities but does so within an impersonal bureaucratic framework. Its impersonality and remoteness are enshrined in Keynesian policy; public expenditures crucial to welfare policy are provided almost as a by-product of general demand management. Recent developments in public expenditure budget forecasting may have reduced this latter factor, but they have not affected the remoteness. The population at large encounters the services either as occasional passive recipients or as continuous but equally passive contributors through taxation; it would be leaning too heavily on the fictions of parliamentary government to claim that everyone shares in actual decision-making by electing governments and local councils which in principle determine policy. Thus the state bureaucracy, by monopolising the role of provider of services, acquires a constantly increasing burden as the only organisation able to respond to needs, while the same monopolisation and remoteness lead to growing public resentment at the cost which has to be borne and at the isolation people feel from services.

As Himmelstrand remarks, it is, ironically, liberalism which creates vast state intervention, because the state is the only institution available within liberal society for expressing public purpose. Or, as Daniel Bell (1976) expresses the point from a quite different intellectual tradition, we all make increasing claims to social rights which cannot be provided through the market and which are therefore addressed to the state, but we lack any agreed rules, moral or otherwise, for determining the appropriate scope and priorities of the state (or, in his terms, public household):

> Today — and this is the distinctive change in the idea of rights, particularly the right to happiness — the satisfaction of private wants and the redress of perceived inequities are not pursued individually through the market, but politically by the group, through the public

household. Liberalism had justified the individual pursuit, free of the *polis*. Classical political theory, and its modern reformulation by Rousseau, sought to justify the primacy of the *polis*. The modern appetite wants to enhance some individuals at the expense of others, and to aggrandize all, through the public household. But the difficulty is that the public household in the twentieth century is not a community but an arena, in which there are no normative rules (other than bargaining) to define the common good and indicate conflicting claims on the basis of rights. The question again is: what can be the political philosophy of the public household? (p. 256).

Some advocates of the 'overloaded government' thesis advocate a simple roll-back of the state's activities as a solution to this problem. Bell, recognising that these activities are not so artificial and superfluous that they can be turned off like a forgotten tap, is more constructive. Rejecting the unthinking preference for the private over the public which economic liberalism requires, yet treasuring the political liberty which that same doctrine brought in its train, he asserts:

> We can reject the pursuit of bourgeois wants, as lacking a moral foundation for society, and insist on the necessity for public goods. Yet we need political liberalism to assure the individual of protection from coercive powers. . .And the arbiter of both cannot be the market — which has to be seen as a mechanism, not a principle of justice — but instead must be the public household. (p.277)

He continues:

> The idea of the public household is, then, an effort, in the realm of the polity, to find a social cement for the society.

> The centrality of the public household does not necessarily mean the expansion of the governmental economy or the administrative sector. It is, to go back to Aristotle, 'a concern more with the good condition of human beings than with the good condition of property.' (p.278)

Bell does not really provide a satisfactory solution to the problem, but his is a theme which has been echoed by other writers under the rubric of 'fraternity' (Halsey, 1978; Crick, 1978). Surprisingly, perhaps, Bell is scathing of the role of participative democracy in tackling the question, while other authors, particularly Halsey, see a crucial link between fraternity, participation and community.

What these writers are describing is an attempt at finding a third system of social regulation other than those of politics and market. This is regulation by normative ties. As a model of an entire society this is hopelessly idealistic, because the mechanism whereby norms become sufficiently strongly binding to render other kinds of constraint unnecessary can never be satisfactorily demonstrated; examples of such models include some of the nineteenth-century Catholic conceptions of corporatism and such utopian sketches as we have of social order under post-revolutionary society. On the other hand, normative regulation is not entirely absent from everyday society: it is particularly important within families, closely knit work groups and residential communities. Writers like Bell and Halsey have in mind the possibility of extending this kind of regulation to somewhat broader spheres — as the names 'public houshold' and 'fraternity' imply. Working from the original base in family and community it can be predicted that such a pattern could only be successful if it were rooted in strong interpersonal ties and in the absence of major conflicts of interests. It is not impossible that we shall see the devolution of areas of the welfare state to community-based organisations in this way, indeed in minor ways the process has started (Pahl, 1976). Governments have an interest in doing this because they want to avoid bearing the total burden, would like to tap sources of voluntary action if only to save money, and need to reduce the size of their own bureaucracy. The results of the development will be varied: at one extreme tokens of participation will quieten discontent and at least temporarily restabilise the system at little cost; but in other cases participation may result in demands for constantly increasing powers, a reduction in the alienation from the welfare state, and a consequent pressure for improved and extended services. This would mark an increase in democratisation and a greater responsiveness of the welfare state to popular demands.

These are all changes which can be seen as possibly emerging within capitalist society and which might result in shifts in the configuration of class interests. It will be argued by Marxists that in fact radical changes of this kind will not be possible, because capital will resist challenges to its domination, resulting in either suppression of the initiative or struggle culminating in revolution. For example, Offe (1975a:p. 140), while arguing on not dissimilar lines that the absence of participation is one source of current state crises, regards widespread participation as an impossible option for a capitalist society. In many cases this may well turn out to be true. The difference between the position adopted in this paper and most established Marxist theories is not an attempt to argue that peaceful social change is always possible. Rather, the differences are the following.

By looking for developments which are likely to take place within a capitalist society one will at least be able to indicate the points of tension over which conflict will arise. This is not a point which in itself causes difficulty to Marxists; indeed, for Marx himself it was an essential part of the dialectical process. The trouble is that in practice function-alist and instrumentalist Marxist theories have difficulty in finding 'space' within their highly articulated model of society in which institutions serving working-class interests can even get off the ground. This explains why, as Harloe notes with reference to the work on urban movements of Castells, the only groups regarded as having any potential for social change are the highly oppositional *groupuscules* working on the fringe of society even though, as research carried out by a group associated with Castells himself has shown (Cherky *et al.*, 1978) these are just one end of a range of groups engaged in similar activities, some of which, *within certain political systems,* have achieved a level of real institutionalised power. The trouble with marginal groups is that they rarely achieve sufficient internal stability to last more than a transitory period; they establish virtually no popular base; they develop few vested interests which will give a range of people a commitment to defending them. They are therefore poorly equipped to wage any real conflict; if they become taken up in a revolutionary movement they are unlikely to develop any independent power base within it, resulting in the familiar phenomenon whereby such groups are easily crushed by the revolutionary elite which eventually manages to seize control of the state. In contrast, groups which do secure a real footing within a capital-ist society are thereby able to acquire characteristics of permanency and strength which, while making them vulnerable to the familiar pattern of incorporation, also put them in a better position to undertake conflict if they have to.

It *may* well be the case that a capitalist society is unable to accom-modate developments which threaten the dominance of capital. But to assert that it will be so as an iron law is to go beyond the predictive ability of social science. As was discussed earlier, Marxist theory has constantly been taken by surprise by capitalism's ability to make adjust-ments previously judged impossible. Judgements as to the possibility or not of a given change being accommodated must be couched in terms of specific variables likely to predispose a particular situation one way or the other. In other words there has to be a short-range level of theory for which the more rigid functional theories cannot provide.

Notes

1. Important examples, from which the following discussion draws, are: Rose and Peters, 1977; Brittan, 1975 and 1978; Huntingdon, 1974; Buchanan and Wagner, 1977; and, to a lesser extent, Bell, 1976 and Lowi, 1975.

2. Writing before the era of economic growth which followed World War II, but in the light of earlier smaller episodes, Laski (1973: ch.2), noting that capitalist democracy 'seeks a reconciliation between the concentration of economic control in a relatively small number of persons and the widest diffusion of power', suggested that this would be impossible unless the economic system was expanding. Speaking specifically of fascism and nazism, but in terms which are apposite to current calls for a roll-back of democracy from such people as Brittan or Buchanan and Wagner, he suggested that in the event of contradiction 'the assumptions of capitalism then contradict the implications of democracy. If the phase of contraction is prolonged, it becomes necessary either to abrogate the democratic process or to change the economic assumptions upon which the society rests'.

3. For a good survey of the field see Winkler, H.A. 1974.

4. Two works standing outside the immediate past period are Beer, 1965, and Shonfield, 1965. More recent analyses include Crouch, 1977 and 1978; Grant, 1977; Schmitter, 1974 and 1977; T. Smith, 1976; Nedelman and Meier, 1977; Panitch, 1977; Lehmbruch, 1977; Anderson, C.W. 1977; Harris, 1972; Winkler, J.T. 1976; and Pahl and Winkler, 1974.

5. So also, only less explicitly, are Grant, 1977, and Shonfield, 1965.

6. Hilferding's theses are scattered in a variety of articles and speeches. H.A. Winkler, 1974, and Kocka, 1974, have reconstructed the core of this argument. His own main work was *Finanzkapital*, 1927, 4th edn.

7. In this discussion, and the rest of this paper, I refer to capital and labour as abstractions in the Ricardian sense. Some attention is given to divisions within capital, but the vast problem of divisions within labour has had to be neglected because it is not the main focus of this paper.

8. This is not to deny the enormous value of the arguments: that capital needs the state to co-ordinate it because, as an inherently fragmented, competitive system, it cannot provide its own co-ordination; and that any particular element of capital may find itself opposed to the measures the state takes in the interests of the overall system. But the liberal democratic institutions thereby constructed do provide the constant risk that forces outside capital will make use of them. It is after all no coincidence that it has been in liberal democratic capitalist societies *alone* that free trade unions, free elections based on universal adult suffrage and widespread civil liberties have developed. At the very least, capitalist interests can never be *sure* that the state will not be captured by labour; hence the extravagant measures they take to leave no areas of the polity uncovered by their own organised activities. Perhaps they would feel more confident of the strength of their position if they followed the Marxist literature on the capitalist state?

9. This is of course not the only purpose of his book, the sub-title of which is *The World's Political-Economic Systems,* and which is in no way confined to liberal democracy.

10. Lindblom (p.133) adopts the list of characteristics of polyarchy given by Dahl (1971), which includes: freedom to join and form organisations, freedom of expression, right to vote, eligibility for public office, right of political leaders to compete for support and for votes, alternative sources of information, free and fair elections which decide who is to hold top authority, and institutions for making government policies dependent on votes and other expressions of preference.

11. To reduce all social relations to class relations, as Poulantzas does, solves some problems of neatness in theory-building, but at a heavy cost. For example, to define power in terms of class relations alone is not unreasonable given the confused state of the usage of power in political science, but it leaves a vast residual category of actions which are normally thought of as constituting acts of power and which would need to be re-labelled, theoretised and related to class power.

12. That is, those of the behaviourists (who tend in practice though not by logical necessity to be 'pluralists'), e.g. Dahl, 1961 and Polsby, 1963, and those who look for evidence of power in forms other than overt political action (Bachrach and Baretz, 1970, Lukes, 1974). While the latter do not usually call themselves structuralists — Lukes, using Poulantzas as his model of a structuralist approach, is distinctly coy about being associated with them (p. 55) — the only way to account for a form of power which does not have to deploy itself in action is in terms of a theory of structural location which confers inbuilt advantages; the interest's goals are secured, not because of exceptional political activity on its part, but because the system operates in such a way that it automatically benefits.

13. As an example of the latter point, one reason for the greater success within polyarchy of the Swedish working class compared with many others was the unique opportunity enjoyed by the Swedish Social Democrats in the 1930s to form an alliance with normally conservative agrarian interests (see Martin in the present volume, p. 98)..

14. This of course means relinquishing the usual agnosticism about the possibility of there being general interests, especially in a class society. *Pace* the recent disillusion with certain forms of economic growth, I believe it can be argued that most cases of expansion in the productive capacity of a society serve a general interest, provided conditions of Pareto optimality are met.

15. That is, within liberal democracy. In authoritarian societies, where there is no polyarchy, elites are recruited from the structurally dominant classes in an unproblematic way.

16. For a useful survey of the different capacities of these three approaches, see Alford, 1975.

17. Sweden constitutes a significant exception, as Martin's essay here shows. Because of the trust the unions felt in the policies of the Social Democratic Party, based largely on close consultation and participation in decision-making, Sweden was for a long time able to pursue both Keynesianism *and* balanced budgets. The government was prepared to intervene in the economy in a more detailed way than through general fiscal policy, and the unions were sufficiently confident in the security of full employment that they developed and supported the active manpower policy. All this made it less necessary to rely on deficit financing.

2 THE DECLINE OF KEYNESIAN POLITICS[1]

Robert Skidelsky

This essay is about Keynesianism as a system of political control over economic life. My concern, therefore, is not with possible logical flaws in Keynesian theory, but with its declining ability to do political work. The analysis will concentrate on Britain; to that extent its general applicability may be limited. The political economies of some other industrial countries seem to work better than Britain's. However, the breakdown of 'world Keynesianism', the subject of a later section of this essay, is bound to have permanent repercussions on the domestic politics of all Organisation for Economic Co-operation and Development (OECD) countries.

The decline in Keynesian politics thus represents a decline in a particular method of control. Before Keynes, control of economic life was commonly discussed in terms of two alternative models — central planning and the market system. Only the second was seen as compatible with economic and political liberty. Hence a split in thought, and politics, developed between the planners and libertarians. Keynes invented a system of control *through* market relationships: his genius was to make the market, rather than bureaucracy or totalitarian parties, an instrument of a certain kind of central planning. He thus promised to make it possible for rulers to achieve politically necessary economic results without sacrificing market and political liberties (or as a Marxist might put it, without sacrificing capitalism). That is why his ideas were appropriated by the democratic elites, and could become the dominent ideology of the postwar Western world.

Today the promised economic results are not being achieved. 'Present economic conditions', notes a recent report of OECD experts, 'are obviously abnormal in terms of capacity utilisation, inflation and international payments equilibrium' (McCracken, 1977:p.11). In recent years, the Western world has experienced high unemployment, high inflation, and a recession deeper than at any time since the 1930s. Some say that this merely represents 'an unusual bunching of unfortunate disturbances unlikely to be repeated on the same scale, the impact of which was compounded by some avoidable errors in economic policy' (McCracken, 1977:p. 14). My own view is that this 'bunching' marks the decline of the Keynesian system of political control over the economy.

The optimistic view assumes that our major difficulties started in the early 1970s. But this is not so. Inflation had appeared as an insoluble and growing problem several years before. Moreover, 'already before the quadrupling of oil prices in 1973, most countries show a clearly marked association between rising inflation and rising unemployment' (Friedman, 1976:p.22). Today it is clear that Keynesian tools unaided are unable to rescue us from 'slumpflation'. Both Keynesians and non-Keynesians agree about this. The Keynesians would reflate the economy to restore full employment, relying on 'orders' to stop wage and price inflation. Non-Keynesians maintain that this would mean the end of the economic and political liberties that Keynesian politics promised to preserve. To put it another way, the trade-off between stagnation, inflation and liberty has been worsening.

My argument will be that the political decline of Keynesianism can be largely attributed to the growing inadequacy of its assumptions. Keynesians thought the only thing needed to secure rational economic policy was to convert the political managers to the new wisdom. But this assumed two things: first, that government economic policy could be insulated from political demands which conflicted with economic rationality; secondly, that, once applied, it could not be undermined by the autonomous actions of trade unions and employers. These assumptions were more or less plausible 40 years ago. They have not been so for many years. The managers have been less and less able to manipulate democracy and the market for the purposes of 'rational' Keynesian management. Specifically, manipulation has increasingly taken the form of bribery, with governments having to 'buy off' potentially hostile voters, and over-powerful interest groups. This situation signifies a more general decline in authority. Keynesian politics themselves can be seen as a stage in that decline: the government attempt to manipulate economic life as a response to the simultaneous growth of collective demands and decline in traditional class, and imperial, authority. To that extent, Keynesianism was perhaps always an unstable, or transitional, stage in the control of economies.

It is unfair to blame Keynes himself for the eventual decline of Keynesian politics. The Keynesian system has been called upon to do more political work than Keynes himself ever promised it could: it has been overloaded with demands from the politicians, themselves subject to the twin pressures of rising expectations and declining authority. On the other hand, these demands have been encouraged by the exaggerated claims of the neo-Keynesians. Keynes himself offered a fairly crude technique of bringing an economy out of a depression. The neo-

Keynesians. Keynes himself offered a fairly crude technique of bringing an economy out of a depression. Keynesians have offered a growth mechanism and a guarantee of a politically acceptable trade-off between unemployment and inflation (the so-called Phillips curve). In combination, Keynesian and neo- Keynesian techniques promised a system of economic management without costs. To be sure, economists and politicians still talked the language of choices. But these choices were seen as marginally different emphases within a framework of painless progress.

The escalation of Keynesian claims was in part a response to growing demands. But it was also the expression of the powerful faith that social science could solve problems which in the past had brought about the downfall of nations and civilisations. Growing social knowledge could be made the basis of ever more ingenious manipulations: feats of intellectual acrobatics which would reconcile not only desirable economic goals, but these with liberty and national independence. Ignored, or assumed away, were the conditions of application. It is from this perspective that I wish to examine the decay of Keynesian politics.

The Logic of Keynesianism

In defining a Keynesian logic of intervention, two points need stressing: first, the government was to determine the level of output, not what was produced, how it was produced, who produced it and to whom it went; secondly, it would achieve its aims by indirect means, through altering market choices not through direct controls. Thus Keynes says in the *General Theory* (1936: pp. 378,379) that the government's job was to secure an 'aggregate volume of output corresponding to full employment'. The market would allocate resources and rewards as hitherto. Moreover, it would achieve its aims mainly by varying disposable income, making it more or less attractive for businessmen to invest and consumers to consume. To be sure, Keynes talked about a 'somewhat comprehensive socialisation of investment'. But all he appears to have meant by this vague and alarming phrase was that the government should be prepared to augment private investment sufficiently to produce full employment. Whether, or to what extent, it would *have* to do so, experience only would show. Also Keynes thought that the state should use the taxation system to redistribute income 'in a way likely to raise the propensity to consume' (Keynes, 1936:p.373). But how much redistribution was needed was seen as an empirical question, and in any case Keynes always envisaged substantial differences of rewards.

Talking about intervention in this way made possible a new politics. Keynes's view that if demand was right, supply could look after itself (the inversion of Say's Law) undermined the socialist case for central planning and public ownership which had rested on the inefficiency and injustice of the allocative mechanism under capitalism. Secondly, the Keynesian system avoided having to choose between capital and labour. Keeping demand buoyant would underwrite both profits and employment, thus easing the conflict over the distribution of wealth. Broadly, the decision for macroeconomic as opposed to microeconomic intervention was a decision for indirect and general, as opposed to direct and detailed, economic control. Fiscal and monetary leverage by government could be reconciled with economic free will by individuals and groups: 'The invisible hand of Adam Smith's *Wealth of Nations* was not to be abandoned, but merely guided by Keynesian economic controllers' (Hirsch, F. 1977:p. 119). These decisions reflect Keynes's own political values. 'The question is', he wrote in 1939, 'whether we are prepared to move out of the nineteenth-century *laissez-faire* into an era of liberal socialism, by which I meant a system where we can act as an organised community for common purposes . . . while respecting and protecting the individual — his freedom of choice, his faith, his mind and its expression, his enterprise and his property' (quoted in Moggridge, 1974:p.69). They also express his conviction that freedom can be saved by thought. The authoritarian state systems, he wrote, 'seek to solve the problem of unemployment at the expense of efficiency and freedom. It is certain that the world will not much longer tolerate the unemployment which is associated with present day capitalist individualism. But it may be possible *by a right analysis of the problem* to cure the disease while preserving efficiency and freedom' (Keynes, 1936:p.381).

This particular way of combining freedom with control proved irresistible to liberal economists and politicians once they had grasped its point. As Galbraith (1977:p.217) put it, looking back on his Harvard days, 'Keynes had a solution without a revolution. Our pleasant world could remain; the unemployment and suffering would go. It seemed a miracle.' In Fred Hirsch's (1977:p.126) words: 'To those equally repelled by the politics of Stalin and Hitler, and by the economics of John Strachey's communists and Montagu Norman's bankers alike, the Keynesian middle way came almost as a deliverance: promising full employment and J.S. Mill too'. Marxists have seen the matter somewhat differently. Keynes's achievement was to 'protect capitalism from the revolutionary political forces capitalism has given

rise to'; Keynesianism 'turned out to be the theoretical-ideological programme that best synthesised the practical requirements of capitalism'
(Linder and Sensat, 1977: pp.244,248).

Keynes's political achievement can be fully appreciated only against
the background of the times. In 1932 Mussolini proclaimed, with some
justice, that 'all the political experiments of our time are anti-liberal'. In
an age of imperialist rivalry, war, and Depression, there was a stampede
away from the market system towards central planning, based on
authoritarian, or even totalitarian, politics. The aspect of the movement
which particularly concerns us is the one derived from the experience
of the Depression.

The most popular general explanation of the failure of the market to
maintain or restore prosperity between the wars started from the
supposed breakdown of its 'disciplines'. The argument went as follows.
The working-class movement, through its political and industrial wings,
had been able to win advances in social services and wages which had
made a large section of capitalist industry unprofitable: hence liquidation
and mass unemployment. The argument could be, and was, given an
international dimension by adding Third World revolts and the spread
of protective tariffs to the list of forces eating into capitalist profits.
This type of explanation was common to both socialist and classical
economists, grounded alike in the tradition of conflict
between the wage earner and employer over the division of income in
industry. Beatrice Webb (1948) talked, in the 1930s, of the incompatibility between 'profit-making capitalism and political democracy';
between an economic system controlled by a minority in its own
interest and a political system which gives 'workers the . . . power to
enforce demands on the national income which capitalism has neither
the ability nor the incentive to supply'. *Laissez-faire* economists like
Pareto and Hayek talked about the 'irrationality' of the masses, their
failure to understand the 'laws of economics', but they meant much the
same. Their basic complaint was that industry had been burdened with
too many costs arising from the action of democracy to make possible
profitable production in an increasingly competitive world. However,
the political conclusions following from such an analysis could take
diverse forms. The extreme left proposed to solve the conflict between
capitalism and democracy by abolishing capitalism. That section of big
business which supported fascism proposed to solve it by abolishing
democracy. Most 'men of goodwill' shrank from such extreme
conclusions. Those on the left thought capitalism should be subjected
to 'planning' and income redistribution, but not too much. Those on

the right wanted to reduce trade union power, the social services, and wages, but not by too much. Both shrank from the political implications of tampering too much with either capitalism or democracy. A whole generation of liberals was paralysed by the apparent incompatibility between effective measures for coping with economic distress and the preservation of the various freedoms — economic and political — which they still cherished. This kept them out of the communist and fascist camps; it did not give them a libertarian solution to the Depression.[2]

For that an entirely different analysis was needed. This was what Keynes provided. If for the socialist the villain of the piece was the Businessman, and for the capitalist, the Worker, for Keynes he was the Saver.

Long before Keynes had worked out a new economic theory, or even before he had recognised the existence of an economic problem, he had developed a personal philosophy which rejected the Puritan ethic of self-denial, or abstinence, in the service of the future. Of Victorian society he wrote (1919: p.12):

> The duty of 'saving became nine-tenths of virtue and the growth of the cake the object of true religion. There grew round the non-conumption of the cake all those instincts of puritanism which in other ages has withdrawn itself from the world and neglected the arts of production as well as those of enjoyment.

Thus, already in 1919, when these words were written, Keynes saw the '*duty* of saving' as the main obstacle to production, consumption and enjoyment. The most scornful passages in his economic and non-economic writings are reserved for the 'hoarding instinct' which, he suggested, future ages would treat as 'a somewhat disgusting morbidity, one of those semi-criminal, semi-pathological propensities which one hands over with a shudder to the specialists in mental disease' (Keynes, 1931:p.369).

By this route, Keynes approached his own explanation of the British — and to a lesser extent the world — Depression. The villain had been identified; it remained to incorporate him into economic analysis. Society, Keynes argued, was saving too much for reduced private invest-investment possibilities. The high propensity to save was partly due to the hold of the Puritan psychology which still enforced abstinence on all classes; it was partly institutionalised in the great inequality of wealth which lowered the propensity to consume, and in government policies which aimed at the smallest possible budgets in order to encourage private accumulation. As an economist, Keynes, of course, recognised the importance of saving for progress, though he thought that its importance even in this respect had been exaggerated. But with the passing of the exceptionally favourable private investment opportunity of the 19th century, social organization for a 19th century level of saving was giving the market system a permanent bias towards deflation and unemployment. Government policy had compounded the trouble by too rapidly reducing public spending from its high wartime levels and by returning Britain to the prewar gold standard which overpriced British exports and reduced home activity by forcing up the rate of interest. Keynes offered a whole outfit of remedies: the stimulation of consumption by transferring wealth from high saving to high spending groups; the stimulation of private investment by bringing down the rate of interest; and the use of public spending to fill any shortfall which remained.

Workers and manufacturers had only walk-on parts in Keynes's play: they were victims alike of a malign interaction between a bloated rentier class and financial institutions geared to vanishing investment outlets.[3] Provided domestic investment and consumption could be propped up, a secure basis would be provided for class collaboration in an increasingly affluent future. There was no need to smash either capitalism or democracy. All that was necessary was for government to create more favourable market conditions which would induce business-men to invest. This could be achieved by manipulating certain key economic variables; it did not require the abolition of any existing institutions, or direct controls over economic activities. Keynes's very different analysis of the problem thus suggested a way of overcoming it without recourse to either communism or fascism.

Marxist and some classical economists had both attributed the Depression to the growing strength of the working-class movement eating into employers' profits. By arguing that both employment and profit were subject to a deflationary tax imposed by 'savers', Keynes had produced a different explanation, showing how the Depression could be overcome without totalitarian politics. But it could be argued that he merely postponed the day when democracy and capitalism would collide. Marxists were forced to admit that there had been more slack in the system than they had allowed, a slack which could be taken up by Keynesian measures. But once 'over-saving' had been removed, then the final struggle for the division of the cake would begin. With resources fully employed, working-class gains could be achieved only at the expense of employers' profits. Keynesian policy might take an economy from an underemployment equilibrium to full employment. But it had yet to show that it could keep it there without direct controls.

The faith that Keynesian measures would be able not only to cure unemployment in the short-run, but also to provide stability in the long-run, rested on two beliefs. The first was that governments, equipped with the new macro-economic tools, would be willing and able to manage demand 'rationally' — that is, not to run the economy at too low or too high a demand. The second was that there would be enough of a market for market manipulation to work. In other words, the political electorate, pressure groups, trade unions and big business must not be able to impede either the formulation or the effects of an economic policy made by Keynesian experts. A strong state and a free economy were indispensable conditions of libertarian Keynesianism. Keynes himself (1936:p.245) took as 'given' the 'social structure' and the 'degree of competition'. These were important qualifications.

Before considering what has happened to them, one further point must be made. Although the *General Theory* was written in 1936, the Keynesian system of political economy was launched during World War II. The association of infant Keynesianism with a 'war economy' is very important, many of the working assumptions of the Keynesians about what could be done in a democracy deriving from this rather special period. War not only produced, for the first time, a budget large enough to act as economic controller, but also eliminated, or greatly minimised, budgetary politics, since there existed clear priorities imposed by the war itself. It brought together Capital and Labour in a spirit of wartime unity and sacrifice. Finally, it replaced the international anarchy of the interwar years by an Anglo-American directorate. These were the real world conditions in which the Keynesian system was first applied. We must now turn to the underlying assumptions.

The Political Context of Keynesianism

Galbraith's chapter on Keynes in his book *The Age of Uncertainty* is headed 'The Mandarin Revolution'. This implies Keynes's most characteristic belief: that public affairs should and could be managed by an elite of clever and disinterested public servants. He shared this belief with eminent contemporaries like William Beveridge. Keynes remained rooted in the Edwardian tradition of reform 'above class' through the agency of a benevolent state serviced by a technocratic elite.

not, because the political, unlike the economic, consumer is not subject to a budget constraint. In the case of collective wants, consumers' preference is established not by individual purchase, but through the voting system. But the voting system does not establish the appropriate revenue basis for the expressed preference. Since spending programmes are popular, and the taxes to pay for them unpopular, a highly competitive political system has an inbuilt tendency to make inadequate budgetary provision for enlarging social expenditures. The result is inflation. To monetarists especially it is political competition which them it is political competition which produces 'excess demand.'[5]

On its own, this theory of how policy is formed is inadequate. Nineteenth-century political systems were competitive but fiscally conservative. It is not competitors for the votes of a largely propertyless electorate which has reversed this tendency. Nor should we overlook the growth of humanitarian sentiment among the wealthy which tended in the same direction. There is a further point. The simple model of economic democracy assumes 'the continuing responsiveness of the government to the preferences of its citizens' (Dahl, 1971:p.1), just as economic entrepreneurs are assumed to be continuously responsive to consumer preferences. But clearly this is not so. Political elites, acting together, often keep issues out of politics. Political leaders will sometimes act against popular wishes for the sake of the 'public good' or for moral reasons, whereas even business monopoly never acts against the wishes of consumers. Then there is the relative autonomy of the professional bureaucracy, and the role of minority pressure groups. Finally, it may be that politicians are unduly timid without cause: that on economic questions they wrongly assume that the people who vote for them are as shortsighted as they are. The picture is therefore considerably more complicated than the simple model of economic democracy would suggest.

Nevertheless, the correlation between the growth of democracy and the growth of public spending is too striking to be ignored. This suggests that the remaining immunity of elites from democratic controls in some areas is purchased by their ability to provide 'bread and circuses.'[6] With the new Keynesian tools, economies can be managed so as to win elections. According to Hutchison (1968: pp.121-2) R.A. Butler's budget of April 1955:

was the first time that the immensely heightened post-war economic power of government has been operated, with such successful timing, in harmony with electoral considerations. . . . The second half of the fifties saw the first, exquisitely timed, example of the political business cycle, bringing to the Conservatives a third electoral success running.

Such a process tends to be inflationary. The argument can be put more generally. With the decline of authority, politicians can govern only through 'bribery'. But control through bribery has economic costs which control based on authority does not. It is a more expensive technique of government, and the expenses are met through printing money.

However, democratic pressures cannot provide the whole explanation for growing social spending. As Lindblom (1977:p.124) has pointed out 'democratic and communist regimes do not differ greatly with respect to public expenditures on health and welfare as a percentage of gross national product'. Where communist regimes score is in their ability to choose between these and other objects of spending, particularly consumer spending. The role of the competitive political struggle in democracies may be less to exaggerate collective demands than to make it more difficult for democratic governments to choose between finite resources.

War has been a powerful stimulus to the growth of public spending. Although, as Peacock and Wiseman have argued, wars create a tolerance for higher taxation, no wars have ever been paid for by taxes alone. As a result of the state of international relations, military spending as a proportion of GNP has been greatly enlarged during this century; in all the big Western nations there exist powerful military lobbies. Theoretically, military spending could and should have been at the expense of consumer spending or social services; but democratic governments have been under almost irresistible pressure to provide both guns *and* butter; the Johnson administration's unwillingness to raise taxes to pay for the Vietnam war is the most striking recent example.

Again, the need of industrial societies for publicly, as well as privately, provided goods seems constantly to grow. This was the basis of the so-called Wagner's Law of Rising State Expenditures, formulated a hundred years ago (Bird, 1971). It can be applied to contemporary conditions. More and more private goods demand complementary public investment, e.g. the growing use of motor cars greatly increases the need for modern highways. Urban concentration calls for large municipal programmes. The increased need for skilled labour places

higher demands on education. The government has to underwrite
advanced technology. In other words, the cost to government of maintaining the national economy — of getting businessmen to perform their
functions, of maintaining a reasonable environment, of facilitating
growth — seems to have been steadily rising, with state policy a prey to
increasing numbers of special interest groups. In practice, democratic
governments have tried to avoid the choices involved through reliance
on growth. Successive British governments have promised increases in
the public services to be paid for out of projected growth rates which
proved totally unrealistic.

Finally, Rose and Peters (1977:pp.6,7) draw attention to what they
call the 'inertia claims of public policy'. As they put it 'The costs of
public policy do not reflect the current choices of the day, but past
decisions. They are commitments embodied in laws authorising and
requiring government to spend annually for stated purposes ... Any
newly elected government is immediately committed to them, unless
it wishes to risk the political odium of repealing measures providing
benefits that millions of citizens have come to expect'. The budget, in
other words, is controlled by history, not by Keynesian managers.
Politicians' promises have to be met by increasing, not redistributing,
spending. And in the absence of adequate growth, governments are tempted
to resort to inflation as an alternative to cutting public spending elsewhere
or raising the necessary taxes.

To sum up this section of the argument, governments have been
driven by electoral competition, by events, and by structural changes
in the economy to take an increasingly active part in economic life.
But this does not make them rational managers in the Keynesian sense.
According to Keynes, fixed rules were supposed to be replaced by
executive discretion in framing economic policy. Instead the budget
has become 'overloaded' with claims. Put another way, this marks a
decline of traditional control mechanisms, thus increasing the costs of
governing. Today's governments have more responsibility but less
discretion than Keynes envisaged.

Problems of Keynesianism

Keynesian politics assume two things: that governments have enough
autonomy to be able to act rationally; and that there is enough of a
market for market manipulation to work. They can break down if
either of these assumptions is false. Either powerful interests can distort
the making of policy; or they can have enough independence from
market forces to disregard policy which does not suit them. In practice,

both occur to produce a malign interaction. Powerful trade unions can price products and labour out of competitive international markets. Businesses and unions can then force governments, afraid of industrial collapse, to subsidise unemployment. Thus a trade union induced inflation can trigger off a 'demand' inflation as governments try to save industries and jobs.

Keynes himself ignored institutions as an independent cause of inflation. 'True inflation' was caused by excess demand. However, he also said (1936:pp.301,303) that 'semi-inflation' might arise short of full employment, due to supply scarcities and a general pressure for higher wages as conditions improved, while admitting that 'they do not readily lend themselves to theoretical generalisations'. In fact, the relationship between 'true inflation' and 'semi-inflation', and the possibly differing causal mechanisms underlying them, was never satisfactorily cleared up. Keynes's own uncertainty did suggest, however, that he might have been prepared to run the economy at less than full employment to retain some element of wage and price discipline. Robinson has argued that it is impossible to know 'what Keynes's personal "trade-off" would have been between high employment, inflation and curtailment of economic liberties' (Hutchison, 1977:p.59). Hutchison has suggested (1977: pp.14,44) that in 1937 Keynes wanted to level off economic expansion with unemployment at 11-12 per cent. Kahn (1974) disagrees: Keynes th(the economy could be safely expanded until the unemployment figure dropped to 6 or 7 per cent; however, both percentages are below what postwar Keynesians would have regarded as a sustainable level of full employment. Basing itself on the Phillips curve, the British Treasury assumed in the late 1950s that stable prices could be achieved with an unemployment level of 1.8 per cent. This was the politically acceptable promise made by the postwar Keynesian managers. It turned out to be illusory. In the mid 1970s, with unemployment in the Western world rising to 5 or 6 per cent, and inflation in double figures, it was clear that the Phillips curve was dead. Clearly the trade-off had worsened, if indeed it had ever existed in stable form. According to Galbraith, Keynes's macroeconomic revolution had run foul of the microeconomic revolution in trade union and corporate power.

There are many variations on this theme. For some left-wing writers, inflation is largely a product of monopoly pricing by multinational corporations. This is part of a more general argument that multinational business has largely escaped from the control of national governments and national policy. Multinational enterprise, it is said, can insulate itself from monetary and fiscal policy by access to the Eurodollar market and by transfer pricing. The apportionment, by multinationals, of production between subsidiaries in different countries according to a long-term plan impedes a nation's efforts to increase exports through devaluation, or retain jobs by special incentives. It has been widely argued that in slow-growing countries, multinationals have become agents for exporting jobs rather than goods (Holland, 1975, especially ch.2 and pp.61-4).

In fact, the situation is more complicated. Keynesian policy was supposed to create market conditions sufficiently attractive to produce a full employment level of profitable investment. If production is being transferred from country A to country B this can only be because country A fails to provide a sufficiently profitable environment to retain domestic business. The flight of capital and jobs no doubt makes the problem cumulatively worse, but it seems perverse to blame the multinationals for the original situation. The explanation for the failure lies elsewhere. No one understands the underlying reasons for the rundown of a national economy, why one society grows faster than another. But a proximate reason for the flight of capital must be the behaviour of the workforce. In particular, inflationary pricing by firms may well be a response to inflationary wage settlements. According to Glyn and Sutcliffe (1972), the inflationary spiral originates not in monopoly pricing but in working-class pressure for higher wages which forces businessmen to put up prices in order to maintain customary profit margins. The greater the wages pressure in a particular economy, the higher its prices relative to other countries', and the weaker its competitive position.[7] The basic point here is that inflationary pricing is a sign of capitalist weakness, not strength. It marks the breakdown of the market and social disciplines that previously restrained wage demands. It is union, not business, power which aborts the Keynesian attempt to secure a non-inflationary full employment policy.

The upsurge of working-class power can be analysed in a number of different ways. Strict economic analysis would concentrate on the growth of monopoly in the supply of labour through greater unionisation, the related growth of industry-wide bargaining, guaranteed full employment, and technological interdependence which enables small groups of workers to 'hold the community to ransom'. But models of monopoly cannot provide the whole answer; as has been pointed out, only a proportion of the workforce is unionised; and of that proportion a large number are members of unions with no monopoly power. Therefore it is not simply the enhanced bargaining power of the unions alone: it is their willingness to use that power to win greater incomes for their members: and the greater militancy of workers as individuals. This in turn stems from changes in social attitudes: the so-called revolution of rising expectations which demands constant wage increases irrespective of productivity gains; the erosion of Puritanism; the breakdown of deference (not least towards collaborationist trade union leaders); the decline of patriotism – a point particularly stressed by Mishan (1974:pp.19ff.); the growth of egalitarian sentiment; alienation; and so on.[8]

Against this, it is sometimes argued that workers' actions are essentially defensive. Each group of workers seeks to defend its relative position. Thus 'changes in the money-wage on one particular group ... could trigger off a leap-frogging type of wage spiral' (Lal, 1977:p.33; Kahn, 1974:p.30). Exogenous increases in the cost of living, whether produced by 'excess demand' or rising import prices, could have the same effect if the expectation was that a particular group of workers would try to maintain its real wage in the changed circumstances. Central to this type of analysis is the view that relative wage rates are fixed not by market bargains but by history. Workers will resist any changes in their relative positions.

There is no logical contradiction between these two mechanisms: in fact they can be, and are, mutually reinforcing. A drive to improve the position of the working class as a whole can quite easily coexist with a defence of historical relativities. Indeed, one could argue that it is precisely this combination of radicalism and conservatism that has given such a powerful inflationary bias to British pay settlements.

Early Keynesian politics had little need to take account of such disturbing long-term trends. Middle-class policy-makers took it for granted that deference would continue to sustain profits. This was reinforced by the wartime spirit of disciplined national unity and postwar working-class acceptance of 'austerity' at the hands of a Wykehamist chancellor of the exchequer. It could not survive the consumption-based, full employment, capitalist economy which emerged in the following two decades. It was the breakdown of working-class 'restraint' that prompted British and other Western governments to start experimenting with pay policies. But it is wrong to see such policies, as radical Keynesians tend to, as natural extensions of Keynesian politics. From the point of view of Keynesian theory it does not matter whether Keynesianism is applied through economic manipulation or political controls. But this ignores the political function of Keynesian ideas. Keynesian politics became generally acceptable because they were manipulative, not coercive. If Keynesianism moves to coercion it loses its basic political function, its ability to provide consensus. Authoritarian Keynesians become planners; libertarian Keynesians become free marketeers. The basic conflict which postwar Keynesian politics seemed to have transcended returns again, as planning and freedom stand once more opposed. And this is now starting to happen.

The Decline of 'World Keynesianism'

The decline of domestic Keynesian politics has its counterpart in the decay of American-controlled 'world Keynesianism'. Authority has decayed internationally as well as nationally. The disarray of the international economy has crucial repercussions on the viability of domestic Keynesian politics. Interwar Marxists added international rivalries — between capitalist nations, and between the metropolis and the periphery — to their list of insoluble capitalist contradictions. Keynes rejected the Marxist explanation of interwar capitalist crisis both in its domestic and international aspects. In place of imperialist rivalries, he substituted, as explanation, a global deflationary tendency brought about by American and French 'oversaving' — their stockpiling of gold. If this could be reversed, through demonetising gold, or other measures for increasing international liquidity, then there would be enough world demand to keep all the nations at full employment. Some international authority had to be established capable of performing these functions. As it turned out, they devolved upon the United States. The decay of world Keynesian politics has been parallel to the decline of domestic Keynesian politics, and for similar reasons. The United States administration has not been able to act as a 'rational' Keynesian manager; and it has lost control over the international economy in much the same way as domestic governments have lost control over their own economies.

To amplify these points we must go back to the origins of the postwar international order. For much of the interwar years Keynes was an economic nationalist. He opposed the restoration of the gold standard on nationalist grounds. He became a convert to Protectionism in the early 1930s for the same reasons. He even offered a qualified defence of mercantilism in chapter 23 of the *General Theory*. One theme runs through all these nationalist writings: the passing away of the special conditions which had harmonised the nineteenth-century world economy. Chief among those conditions was Britain's supremacy. Britain had 'managed' interdependence to its own and the world's advantage; had 'conducted the international orchestra' as Keynes put it (1930:p.307). World *laissez-faire* was made possible by British leadership.

Kindleberger has elaborated this argument. An international economy is harmonised not by free trade and capital movements, as in classical theory, but by the ability and willingness of a preponderant power to 'underwrite' it. This underwriting, or leadership, consists of four elements: maintaining an open market for imports, providing counter-cyclical lending, co-ordinating macroeconomic policies, and discounting in crisis; in short, preventing deflation (Kindleberger, 1976: p.32). From this follows an explanation of the disorders of the interwar years:

> The world economic system was unstable unless some country stabilised it, as Britain had done in the nineteenth century and up to 1913. In 1929, the British couldn't and the United States wouldn't. When every country turned to protect its national private interest, the world public interest went down the drain . . .

In other words, an economic harmony maintained by the exertions of single power gave way to economic anarchy, which in turn spilled over into political anarchy (Kindleberger, 1973).

As an explanation of why the world economy broke down between the wars this is broadly acceptable, with one modification. Something more than just American reluctance was involved in its failure to assume leadership in this period. The power vacuum to which Kindleberger alludes reflected a genuine fragmentation of power. This had its roots in the spread of industrialisation, nationalism, and imperialism in the last quarter of the nineteenth century. Between the wars, the United States, the British Empire, France, Germany, Japan, and Italy all functioned as independent great powers in the capitalist world; by which I mean powers capable of conceiving their future in terms of independent empires or blocs, supported by their own industrial and military weight. It was World War II which tested, and put to an end, these pretensions for all but the United States, thus making possible an American hegemony over the capitalist world. It is against this background that Keynes's economic nationalism — and his rediscovery of internationalism — has to be set.

It was the war which created the opportunity to 'apply Keynesian thought on a world scale' (Harrod, 1951: pp.525,526). The outcome of the war had concentrated military, political, industrial, and financial power on the Anglo-American alliance. This made possible a 'single act of creation' to restore internationalism. A World Central Bank would become, in Keynes's words, a 'genuine organ of international government', the 'embryonic economic government of the world' (Gardner,

1969:p.xxix) Keynes, of course, recognised that American was the predominant partner, but he hoped that British expertise and authority would counterbalance American power. Specifically, British 'brains' were to manage American 'money' for the public good in an updated version of the *Pax Britannica*.[9] The seat of the new world government was to be London. It was a fascinating vision, very much in the Roman tradition of British imperial statesmanship.

The famous Keynes Plan of 1942 called for an International Clearing Bank to keep accounts for central banks in much the same way as the central bank of each country keeps accounts for the commercial banks. The new bank would make available large overdraft facilities to its members related to their countries' share of world trade. The total overdraft facilities would be the total surpluses of member nations on their balance of trade. Surpluses and deficits in member countries' balances would be registered as credits and debits in the accounts of the Clearing Bank, denoted in an international currency 'bancor'. No country could draw more than its quota, but debtors would be automatically provided with temporary overdrafts, while they (hopefully) put their houses in order. Thus deflation could be avoided, and the capitalist world kept on a fixed-exchange, but full-employment, standard.[10]

Like domestic Keynesianism, this was a political programme to be achieved by economic means. Bancor was Keynes's answer to Stalin, to war, and to formal empire. It epitomised his philosophy of indirect control. And the general concept (though not the details) was taken up precisely because it promised to harmonise the interests of nations, just as domestic Keynesianism promised to reconcile the interests of classes.

The flaw in the system was that the concentration of power produced by the war was a purely temporary reversal of a longer-term decline of European imperialism in particular and the authority of the white races in general. The Communist bloc (soon to be enlarged) withdrew from the American-dominated arrangements, thus preventing them from ever achieving an ideological hegemony. The old European colonial empires were in full dissolution. American policy encouraged this process, failing to realise that imperial authority had provided the essential political framework for world capitalism, which itself was unable to establish any acceptable structure of international authority. Dollar imperialism or even military protection was never an adequate substitute for the 'archaic' imperial cement, because its benefits were too unevenly spread to provide a basis for harmony. Keynes's international vision, like his domestic vision, was based on assumptions already becoming obsolete.

The decline of 'world Keynesianism' can be considered in two aspects. The first was the failure of the United States to play its allotted role as disinterested midwife. Keynes had hoped to divorce American surpluses from American power, making them automatically available to debtors like Britain. The Americans intended to use their surpluses as instruments of their power, supplying dollars on such terms, and in such amounts, as would suit their security and business interests. This was the meaning of Harry Dexter White's successful counterproposal at Bretton Woods for an International Monetary Fund, under which both America's liabilities and debtors' drawing rights were drastically pruned. With the 1946 Loan to Britain, and Marshall Aid, the world economy was refloated on a dollar, not a bancor, standard. Keynes's attempt to multilateralise reserve and liquidity creating functions on a purely technical banking basis had failed. World prosperity was tied to the strength of the dollar, domestic American politics, and the political-military role of the United States. But America was simply not a dominant enough force in world economics to sustain indefinitely such a *tour de force*. In fact, and here we come to the second aspect, its economic capacity to sustain its world role progressively weakened, as old centres of economic power revived, and new ones developed.

The index of this weakening was the structural deficit which started to develop in the American balance of payments following the currency realignments of 1949; a deficit which gave its economic management an inflationary bias. The technical feature which made this possible was the position of the dollar as the universal 'intervention' currency. America alone was on the gold standard; other countries' international reserves were held mainly in dollars. Thus as long as those countries were willing to hold dollars, America had the right to create as many of them as it wanted. The substantive reason for the deficit was that America's political-military role as 'leader of the free world', plus the overseas expansion of American multinationals, produced a level of foreign spending in growing excess of America's receipts from its exports, or other sources.

Here its position was very different from Britain's in the nineteenth century. Britain underwrote the nineteenth-century economy from a position of surplus, even though the pound was as 'good as gold'. But Britain had two advantages which America lacked. As the major manufacturing nation, for most of the century, in a world of primary producers, Britain's surplus tended to be self-sustaining, its foreign loans financing the export of British goods. Secondly, Britain was able to raise taxes from its empire, especially India, to sustain its world role. (British military spending was, of course, proportionately much lower than that of the United States after 1945.)

America's hegemony was never so securely based. In a world of manufacturing economies, America's surpluses were self-liquidating, foreign investment simply building up competitive manufacturing capacity in other countries. Nor, without a direct empire (or perhaps more importantly, imperial legitimacy) could it impose an imperial tax to pay for its overseas military spending. Thus an economy weakening in international terms found itself meeting its global commitments (and aspirations) by exporting not goods but increasingly worthless paper money. The situation was allowed to develop because there was no obvious alternative. On the one side, American outflows, as Kaldor (1971) has remarked, 'provided the rest of the world with a steady increase in international purchasing power', thus fuelling postwar prosperity, albeit at some inflationary cost. On the other side, they financed an American military protectorate which was regarded as highly beneficial. Any drastic cut in American foreign military spending would shift the defence burden on to such surplus countries as Germany and Japan, neither of whom, in view of their past record, were acceptable as political and military leaders. While, therefore, the postwar system weakened America, it did not throw up any obvious heirs-apparent.

The policy of 'benign neglect' was generally acceptable as long as the inflationary costs were limited, and the Russian threat remained credible. Both these conditions changed in the 1960s. From 1965 onwards, the American deficits increased sharply as the foreign exchange costs of empire escalated with the Vietnam war. Parallel with this, France's De Gaulle took advantage of the East-West 'thaw' to challenge the American hegemony over Western Europe. By attacking the right of seigniorage, and by converting dollars into gold, France undermined the ideological and financial basis of American control. Even more significant in the long term was the growing restiveness of the developing world. Here again, America had given the decisive push with its anti-colonialism and its championship of economic growth. Lacking an ideology of empire, the United States could create neither a domestic nor an international framework compatible with its own continuing hegemony.

It was American-European rivalry which brought about the downfall of the Bretton Woods system. As the dollar weakened, a massive flight from the currency developed. In 1970, the reserve transactions deficit shot up to $10b (US); in 1971 to $30b. In face of this, Nixc devalued the dollar in August 1971. The new Smithsonian parities of December 1971 failed to stick, and since 1973 the world has been on a regime of floating exchanges. These currency realignments registered the shifts in economic power without rejuvenating the American position. By providing for a devaluation of the dollar and a revaluation of the strong European countries they were intended to restore the economic basis of American leadership. But they failed to solve the problem of American uncompetitiveness. Monetary power continued to accumulate in Germany and Japan, while military power remained concentrated in the United States. The result was a stalemate system, with no leadership to harmonise or overrule conflicting interests.

The emergence of the OPEC cartel in 1973-4 opened up a second field of international conflict — over the price and supply of raw materials. Western industrial civilisation has depended crucially on access to cheap food and raw materials, which Western power guaranteed. The great oil companies were typical institutions of informal empire, able to combine high profits and selling prices favourable to the West. The formation of the Organisation of Petroleum Exporting Countrie (OPEC) cartel, and its willingness to use its bargaining power, mark an important stage in the loss of control by the West over its economic environment, paralleling the rise of organised producer interests within domestic economies.

The growth of these independent centres of power has already hugely complicated the task of macroeconomic co-ordination. The speculation against the dollar was partly responsible for the hectic inflationary boom of 1972-3; the OPEC price rise of 1973-4 produced the worst recession since the 1930s, while exacerbating a 'cost push' inflation as Western businesses and trade unions tried to maintain profits and wages in face of escalating energy prices. Selfish initiatives by the Europeans and Arabs can be said to have jeopardised the world public good; but the point is that nations or groups of nations are now in a position to take such initiatives, and also veto any steps to re-orchestrate the world economy. With the world economy torn asunder by short-term conflicts of national interest, as well as by the growing North-South split, the ideological basis of such reorchestration is not very apparent. Meanwhile, the American-dominated international system limps on in a kind of limbo between inflation and depression; poised between 'a decaying hegemony and a reluctant pluralism' (Calleo, 1976:p.xv).

Conclusions

The decline of Keynesian politics seems to me demonstrable; it is foolish, because impossible, to predict what will take their place. So I will end by summarising my argument, developing it at one or two points and listing (somewhat summarily) the various possible types of 'new politics'.

Many thoughtful pre-Keynesians attributed the interwar crisis to the class struggle. The extreme left wanted to resolve it by abolishing capitalism; the extreme right, by suppressing the democratic movement. Liberals who saw both capitalism and democracy as bulwarks of liberty shrank from extreme solutions, but had none of their own. Keynes suggested a different way of analysing the problem. He attributed the crisis to 'over-saving' by rentiers and financial institutions; by proposing to remedy this through fiscal and monetary measures alone, he suggested a way of restoring profitability and full employment without sacrificing economic or political freedoms. That is why the Keynesian system could become the basis of a new politics. Today, this system is in decay, unable to overcome 'slumpflation', domestic and international.

Once more, many Marxist and non-Marxist economists find themselves in diagnostic alliance. A further shift in class power away from capitalism and imperialism is making capitalism unprofitable and therefore unworkable. For example, one Marxist writer has written of 'the fundamental decline in profitability which occurred in several countries in the 1970s, itself a reflection of growing labour strength at a time of heightened international competition' (Gough,1975:p.87) — a thought which is certainly present in the minds of many capitalist spokesmen. So one side looks once more to 'democracy' to abolish capitalism; the other looks to the state to limit 'democracy'. In between stand the 'men of goodwill' who hope for miracles of international co-operation to pull us through, much like Ramsay MacDonald did in 1933.

My survey suggests that class struggle is secondary in the Keynesian decline. That the industrial malaise often takes the form of capitalist unprofitability and worker militancy is not itself surprising. One would still need to establish that working-class militancy was directed against capitalism as such, and give grounds for believing that a libertarian non-capitalist system would organise production more successfully. The evidence for the first proposition, at least, is shaky. For example, in their empirical survey of British political attitudes, Butler and Stokes (1971:pp.126-8) found that while class identifications

were still strong, the image of politics as representing *opposing* class
interests has declined.[11]

British capitalism has also had to carry a unique burden of cumulative economic failure. This has undoubtedly worsened class relations.
There has not been enough growth to satisfy rising claims. Capitalism
has been blamed. But to attribute the historical decline of Britain to
the class struggle, as Marxists have done, is to go much too far. A
society's success or failure cannot be identified with one institution,
one set of social relationships, however important. One of the striking
features of modern British history has been the hold of pre-capitalist
attitudes and social relations among all sections of the community.
These, even more than market benefits and disciplines, held British
society together. It is their sudden breakdown under the impact of
affluence which, arguably, has created the authority crisis of British
society. As I shall argue in a moment, there is no obvious sociological
or ideological heir-apparent.

Marxist writers incline to attribute the 'fiscal crisis' of the modern
state to the 'contradictions' of capitalist production. The growth of
monopoly capitalism intensifies the tendency to over-production,
leading to unemployment and crisis. To legitimise capitalist relations,
the state has to plug this growing gap by increasing state expenditures:
hence the 'warfare-welfare' state. Since this spending is largely unproductive of further revenues, the budget deficit tends to grow
(O'Connor, 1973). This type of argument goes back to Rosa
Luxembourg. Gough (1975) has challenged the emphasis on the
structural tendency to over-production, highlighting instead the role
of the class struggle. Both interpretations ground the 'fiscal crisis' in
the economic base, rather than in the political superstructure. However,
the problem may be caused by democratic politics as such. Political
demands have always been largely economic demands — claims on
resources which cannot go round. In the absence of political (and
industrial) democracy, such demands can be suppressed or rationed
by the powerholders. In democratic societies this rationing process is
much more difficult. Communist societies can hold down consumption
not because they have abolished capitalism, but because they have
abolished the multi-party system, the free press, and the right to strike.
They have established political conditions for capital accumulation not
dissimilar from those which existed in the nineteenth century. The
Utopian element in much contemporary socialist analysis comes from
believing that if the economic base were changed accmulation could be
restored or increased consistently with democratic freedoms. My own

view, rather, is that if socialism does solve the economic problem, it will do so as a power system, promising Utopia, while dismantling the possibilities for opposition.

The view that the present crisis arises from the class struggle can be challenged on different grounds. In the Marxist picture, capitalist civilisation will succumb to a growing and unified working class, with a coherent and explicit revolutionary ideology. Neither of these conditions applies in most Western societies.

The working class, too, is subject to dissolution. The further progress of the division of labour produces not a Marxist simplification into proletarians and capitalists, but increasing occupational diversity, leading to growing conflicts of interests, values, understandings, and life-styles. Populations today are much more heterogeneous than they were even 20 or 30 years ago. This makes it much more difficult to 'aggregate' them into political or industrial units. The expansion of the trade union movement under such conditions is deceptive. Trade unionism becomes not an army organised for battle against capitalism, but an arena where group conflicts are fought out. The same is true of the big political parties, which either become incoherent or start splitting up. There is something of a paradox here. The immediate beneficiaries of weakening class politics have been new political groupings based on religion, nation, race. But barring some catastrophic disorganisation in the productive system, these cannot be permanent beneficiaries; nor can class regain its former political importance. The factory proletariat is now too narrow a social base on which to erect an alternative authority structure; and working-class leadership is subject to the same process of eroding authority as are other elites. In fact, it is not easy to detect any new stable bases of political allegiance. The difficulty of making modern societies work arises more from the breakdown of cohesion than from any expansion and solidification of an anti-capitalist proletariat.

It is perfectly true that modern bourgeois societies have what Daniel Bell calls an 'adversary culture', one hostile to accumulation. But it is far from being a 'counter-ideology' in the traditional Marxist or socialist sense. Rather, it rejects all technocratic-rationalist goals, whether capitalist or Marxist. The adversary culture is anti-rationalist, subjective, hedonist, geared more to radical life-styles than radical causes. These in turn have been packaged for mass consumption by the entertainment industry, whose film and pop stars, television and showbiz personalities have replaced politicians and philosophers as the chief gurus of our time. Such genuine political protest movements as have arisen since the war, particularly the ecology and environmental movements, explicitly reject the materialist premises of both classical capitalist and Marxist philosophy. Even political violence has become largely a mode of self-expression rather than a rational means to political ends. No doubt these developments increase the 'contradictions' of capitalism; they will produce equal contradictions in successor regimes of the extreme left which preserve bourgeois liberties.

It may nevertheless be argued that non-capitalist systems will reduce some of these tensions by abolishing one major source of irrationality and injustice: private production for profit. But judging from quite recent historical experience they will substitute others: the irrationality of central planning, the injustice of bureaucratic privilege. These will cause equal resentments, which will have to be suppressed if the system is to work.

Thus socialism's credentials as a libertarian solution to the Keynesian decline are not impressive. But this is because there is no libertarian solution obviously in sight. The continuing, and unsolved, problems of economic growth, plus the new survival problems of nuclear proliferation, resource shortages, and environmental pollution, confront a culture increasingly less responsive to traditional leadership, or perhaps to leadership of any kind. A complex society demands more discipline, while undermining its possibility by destroying the cohesion on which discipline must ultimately rest.

Marxist as well as non-Marxist thought often seeks a new basis of authority in science. In the West, science is sometimes seen as an escape from politics; in the Communist bloc, as an escape from ideology and repression. A number of proposals have been advanced for reducing the 'irrationality' of economic policy by entrusting it to technical experts, much in the Keynesian tradition (Jay, 1976;IEA, 1975:pp:24,41,64,81). There are two grounds for believing that science cannot itself form an authority system. First, since, in the present state of knowledge, there is no way of constructing a 'social welfare function', there is no way of taking the problem of choice out of politics.[12] But this brings us back to the original problem: political bargaining in the absence of sufficient authority to ration demands is an increasingly expensive technique of government. Each group has to be bought off at growing cost. Communist systems sometimes claim to be based on scientific plans of economic and social development. But assent to such plans is secured only by massive indoctrination and the suppression of alternatives and comparisons. They are power systems which use science, not scientific systems which use power. Secondly, rule by a scientific class is in conflict with demands for participation, self-fulfilment and equality, arising from the political and cultural spheres. There is also a sharp discontinuity between the experience and sympathies of the scientific and non-scientific elites, as well as between elites of all kinds and non-elites. If Keynes's attempt to establish the rule of philosopher-kings failed when social authority was still relatively secure, it has even less chance today. For these two reasons, it seems unlikely that science will, in the foreseeable future, be able to confer political authority, though it can reinforce it.

One of the main remedies for ungovernability currently being canvassed is democratisation. This is advanced as a value in its own right, but also as a remedy for economic irrationality. Its essential purpose is to impose the discipline of responsibility on those who can now prevent or disrupt economic policy at any level of the economy. Its main targets are over-large bureaucracies which make insatiable demands on the public purse, but which cannot maintain order lower down. Antibureaucratic tendencies are to be found in various combinations in all sections of politics, but two main, and largely alternative, models of change have emerged.

One version of the anti-bureaucratic programme takes the form of devolving power to the grass roots, giving people control of their immediate industrial and political environments. Tony Benn (1970:p.17) has written: 'Workers now have, through interdependence, enormous negative power to dislocate the system. Workers' control . . . converts that existing negative power into positive and constructive power. It thus creates the basis of common interest with local managers struggling to make a success of the business . . .'. The first problem with this is to work out what genuinely autonomous functions can be devolved to what levels without disrupting a 'chain of command' which often originates at the supra-national level. As Bell (1976:p.160) has pertinently remarked: 'the greater the number of (participating) groups, each seeking diverse or competing ends, the more likelihood that these groups will veto each others' interests, with the consequent sense of frustration and powerlessness as such stalemates incur.' Another problem is how to create a genuine sense of involvement in large organisations. Rousseau thought that democracy was possible only in small, self-sufficient communities. In large organisations, decision-making is necessarily confined to a minority. Would making the managers responsible to the workers in a given firm increase the latter's feeling of power and responsibility? In both factories and universities, the most genuine expressions of participation have been direct action to disrupt routine administration. Once participation is itself routinised in a system of elected councils or committees, the democratic sense of involvement recedes sharply. It cannot be claimed that in societies of large interlocking units any convincing way has been suggested for integrating into a working system the genuine energies which spontaneous disruptive action can release. Without it, the aim of developing a commitment to the success of the undertaking is lost.

A more logically satisfying anti-bureaucratic programme would be to restore the authority of the market. The workers' control movement wants to democratise the top-heavy structures which monopoly capitalism and state socialism have created; the market programme wants to break them up. Ailing enterprises would no longer be rescued by public funds; state industries and services would be forced to compete with private ones; cases of real need would be met wherever possible by cash payments to individuals rather than the provision of state services. The main aim of what is often called the 'social market economy' is to make markets function more efficiently and humanely, rather than supersede them by public or private monopolies, or by central planning or corporate bargaining. Its basic value is a belief in individual freedom, and the market as a condition for it; but two practical benefits are claimed. First, by restoring many economic decisions to the market, such a programme would depoliticise large areas of contemporary conflict, thus reducing the burden on politics to allocate resources and keep the peace. Secondly, the market mechanism provides a much better method than workers' control for co-ordinating the different levels of economic policy: Keynesianism would once more have a market to manipulate, rather than democracy or overpowerful interests to manage (Brittan, 1977: ch.14; Conservative Centre for Policy Studies, 1975). Whether such a programme is politically practicable is another matter. Electorates have been voting against market 'rationality' for 50 years now. Perhaps under affluent conditions, they may be more prepared to pay the price of greater insecurity for enlarged personal choice. But continuing or deepening recession is more likely to strengthen the demand for protection against market forces. However, the success of Glistrup's anti-tax Progress Party in Denmark, which came from nowhere to win 16 per cent of the votes in December 1973, shows the potential appeal of a market philosophy to a prosperous citizenry fed up with bureaucracy and red tape.

How much further progress is possible along the path of economic manipulation on which Keynes embarked? Here there appear to be as yet unrealised possibilities. Lindblom (1977:p.98) has mooted the

possibility of a 'planner sovereignty market system' in which government uses its power of purchase — currently running in many countries
at about 10 per cent of GNP — to restore control over overpowerful
private interests, and to direct the economy into centrally approved
channels. Pahl and Winkler (1974) have argued that a similar system,
which they call 'corporatism', is coming to Britain. The state will use its
economic and legal powers to direct a predominantly privately owned
economy towards the goals of order, unity, nationalism and success. In
a 'corporatist financial strategy' the state employs its multiple financial
powers to modulate the private sector's cash flow, then uses this as a
bargaining lever to extract all manner of 'agreements' from industry:

> The twin practical outcomes of this strategy are that we may in
> future expect to see private industry's apparent profitability increase
> while its discretion over the use of that profit diminishes, and,
> obversely, that the state's capital transfers will diminish while its
> control over the allocation of resources increases.

The logic of the strategy, according to J.T. Winkler (1977:p.86) is that 'it
works through the internal financing of individual companies and not,
in the Keynesian manner, through manipulation of national aggregates'.
At the same time, corporatism ensures 'the very effective co-optation
of the union movement into a corporatist economic structure'. Britain's
Labour government has certainly attempted action along these lines —
for example, tax concessions in return for wage restraint, and the black-
listing of firms for government contracts which break the pay guidelines.
As a recipe for restoring 'order', the corporatist strategy has two main
weaknesses. The first is the assumption by Pahl and Winkler that in the
bargaining between governments and the big producer groups, the
balance of advantage lies clearly with the state. However, this is far from
clear. In Britain, it is not obvious that the present ascendancy which the
government has established over the trade union movement could survive
either the advent of a Conservative administration, or the ending of
large-scale unemployment. Secondly, to what extent can the big
monopolies guarantee 'order', 'unity' and 'success' lower down? Agreements made at the top can be broken below unless additional powers are
taken, which would give corporatism an uncomfortable resemblance to
fascism.

Is more equality the answer? If liberty and opportunity, income and
wealth, and the bases of self-respect were 'to be distributed equally
unless an unequal distribution of any or all of these goods is to the

advantage of the least favoured' (Rawls, 1971:p.303) perhaps authority would shed the resentment which attaches to privilege? This may be doubted. First, the process of equalisation breeds more resentment at remaining inequalities: the 'Tocqueville effect' (Bell, 1976:p.451). Secondly it points the way to 'mass' society and administrative despotism. The historic connection between authority and hierarchy has been very close; it is an act of faith, no more, to suppose it can be broken.

Domestic outcomes to the present crisis will depend to a large extent on what happens to the international economy. Here the prospects are not too bright. The main alternatives appear to be a revival of effective international leadership, or a move to protectionism. The first is very much in the interest of the fast-growing countries and multinational corporations wherever they are located; the second is attractive to slow-growing countries and slow-growing sectors of national economies hit by competition from more successful rivals. The outcome will depend partly on whether the strong expansionist phase of recent economic history, which seems to have existed independently of Keynesian policy, has or has not come to an end. In an expansionist period, when everyone is gaining, even though unequally, it is much easier to reconcile conflicts, than in a static or contractionist period, when gains can only be made at the expense of others.

Writing in the early 1970s, Kindleberger (1973:pp.307 ff.) looked forward to revived American leadership of a liberal world economy. But this is challenged both by strong protectionist pressures within the United States, and the growth of new centres of economic power outside. It may be possible to co-opt some of these new centres into the American hegemony. In 1976, Kindleberger (1976:p.36) was considering a 'tripartite leadership in which, say, Germany, Japan and the United States combine to give stability to the system'. However, the parochial interests of the three nations conflict; and as economic power becomes more evenly distributed between them, it is increasingly difficult for any of them to recapture, or develop, a strong sense of responsibility for the free world economy as a whole. Beyond this, the place of the OPEC cartel in any system of global economic management remains highly ambiguous; while the North-South conflict offers a fertile field for the revival of the West-East conflict, as the United States and the Communist world compete for control of the Third World. After exploring the hopeful possibilities, Kindleberger (1976) gloomily concludes:

The system will limp along until it produces in evolutionary
Darwinian fashion a new system in which the rules of the game,

however devised and promulgated, are asymmetrically enforced and their costs asymmetrically shared . . . The transition to the choice of such a leader, made implicitly rather than by an election process, will be dangerous. The present restraint will be constantly jeopardised by thrusting short-run maximisers or the spread of free riding.

Protectionism and possible military conflict are built into this evolutionary transition. The model here is that of the 1930s: one can argue that World War II was fought over the 'transition'. It is generally assumed that protectionism is bound to spill over into war as nations struggle for access to 'closed' markets and raw materials. The unanswered question is whether a successful international economic system can be established on the basis of a genuine, but shifting, balance of power. Can national interests be peacefully reconciled through 'rules of the game' which do not have to be enforced 'asymmetrically'? If so, it would be an unprecedented historical achievement.

If an authority system breaks down irretrievably it is hard to see what is to follow except a power system, which can be defined shortly as a system resting on a mixture of coercion and indoctrination. It was Plato who first sketched a complete historical cycle, from monarchy to despotism, with democracy as the penultimate phase (*The Republic*, Part 9). The fundamental problem of democracy in a situation where authority has broken down is that it carries with it increasing economic costs (in time, energy, resources) which in the end threaten the system of wealth-creation. Even in a scientific civilisation the point can come when there is no longer sufficient growth to absorb the costs of democratic conflict. If this happens, then the only alternative known to history is a power system, which restores order through regimenting society. This itself is far from stable. At best it can 'freeze' the historical situation for a period by creating a garrison state: at worst, such systems can usher in an era of perpetual war. Twentieth-century history is too full of examples of power systems for us to banish the possibility that they might recur, even in the most highly advanced industrial societies. If they do, Keynesianism may turn out to have been the last bold intellectual attempt to equip democracy with the tools to ensure its own survival.

These are the possibilities which will most probably make up the agenda of serious politics in a post-Keynesian world. What recent developments have done is to cast serious doubt on the Keynesian faith that a permanently successful 'new politics' can be built on

technical manipulation by economic experts. The social and international foundations for such wizardry have proved too insecure. But it
can hardly be claimed that an acceptable 'new politics' is in sight.

Notes

1. I am particularly grateful to Mr Peter Oppenheimer for the care with which he
read and commented on, the manuscript version of this essay. Other debts are too
numerous to acknowledge individually.

2. The failure of the New Deal to cure unemployment is well known. Sweden
did recover, but not because of unorthodox finance (Berman, 1974).

3. See M. de Cecco's suggestive essay (1977).

4. This has nowhere been more graphically expressed than by Marx: 'The
bourgeoisie, wherever it has got the upper hand, has put an end to all feudal,
patriarchal, idyllic relations. It has pitilessly torn asunder the motley feudal ties
that bound man to his "natural superiors", and has left remaining no other nexus
between man and man than naked self-interest, than callous "cash payment". It
has drowned the most heavenly ecstasies of religious fervour, of chivalrous
enthusiasm, of philistine sentimentalism, in the icy water of egotistical calculation.
It has resolved personal worth into exchange value, and in place of the numberless
indefeasible chartered freedoms, has set up that single unconscionable freedom —
Free Trade. In one word, for exploitation, veiled by religious and political
illusions, it has substituted naked, shameless, direct, brutal exploitation'.
'Manifesto of the Communist Party' (1848) in Marx-Engels (1962:p.36).

5. The best-known British exponent of this view is Samuel Brittan (1975,
1977).

6. This is the theme of Pinto-Duschinsky (1970:p.59): 'A large share of the
blame . . . must be assigned to the political system which produced such a close
party battle in the 1950s, to the intellectuals who were unproductive in ideas or
advice, and to the mass electorate which refused to forgo comforts while a
solidly based prosperity was being created'.

7. Their basic argument is that since 1950 wage pressure has forced up prices
which weakened British capitalism's competitive position, thus destroying profits.
The share of profits in the national income (defined as the sum of wages and
profits) fell from 25 per cent in 1950 to 12.1 per cent by 1970 (p.58). Between
1964 and 1970, the rate of profit (defined as 'the relation of profits to the amount
of capital invested') fell from 11 per cent in 1964 to 5.8 per cent in 1970 before
tax, from 7.1 per cent in 1964 to 4.1 per cent in 1970 after tax (pp.65-8). They
concluded that since 1950 there had been a marked fall in the profit share in
Belgium, Italy and the Netherlands; that in Canada, France, Germany and the
USA there had not been much change; and that in Japan the profit share had
moved sharply upwards (p.74).

8. Bell (1976:p. 156) has made the point that the vastly expanded
service sector in contemporary industrial economies is one of the main structural
causes of inflation: workers there demand to keep up with those in manufacturing
industry, but few productivity gains are possible.

9. Gardner, (1969:p. xvii), reproduces the delightful jingle:

> In Washington Lord Halifax
> Once whispered to Lord Keynes
> 'It's true *they* have the money-bags
> But *we* have all the brains.

10. It is generally agreed that the 'overdraft' facility would have made the

Keynesian plan inflationary. It was weighted towards creditor adjustment through provision for periodic liquidation of credit and debit balances. The White Plan, by contrast, was weighted towards debtor adjustment.

11. However, 39 per cent of working-class Labour voters still think of politics as the 'representation of opposing class interests' (Butler and Stokes, 1971:p.68).

12 Even if a utilitarian calculus of this kind could be devised, people in a free society would no doubt still argue about ends.

3 THE DYNAMICS OF CHANGE IN A KEYNESIAN POLITICAL ECONOMY:THE SWEDISH CASE AND ITS IMPLICATIONS

Andrew Martin

The idea that the Keynesian era is over is now a commonplace. There is much that lends substance to the idea. Framed in response to the inter-war great Depression, Keynesian policy seemed to provide an effective means for managing capitalism during the postwar decades of growth as well. Now it no longer seems to work. The severe and protracted disruption of growth in the 1970s has evidently called it into question as profoundly as the great Depression challenged pre-Keynesian orthodoxy. In all the countries where governments had come to rely on Keynesian policy, it has come under attack from sharply divergent political perspectives. No government seems willing to apply the Keynesian prescription for reducing the highest levels of unemployment since the 1930s lest it trigger a new surge of inflation. Thus, the remedy for the earlier crisis apparently provides no solution to the present one: on the basis of Keynesian policy, so it seems, there is no way out of staglfation (Skidelsky, 1977, and in this volume).

Whether this is really so, however, may depend on what is meant by Keynesian policy. There is, after all, a wide range of ways in which it can be interpreted. All have in common the fundamental proposition that, left to itself, capitalism cannot be counted on to provide full employment. This is essentially what marks Keynes's break with what he referred to as the 'classical' position. The heart of the argument underlying this proposition concerns the behaviour of investment. It is that investment decisions in a capitalist economy have an inherent tendency to produce fluctuations in economic activity and with it recurrent unemployment. The only way that full employment can be maintained therefore is intervention by the state to counteract this tendency of investment behaviour.

The differences among the various meanings attached to Keynesian policy concern the ways in which the state's intervention is conceived. These range from a narrow conception, in which the state's role is confined to influencing private investment indirectly by managing aggregate demand, to a broad conception, in which the state's role extends to supplanting private investment as the principal motor of economic activity.

The narrow conception is the conventional one. In effect, it equates Keynesian policy with the particular form of intervention Keynes urged under conditions of the interwar great Depression, which it then applies with a kind of simple symmetry under the conditions of postwar inflations. Thus, when demand is too low to elicit enough private investment to produce full employment, expansion of demand, mainly by taxing and spending decisions adding up to a budget deficit, is called for to stimulate investment. Similarly, when demand is excessive, eliciting so much investment that inflationary 'over-full' employment and supply bottlenecks of all sorts result, restriction of demand, mainly by budget surpluses, is prescribed.

However, the fundamental argument concerning the tendency of private investment to produce unemployment on which Keynesian policy rests does not seem to warrant the assumption that demand management will suffice to counteract the tendency indefinitely and under all economic conditions. On the contrary, the argument seems to point towards the much broader conception of the state's role. In this conception, full employment can ultimately be maintained in a political economy in which the state remains democratic and trade unions retain their autonomy only through forms of intervention that successively reduce the dependence of employment on private investment by an increasing 'socialisation of investment'. If Keynesian policy is viewed as embracing such forms of intervention, and if they are in fact what is now required to restore full employment under current economic conditions, Keynesian policy might still offer a way out of stagflation.

The Keynesian era might nevertheless be over, but then the reason would not be that Keynesian policy no longer offers any potentially effective policy options. Instead, it could be that the political conditions for implementing those options are no longer present. That this may indeed be the case is what this essay attempts to suggest. It does so by exploring the political conditions for implementing Keynesian policy, broadly conceived as policy designed to counteract the tendency of private investment to produce unemployment, as the forms of the policy vary under different economic conditions.

It seems obvious that such variation in the forms of the policy is to be expected. To maintain full employment seems bound to require a pattern of policy that differs in significant respects from the one that is necessary to move from mass unemployment to full employment. Moreover, to maintain full employment must presumably require not merely a pattern of policy that differs from that through which the initial shift to full employment is brought about, but a succession of different patterns of policy. For in the process of maintaining full employment, the particular way in which the state does so can be expected to create new economic conditions. This may well diminish the effectiveness of a particular pattern of policy, which must then undergo further modification in order for full employment to be maintained under the new conditions.

Accordingly, a Keynesian political economy can be conceived as evolving through a succession of stages. In each, full employment is maintained by a different pattern of policy, provided that the political conditions for moving from one stage to the next are present. They obviously need not be. While the political conditions for doing what has to be done to reach or maintain full employment at one stage may be present in a particular country, the political conditions for doing what has to be done in the next stage may not be. For one thing, the configuration of power capable of implementing the needed pattern in one stage may be eroded as a result of the pattern's declining effectiveness before a new pattern can be worked out. Alternatively, the various components of the configuration of power which had a common stake in the initial pattern of policy may come into conflict over various elements of the pattern needed in the following stage, thereby precluding its implementation unless some alternative configuration with sufficient power can be brought into existence.

By the same token, the pattern of policy in any given stage can be expected to vary from country to country, because of differences in not only economic but also political conditions. Thus, the degree to which full employment can be approximated presumably varies, depending on the extent to which the pattern of policy for which political support can be mobilised meets the requirements for maintaining full employment under prevailing economic conditions. For the same reason, the choice among alternative combinations of policy instruments for attaining a given approximation to full employment may vary, resulting in different distributions of other benefits and burdens. To be sure, there may be some systematic connections between the degree to which full employment is approximated and the way it is done. The political conditions for a close approximation to full employment may also entail a combination of instruments that is quite different from the one resulting from the different political conditions under which a lesser approximation to full employment is established.

In addition, the succession of different patterns of policy is likely to have a cumulative character. What is done in one stage can be expected to affect what is necessary and possible in the next — keeping in mind that what is necessary may not be possible. The extent and direction of the cumulative effects presumably depend in some way on the degree to which full employment is approximated and how it is done. Variations among countries in these respects can accordingly be expected to result in differences in the ways in which their political economies change over time. If the political conditions for maintaining full employment continue to be met under changing economic conditions, so that the political economy continues to evolve through the successive stages marked by different patterns of policy required for full employment, the cumulative effect could be a very substantial transformation of the political economy. Conceivably, the capitalist character of the economy itself might become highly attenuated, possibly resulting in something like a transition to socialism. If that is the likely consequence of continued maintenance of full employment, there is bound to be substantial resistance to the patterns of policy producing such effects. The strength of that resistance may be sufficient to arrest the evolution of the political economy at a stage where the attenuation of its capitalist character is still limited. Thus, entry into the next stage, in which the pattern of policy required to maintain full employment under new economic conditions is one that transcends the limits of capitalism, is blocked.

While full employment appears to be made compatible with capitalism by Keynesian policy in its initial stages, it may become incompatible with capitalism as Keynesian policy undergoes the modifications required to maintain full employment in later stages. Keynes himself (1936:p.378) caught a glimpse of this possibility, anticipating that in the long run, 'a comprehensive socialization of investment will prove the only means of securing an approximation of full employment'. Among other things, this is a clear indication that Keynes himself did not conceive of the simple management of demand by fiscal and monetary policy as indefinitely sufficient to maintain full employment, as did those who subsequently gave Keynesian policy this restricted meaning. It is also an indication of Keynes's recognition that what had to be done to maintain full employment was likely to require some fairly significant institutional changes, although he was certainly not a socialist, rejecting what he understood as socialism at the time.

Michael Kalecki, who had simultaneously and independently 'worked out all the essentials of what became known as Keynes's theory, (Robinson, 1977: Feiwel, 1975). I also expected the maintenance of full employment to precipitate institutional change:

'Full employment capitalism' will have, of course, to develop new
    social and political institutions which will reflect the increased power
    of the working class. If capitalism can adjust itself to full employ-
    ment a fundamental reform will have been incorporated in it. If not,
    it will show itself an outmoded system which must be scrapped.
    (Kalecki, 1943:p.331).

If capitalism would consequently be replaced by socialism, that would
be an outcome that Kalecki, in contrast with Keynes, would have
welcomed.

    Addressing himself primarily to the immediate problem of reducing
unemployment, Keynes did not spell out in any detail his expectations
concerning the kinds of policy needed to maintain full employment at
a stage when it had already prevailed for some time. The basis of his
expectations in what we take to be his underlying argument was largely
obscured in the 'neo-classical synthesis' through which Keynes's specific
response to the great Depression was absorbed into mainstream
economics. While this orthodox version of Keynesian economics has
been increasingly called into question in the light of the contemporary
economic crisis, the few Keynesians who had held out against it have
been elaborating a more far-reaching conception of Keynesian policy
of the kind to which we refer. This 'post-Keynesian' school, for which
Kalecki is an important source as well, insists that what is essential in
Keynes's analysis of capitalism is incompatible with the neo-classical
mode of analysis, and has been attempting to work out more fully and
consistently than Keynes did what it deems essential to his analysis
(Eichner and Cornwall, 1978). This alternative view of the economics
of a Keynesian political economy has emerged as one of the principal
challenges to the neo-classical synthesis, along with Marxian and
essentially pre-Keynesian conservative challenges.

    Our purpose in this essay is not to present yet another summary of
that view, however, nor to proceed on the assumption that it is
necessarily valid. Our concern is rather with the politics of such a
political economy. This, of course, has not been the focus of the post-
Keynesians' attention since it is the issues of economic theory involved
with which they are concerned. Even so, they have tended to be more
attentive to the class and group conflicts at stake in economic policy
than mainstream economists (and political scientists, for that matter).
In particular, Kalecki's idea of a 'political business cycle' is a major
contribution to the analysis of a Keynesian political economy. This
idea has recently been taken up by some economists (and political
scientists) in a belated recognition of the political sources and conse-

quences of economic policy. But even when it is more fully elaborated, as it must be, the notion of a political business cycle is primarily concerned with short-run changes, or a succession of them that fall into a recurring pattern. This leaves open the question of how a Keynesian political economy, whatever the extent to which it is subject to such a cycle, develops over the long run, just as economic business cycle theory leaves open the question of economic development over the long run. It is this question of how such a political economy develops over the long run to which this essay is addressed. In particular, it is focused on how the political conditions for maintaining full employment may continue to be met under changing economic conditions and the consequences this may have for the political economy's evolution. All that will be attempted here is a preliminary sketch of what the long-run dynamics of change in a Keynesian political economy might be. This will be done primarily on the basis of a discussion of the way in which a close approximation to full employment has been maintained in Sweden.

The Swedish case offers a promising point of departure for exploring those dynamics of change for several fairly obvious reasons. Sweden was the first country in which a Keynesian pattern of policy was implemented. The Social Democratic Party that did so after coming into office in 1932 remained in office virtually without interruption until 1976. The fact that it is a labour movement party has given it a particularly strong stake in maintaining full employment, as will be argued more fully later on. It would therefore seem that the political conditions for maintaining full employment have been continuously met in Sweden longer than anywhere else. The evolution of the Keynesian political economy established in Sweden may consequently have proceeded further than in any comparable case, although this is not necessarily so.

On the basis of the Swedish case, we will suggest that the evolution of a Keynesian political economy can be divided into three stages, each of which is characterised by a distinctive pattern of policy. At the point at which the long era of Social Democratic rule came to an end, Sweden had passed through the first two stages and appeared to be in the process of transition to the third. Whether that transition will take place or not, or if it does in what form, is now problematical. For while it is likely that the Social Democrats will return to office after the next election, that will not necessarily satisfy the political conditions for implementing the pattern of policy required to maintain full employment in the third stage. Why this is problematical can be best understood after reviewing the evolution through the first and second stages.

Labour Movement Parties and Full Employment

If the political conditions for approximating full employment have been met in Sweden throughout the period during which the state was controlled by the Social Democratic Party[1], the fact that it is a labour movement party would seem to be a large part of the explanation. The party's main organisational and financial resources are provided by unions covering a large part of the labour force, the members of those unions comprise the core of the party's electoral constituency, and the party and unions identify themselves as parts of a single, unified social democratic labour movement. The unions to which the party is linked, formally in many cases at the local level but informally at all levels, are those organising blue-collar workers. The central federation to which they are affiliated is the LO. There is a separate federation of white collar unions, the TCO, which has no formal links with the Social Democratic or any other party, and within which there is substantial competition among activists committed to different parties. LO unions today cover just under half of the labour force, including virtually all industrial or blue-collar workers, while TCO unions' membership amounts to a little over a fifth of the labour force. The extent to which LO members constitute the Social Democratic Party's core constituency is reflected by the fact that 71 per cent of LO members voted for the Party in the 1973 election (Petersson and Sarlvik, 1975). In contrast, only 35 per cent of TCO members voted Social Democratic in that election, though this was a larger portion than voted for any other party. Except for 3 per cent that went to the Communists, the rest of TCO members' votes, i.e. a majority, were spread among the three so-called bourgeois parties, with 33 per cent going to the Centre Party, 12 per cent to the Liberals and 14 per cent to the Conservatives. Neither organisationally nor in the voting behaviour of its members, then, is TCO part of the social democratic labour movement. Its rapid growth has consequently posed increasingly pressing strategic problems for the movement to which we will return.

The links between the Social Democratic Party and blue-collar unions go back to the origins of both. Indeed, during the years following its founding in 1889, the party played a decisive role in the early growth of the unions, even performing the functions of a central federation. This was an effort to create an explicitly socialist labour movement, but the unions' need to organise non- or anti-socialist workers led to the organisational separation of the political and labour market functions of the movement through the establishment of LO in 1898. However, a large portion of LO unions continued to provide what was in effect the local organisation of the party, and their leaders at all levels have typically been committed Social Democrats. At the same time, the conception of a single movement whose political and labour market struggles are completely interdependent has continued to pervade Social Democratic and LO union ideology.

In more general terms the ideology is rooted in the nineteenth-century socialist critique of capitalism. However, like virtually all the parties that grew out of the Western European socialist movement and which participated in the democratisation of parliamentary institutions, the Swedish party became committed in the process to parliamentary, reformist politics, and its ideology underwent an implicit accommodation to the indefinite persistence of capitalism. This accommodation was decisively reinforced by the approximations to full employment that proved possible through the first and second stage patterns of Keynesian policy. By the same token, the accommodation is evidently being severely strained as the continued maintenance of full employment becomes contingent on the introduction of third-stage patterns of policy. Thus, the consistency between the ideological orientation and structural character of labour movement parties like that of Sweden seems to be contingent on the viability of what Kalecki called 'full employment capitalism'.

Accordingly, it would seem that such parties would be more likely to place top priority on maintaining full employment than other parties – at least those whose organisational and electoral base is not primarily in unions and their members. The stake in full employment built into labour movement parties by virtue of their links to the organised working class seems obvious. The stake would seem to be especially strong to the extent that union members are more vulnerable to unemployment than others. There are indications that this may no longer be the case as much as it probably was in the past, as unions win increased employment security and the labour market becomes increasingly segmented. On the other hand, the larger the proportion of the labour force covered by unions, the more unlikely it would seem that union members can escape unemployment. Moreover, unions have a stake in full employment because their bargaining power depends on it. This has certainly been the case in general and probably continues to be so even where considerable labour market segmentation occurs.

In addition to the organisational stakes of the unions that provide labour movement parties with important political resources, the parties' ability to mobilise electoral support evidently depends more generally on their capacity to maintain full employment when they control or participate in government. Their performance in office in this respect probably determines in large part the credibility of their claims to represent the working class, including employees who are members of unions not identified with the parties but whose votes are nevertheless needed.

The supposition that labour movement parties are therefore more likely than others to strive for full employment is certainly consistent with a good deal of evidence. In what is probably the fullest and most careful study of the subject, Hibbs (1977) related unemployment (and inflation) levels to the strength of labour movement parties in twelve Western European and North American countries. His measure of those parties' strength is the percentage of years between 1945 and 1969 that 'Socialist-Labour parties' have participated in the executives of those countries. This is shown to have a strong inverse correlation ($r = -.68$) with mean percentage unemployment (adjusted for comparability) in the period from 1960 to 1969. Over the same period, in which there seems to have been a pretty clear 'trade-off' between unemployment and inflation, there is an even stronger positive correlation ($r = +.74$) between labour movement party strength and mean inflation rates. These findings do not leave much room for doubt that labour movement parties tend to place a higher priority on reducing unemployment than inflation, and that the priorities of other parties tend to be more nearly the reverse. Moreover, even when labour movement parties are not in office, provided that they maintained low levels of unemployment when they were previously in office, their presence in the political arena seems to compel the parties that are in office to approximate full employment more closely than they would otherwise be likely to.

While it does therefore seem that the political conditions for full employment are more likely to be met when labour movement parties control or participate in governments, or are strong enough in opposition to constitute a potential replacement for the parties in power, we cannot assume that this will necessarily be so. Even labour movement parties may put a higher priority on other goals, for which they may be willing to tolerate increased unemployment. The performance of the British Labour Government from 1964 to 1970 offers a striking example. Alternatively, even if they do put top priority on full employment, they may not know how to achieve it under prevailing economic conditions, or to find a pattern of policy for doing it that is at the same time politically viable, given the existing configuration of political power. The responses of the British Labour Party and German Social Democratic Party to the interwar great Depression may be seen as examples. It was, of course, the contrasting response of the Swedish Social Democratic Party that led Sweden into the first stage of a Keynesian political economy earlier than any other country. A closer look at these different responses can serve as a point of departure for exploring in more detail the political conditions under which a Keynesian political economy is established and goes through successive stages of development.

The First Stage

The deep crisis of capitalism that began in 1929 faced all the reformist labour movement parties with a critical challenge, and also opportunity. Obviously, their working-class core constituencies were hard hit by massive unemployment, posing a clear test of the parties' ability to protect the interests they claimed to represent. Since the parties had long since abandoned any real intention of replacing capitalism by socialism, at least for the relevant future, they could only meet that test if they found a way of combating unemployment despite capitalism's apparent tendency to create it. This implied a degree of control over the very operation of capitalism that went considerably beyond the kind of welfare state reforms on which their claims to working-class support had come to rest. However, there was no way of doing so within the framework of the economic conceptions in terms of which the German Social Democratic and British Labour parties' options were defined by their respective leaders. In the former case, the leaders invoked a fatalistic version of Marxism that ruled out any solution short of the replacement of capitalism, which could only happen when the laws of capitalism's operation made it happen. In the latter case, the leaders insisted on orthodox liberal grounds that there was no alternative except to help the business cycle go through its necessary course by conforming to its requirements with balanced budgets, achieved by tax increases and spending cuts, and reductions in wages and prices.[2]

Both perspectives came to the same thing, leaving non-revolutionary labour movement parties with no way of protecting the interests of their constituencies. At best, the parties could attempt to shift the burdens of the depression from the working class to other groups, which formed the core constituencies of other parties. But the support of one or another of these other parties was necessary to implement any

policy whatsoever, for in no case did the labour movement parties have
parliamentary majorities. The latter could obviously not expect any of
the other parties to join them in shifting the burdens from the working
class on to their own supporters. Thus, as long as labour movement
parties accepted the premise that capitalism was not about to be
replaced by socialism, and that budgets had to be balanced in order for
the capitalist economies to recover, they were boxed into a zero-sum
game they could not win.

If the balanced budget requirement is abandoned, however, the
political as well as economic possibilities are transformed. Since deficit
financed government spending can expand demand and thereby reduce
unemployment, without any increase in taxes or cuts in spending,
prices or wages, it becomes possible to form coalitions around the
shared easing of burdens such a policy permits. German union leaders,
without ever having heard of Keynes, and British union leaders, who
did happen to know what Keynes was already arguing at the time,
both called upon their party counterparts to pursue such expansionary
policies. In both instances, the party leaders refused, closing off
whatever possibilities for politically viable responses there were. By
adopting precisely such a policy, on the other hand, the Swedish Social
Democratic Party laid the political as well as economic basis for
remaining in office, although they too had fallen short of a parliamentary majority in the 1932 election, and also for nearly half a century
thereafter.

When the Social Democrats took office in Sweden in 1932, the
leaders of the bourgeois parties — conservatives, liberals and agrarians —
opposed the new government's proposal for an expansionary budget.
However, the Social Democrats picked up the needed margin of support
by striking a bargain with a dissident wing of one of the parties, the
agrarians. In exchange for support of their economic policy, the Social
Democrats abandoned their earlier opposition to tariffs and other
measures to bolster prices of agricultural commodities. Having won
these gains for the agrarian party's core constituency, the dissidents
succeeded in taking over the party, which then supported the Social
Democrats not only at that time but repeatedly until the late 1950s.
A configuration of political power capable of establishing and sustaining a Keynesian political economy was thereby created, but it took
a Keynesian pattern of policy to make it possible in the first place.
The coalition comprising that configuration could hardly have been
forged if either of the parties involved had insisted on balanced budgets,
wage and price cuts and all the rest, for under those circumstances their

core constituencies had conflicting stakes. An expansionary budget deficit rendered those stakes compatible (Rustow, 1955:pp.99-110).

On the basis of that kind of policy, the labour movement parties in Germany and Britain might also have been able to put together coalitions capable of implementing it, although this was perhaps more certainly the case in the latter than the former. In general, it would seem comparatively easy to meet the political conditions for implementing the kind of Keynesian policy that suffices when there is massive unemployment and under-utilised capacity. To move towards full employment under these circumstances simply calls for the stimulation of demand. A pattern of policy essentially limited to such demand management is what characterises the first stage of a Keynesian political economy. Within that stage, demand management may take varying forms, depending on the particular configuration of power through which one form or another can be implemented. Thus, expansionary deficits may be produced primarily by increasing expenditures or decreasing taxes, accompanied by different distributions of burdens and benefits.[3] But the resulting expansion provides scope for gains that are nevertheless widely diffused, so that political conflict over alternative forms of Keynesian policy in its first stage is essentially a positive sum game. Hence the irony, and tragedy, of the British and German labour movement parties' failure to recognise the policy options open to them in the context of the great Depression.

The lasting political consequences of the Swedish Social Democrats' success in mobilising a coalition around the implementation of first-stage Keynesian policy were in fact more significant than its immediate economic consequences. Innovative in principle, the policy carried out was too little and too late in practice to have much impact, which was delayed by a long construction strike and outweighed by revived demand for Swedish exports. A major factor in that was the devaluation of the crown in 1931, following the devaluation of the British pound. As the recovery proceeded, domestic demand became more important in sustaining it. However, the Social Democrats' budget policy became increasingly and prematurely cautious, betraying less than full confidence in the policy innovations for which they claimed credit. The result was that full employment was not as closely approximated during the 1930s as it might have been (Arndt, 1944:pp. 207-20; Lundberg, 1957). Nevertheless, the reduction in unemployment that did occur seemed to confirm their claims, and they were rewarded by substantial gains in the 1936 and 1940 elections, the latter being one of just two in which they won absolute majorities in the directly elected

Second Chamber. By then, however, the onset of World War II over-shadowed everything else. A four-party coalition was formed to administer neutral Sweden's 'siege economy', relying heavily on direct controls as in the belligerents' war economies.

For our purposes, what was most important about the Social Democrats' wartime experience was the conclusions they drew from it concerning postwar economic policy. Throughout the West, it was generally expected that the danger of unemployment would again loom large after the war. Programmes for postwar reconstruction stressed the need to avert that danger, not only because of its social costs but also as essential to the preservation of peace. This contributed substantially to the political conditions for establishing Keynesian political economies in a large number of countries. But much of anticipated postwar policy went beyond the management of demand characterising first-stage Keynesian policy. Particularly on the left, the call was for economic planning, including various degrees of nation-alisation. While the notion of planning embraced a rather wide spectrum of policies, including even the most limited macroeconomic demand management, it typically referred to a whole range of fairly dis-aggregated sectoral policies, to be co-ordinated within the framework of an overall conception of their interrelationships and desired path of economic development over a period of several years – i.e. a plan.

There was a clear thrust in this direction by the Swedish Social Democratic labour movement, expressed in 1944 in a joint Party-LO 'Postwar Programme'. From the siege economy experience, it was concluded that much more could be done to achieve full employment and meet social needs than had been done through cautious fiscal management of the economy in the preceding decade. Unemployment could be more nearly eliminated and a higher level of activity attained if, instead of relying primarily on general stimulation of private invest-ment, the state played a much larger and more selective role in shaping the pace and composition of investment. A variety of techniques for doing so were set forth in the programme, including some national-isation, increased control of credit, and co-ordination of rationalisation in the private sector (LO, 1948).

However, the programme could not be implemented. The actual course of economic events confounded the expectations on which the programme was based, as it did the expectations held all over the West. It turned out that the prevailing tendency, as is well known, was towards inflation rather than unemployment. Moreover, the political conditions for moving well beyond first-stage Keynesian policy in ways outlined in the programme rapidly disappeared. The Social Democrats lost their absolute Second Chamber majority in the 1944 election, though it was then the Communists rather than the bourgeois parties that made the major gains, contributing to the Social Democrats' programmatic radicalisation. After the wartime coalition broke up, however, organised business launched an intense ideological offensive against the Social Democrats, charging that they were bent on establishing a centralised planned economy in which freedom would be destroyed. This 'anti-planning campaign' was joined by the bourgeois parties, and in combination with the atmosphere engendered by the cold war, it contributed to further losses for the Social Democrats as well as a sharp setback for the Communists in the 1948 election, though the Social Democrats managed to retain a two-seat lead over the three bourgeois parties. All the more vulnerable to attack under economic conditions to which it was not geared, the postwar programme was abandoned. In the context of inflation, the Social Democrats were compelled to go beyond the demand management to which the first stage was essentially limited, but in a different way.[4]

Labour Movement Parties and Inflation

Within a generalised Keynesian framework, the problem of maintaining full employment in the context of inflation accompanied by growth has been understood as one of supplementing demand management with some additional techniques by which the rate of inflation can be made lower than it would otherwise be at a given level of demand. Inflation rates can of course be lowered if demand is depressed enough but full employment is then sacrificed. This is obviously the familiar notion of a 'trade-off' between unemployment and inflation, that has typically been expressed in terms of the Phillips curve and its various derivatives and refinements. Except in the most naive conceptions, what the trade-off is in a particular country and period is understood to be a function of the whole range of institutional and cultural factors that enter into the behaviour of economic actors. To improve the trade-off, the operation of such factors has to be influenced. The combination of techniques for doing so with demand management characterises the pattern of policy in the second stage in the development of a Keynesian political economy.

Whether, when, and in what form Keynesian political economies have entered the second stage has varied from country to country. This has depended partly on differences in economic structure which make it more or less difficult to maintain full employment without exceeding a given inflation rate. Particularly important in this respect is the degree of openness of an economy. This affects both the relative importance of domestic and external sources of inflation and the effects on employment of domestic inflation rates relative to those in a country's trading partners.

Entry into the second stage has also varied with differences in political structure. In particular, this has depended on how high a priority the political formations controlling the state place on maintaining full employment. As we saw, a high priority is more likely to be placed on it to the extent that labour movement parties control the state and less likely where other kinds of parties do so. In the latter case, and if a first-stage Keynesian political economy has come into being at all, it is likely to be easier to remain within that stage. Aggregate demand management is more adequate to curb inflationary pressures the higher the average level of unemployment that is politically enforceable. Where the kinds of parties controlling the state are non-labour movement parties, more than one of which may alternate in power, party competition may still attach some electoral risks to high unemployment. These would seem to be the political conditions under which a political business cycle is likely to be most pronounced, resulting in substantial fluctuations around a higher average level of unemployment. But even in countries with configurations of power that permit this, economic conditions may compel governments to enter the second stage. Demand may not be managed effectively, because of its inherent difficulties or the consequences of other political objectives. A well-known example is the failure to prevent escalation of the Vietnam war from generating inflation in the United States.

Where labour movement parties control the state, entry into the second stage appears to be unavoidable. Their built-in stake in the closest possible approximation to full employment on a continuing basis makes it all the more difficult for them to curb inflation by demand management alone. The issue confronting such parties then is what kind of additional techniques are politically viable, particularly in terms of preserving the political resources provided to them by the unions. The techniques typically relied on in second-stage patterns of policy have been designed directly to prevent prices, including the price of labour, from rising as fast as they might under prevailing demand and market power conditions; that is, some version, strong or weak, of a 'repressed inflation' policy, generally promulgated in the form of an 'incomes policy'.

It is widely assumed that labour movement parties are best able to implement incomes policies. Their ties to unions are supposed to enable them to elicit the wage restraint which is an essential element, if not the whole point, of such policies. At the same time, such parties are believed to be more likely to pursue the policies unions tend to want in exchange for restraint. This includes not only the full employment which occasions the need for incomes policy but also tax and transfer policies on distributive terms acceptable to the unions. The latter are in turn expected to be more likely to comply, not only because of ideological and personal links to the parties but also because of their organisational stake in full employment. Thus, unions have a stake in helping the parties most likely to deliver full employment succeed in managing a full employment economy, thereby enhancing their chances of staying in office and continuing to maintain full employment.

However, these expectations overlook major obstacles to incomes policies even when labour movement parties attempt them. The possibility of satisfying the distributive terms acceptable to unions is very limited with respect to non-wage incomes and wealth, particularly in upper income groups. Moreover, the income distribution is itself made more salient by the very attempt to implement incomes policies. So even if non-wage incomes could be restrained as effectively as wage incomes, this may not suffice precisely because the very distribution that is thereby kept unchanged is not accepted as fair. Also, wage incomes alone are bound to be restrained with varying degrees of effectiveness, with the result that existing differentials are disturbed. If union federations or individual unions resist resulting demands for increases to restore differentials, they jeopardise cohesion within the federations or unions. On the other hand, if they refuse to comply with incomes policy or, having complied, relax or abandon compliance, they risk a breakdown of cohesion in the labour movement as a whole if the party continues to insist upon the necessity of incomes policy. (The tensions between the British Labour Party and the Trades Union Congress in the late 1960s provide an obvious case in point.)

The calculus of risks is bound to vary under different economic conditions and with differences in the forms of incomes policies and the terms offered in exchange, as well as the political risks attacked to failure to agree on an incomes policy. In general, however, incomes policies are likely to threaten labour movement parties with serious risks to internal cohesion. If so, they are not ordinarily a politically viable option for such parties. The parties are accordingly compelled to seek alternatives. This is the situation the Swedish Social Democrats found themselves in during the early 1950s.

The Second Stage

The initial version of second-stage policy adopted by Sweden's Social Democratic Government was a fairly strong form of repressed inflation policy. Controls left over from the war were used and others reintroduced. In addition, the government got an agreement among all the organisations of producer groups, including LO, to freeze incomes at existing levels during 1949 and again in 1950. Any further extensions were made impossible by the inflationary pressures associated with the Korean war. The resulting termination of the freeze was followed by a wage explosion that just kept pace with the increased cost of living. Viewing this as an unavoidable 'one-time' adjustment to higher price levels, the government sought to re-establish price stability by calling for a renewal of wage restraint though not a new freeze, in 1952. This time, however, LO refused. Instead it called upon the government to pursue an alternative strategy that had been worked out by its own economists. Referred to as the 'Rehn model' after one of the economists responsible for its formulation, this strategy was adopted as LO's official policy at its 1951 Congress.[5]

LO's rejection of any strategy that relied primarily on wage restraint to prevent a wage-price spiral was based on the kind of inter-class distributive and intra-class organisational considerations referred to above. Its alternative rested on an analysis stressing differences in profitability in different parts of the economy and fragmentation of the labour market into partially separate submarkets. From this the conclusion was drawn that the full employment goal had to be disaggregated, relying on 'general' fiscal policy to maintain full employment in most of the economy and 'selective' manpower policy in the remainder. While these two kinds of policy were carried out by the government, union wage bargaining would be co-ordinated by LO in accordance with a 'solidaristic wage policy'. In principle, this was conceived as a policy of equal pay for equal work, regardless of an employer's ability to pay, and a reduction of differentials between different kinds of work. The interaction of government and union policies was expected to result in non-inflationary full employment in the following way.

First, fiscal policy would be more restrictive than in the postwar years, keeping demand high enough to assure full employment in most of the economy but not in the least profitable activities. Part of the increased restrictiveness would be achieved through the introduction of indirect — i.e. sales — taxation. This was expected to diminish the scope for price increases to compensate for increased wage costs, shifting the burden of restraining wages back to employers. The combined effect of such fiscal policy and continued wage pressure would be a squeeze on profits. Because wage pressures would be shaped on the basis of a solidaristic wage policy, however, the profits squeeze would have a differential effect on different firms, hitting them harder the less profitable they were. The least profitable firms would be forced to become more efficient or shut down. The workers threatened with unemployment as a result would be guaranteed alternative job opportunities — at standard rates — by a vast expansion of selective manpower policy, including information, retraining, and financial support during the process of transition from old to new jobs. In this way, a process of structural change in industry would be encouraged, increasing the proportion of efficient, low-cost activities capable of paying standard rates without putting increased pressure on prices. At the same time, manpower policy would ensure that the costs of structural change would be shifted from the workers involved to the society as a whole.

While non-inflationary full employment would therefore supposedly be accomplished primarily through a profits squeeze that accelerated structural change rather than through direct restraint of wages and prices, LO's co-ordination of wage bargaining was expected to prevent the kind of inter-union wage rivalry that might otherwise act as an autonomous source of inflation. In this limited respect and under the specified conditions, then, there was an element of restraint in the LO strategy.

The profits squeeze was also expected to reduce business savings. Since accelerated structural change presupposed increased investment in the efficient parts of the economy capable of expansion, the decline of business savings would have to be more than offset. This would be done by an increase in public-sector savings, which a more restrictive fiscal policy would make possible. Over the long run, in addition, the combined effects of the profits squeeze, solidaristic wage policy, and growth in the public-sector share of savings would decrease economic inequality. Summing up, LO's strategy was expected to contribute to the Social Democratic labour movement's long-run egalitarian goal at the same time that it provided a way of maintaning full employment that was also consistent with the movement's organisational cohesion. This was in turn a prerequisite for the political power on which the continuation of full employment depended.[6]

As it turned out, the political conditions for implementing the LO strategy were not met for most of the 1950s (Hancock, 1972:pp.214-24). Partly this was because the Social Democratic government's economic policy decision-makers were not initially convinced of its validity. Even if they had been, though, they could not have implemented it. The party's postwar electoral decline had made them once more dependent on parliamentary support from the Agrarian Party, which participated in a coalition government from 1951 to 1957. The agrarians were not willing to support reintroduction of indirect taxes and increased expenditures on manpower policy except during recessions, both of which were key elements in the strategy. However, under the economic conditions that prevailed from the end of the Korean war through most of the decade, inflationary pressures remained relatively low, thereby minimising the need to find a politically viable way of dealing with inflation.

To all intents and purposes, economic policy during the mid-1950s reverted back to the pattern characteristic of the first stage in the evolution of a Keynesian political economy. The main innovations resulted in the refinement of fiscal policy as an instrument for stabilising demand. Specifically, an investment reserve fund system was put into operation (Eliasson, 1965; Bergstrom, 1971). This was designed to shift investment from boom to slack periods. It allows firms to set aside some of their profits, a portion going into blocked accounts in the central bank. If the firms then use some of the profits set aside in this way for investment at times specified by the government, they never have to pay any taxes on the amounts involved, as they must if they withdraw and use the funds at any other times. While this increased the government's ability to influence the timing of investment for stabilisation purposes, it also introduced a marked pro-investment bias into the corporate tax structure. This raises a distributive issue which did not emerge at the time but has become more salient since, as we shall see later on.

During this period, the main focus of Social Democratic policy shifted to expansion of the welfare state within the framework of first-stage Keynesian economic policy. However, this laid the political basis for a transition to a second-stage policy more like LO's than the initial version. The most important welfare state reform was the introduction of a compulsory scheme providing generous income-related pensions to supplement the already existing Beveridge-style flat-rate national pension system. Included was a national pension fund in which a large surplus was to be built up over a transitional period during which the scheme would gradually be implemented. The fund was based on a gradually increasing payroll tax paid by employers. It was argued that this was necessary to compensate for a decline in household savings expected to result from the introduction of the scheme. But the proposed remedy amounted to an increase in public-sector savings, which was precisely what the LO strategy prescribed, although the fiscal mechanism involved was not the same.

While the basis for meeting a key requirement of the Rehn model would be laid in this way, provided that fiscal policy did not offset the public-sector surplus in some other way, the immediate effect of the proposal was political. The business community, as well as the liberal and conservative parties, attacked the national pension fund on the ground that it would give the state control over the credit market. They thereby precipitated a sharper ideological controversy than at any time since the late 1940s. In this case, however, the pension reform provided the Social Democrats with an issue around which they were able more effectively to mobilise their core constituency as well as some additional support in the growing white-collar component of the labour force. This proved sufficient to offset the loss of support from the Agrarian Party, which left the coalition over the pension issue. They did so less because of the substance of the issue, on which they did not join with the other two bourgeois parties, than in an ultimately successful effort to redefine their identity, symbolised by changing their name to Centre Party and by carving out a new constituency in order to survive in the face of their traditional constituency's decline.

The outcome was that the Social Democrats gained the parliamentary basis for governing alone after the 1960 election. This made it possible to introduce the two elements of the Rehn model blocked earlier, indirect taxation and a large expansion of manpower policy. Meanwhile, LO's co-ordination of wage bargaining was being firmly institutionalised in a system of centralised negotiations with the Swedish Employers Confederation (SAF), that has now been continuously in operation since 1956 (von Otter, 1975; Fulcher,1973;Edgren *et al.*, 1973; Calmfors 1977). The principal elements required by the LO strategy were now apparently in place, and it seemed as if it was indeed being put into operation with considerable effectiveness during the second half of the 1960s.

Thus, a shift into the second stage of a Keynesian political economy had apparently taken place in Sweden in a form consistent with union and hence union-party cohesion. In this form, a close approximation to full employment could be maintained not simply because inflation could be curbed without sacrificing full employment, but because it could be curbed in a way that made it possible to preserve the political resources enabling a labour movement party to retain control of the state. As long as it did so, it could go on using the state to manage capitalism according to the labour movement's priorities, the highest of which was full employment.

Limits of the Second Stage

By the middle of the 1960s, doubt was already cast on the political viability of the form taken by this second stage. In important respects, the economic strategy on which it rested was not being carried out with sufficient effectiveness on its own terms. But even if the strategy could have been carried out as prescribed, there were evidently features of it that left it vulnerable to attack, from within the social democratic labour movement as well as without.

The effectiveness with which the strategy was implemented was impaired by faulty timing of changes in the direction of demand management. In particular, the restrictiveness of fiscal policy was increased too late in the expansion that was taking place during 1964 and 1965. The result was an acceleration of inflation and a relaxation of the squeeze on profits. This meant that an essential condition for LO's co-ordination of wage bargaining was undermined. The extent to which profits are squeezed affects the level of wage drift — that is, wage increases in excess of those provided for in contracts negotiated by the unions. Over the postwar period, wage drift has averaged out at about the same level as contractual increases, reflecting the limits on the extent to which the centralised bargaining system actually determines wages. Some drift is an unavoidable consequence of local piece-rate negotiations and other factors, and provides both flexibility for management and a kind of safety valve for the unions. However, high levels of drift imply a failure by the unions to press their members' claims for anywhere nearly as much as they could get. Moreover, they imply an inability to enforce a solidaristic wage polciy, insofar as drift tends to vary with employers' ability to pay. LO's ability to retain support for its co-ordination of wage bargaining on the basis of such a wage policy is accordingly impaired. This is just what happened in 1964 and 1965 when wage drift substantially exceeded the contractual increase provided for in a two-year agreement reached in 1964. Workers who benefited least from drift consequently saw centralised bargaining as a mechanism that simply made them fall behind other workers, leading two unions to refuse to participate in the next round of centralised negotiations.

In addition to the difficulty LO had in preventing wage rivalry among unions affiliated to it as a result of the government's failure to

maintain the profits squeeze, there was no way that LO's co-ordination
of wage bargaining could inhibit wage rivalry between its own affiliates
and those outside LO. The rapid growth of TCO unions aggravated the
problem, revealing a fundamental weakness in the LO strategy which it
has been trying to overcome ever since. Under the circumstances, LO
was under great pressure to demand very substantial wage increases to
make up for settling for too little in the previous round, just to be able
to continue co-ordinating the bargaining, not to speak of restoring some
credibility to its wage policy. As a result of the significant increases it
succeeded in getting, combined with a downturn in activity which was
partly due to the government's belated tightening of fiscal policy, there
was a marked restoration of the profits squeeze.

This in turn produced a sharp acceleration of structural change,
particularly during the 1967-8 recession in Sweden. But while there was
an increase in plant closures, there was not enough expansion in the
more profitable activities to offset the job losses in the high-cost
activities. In fact, the investment that was taking place was increasingly
in labour-saving equipment rather than the capacity expansion that
could increase employment. The burden of providing alternative jobs
was therefore shifted to the public sector, where the government's
commitment to full employment led it to increase employment at a
more rapid rate. At the same time, the regional concentration of plant
closures was forcing increased geographical mobility, arousing dis-
contents in both declining areas and the urban conurbations where
industrial activity was growing. For some who lost their jobs, even
geographical mobility and all the assistance provided by manpower
policy did not suffice to secure alternative employment. And among
those who retained their jobs, intensification of technological change
and rationalisation was creating increased stress and insecurity (Martin,
1977b).

All these phenomena raised the issue of how the social costs of
structural change were actually being distributed. Instead of being
borne by the society as a whole, as anticipated in the Rehn model, they
were apparently being borne to a considerable extent by those directly
affected. The outcome might well be an increase in inequality rather
than a decrease. The acceptability of structural change was declining
in this context, particularly as it was seen as taking place on inequit-
able terms — as well as sacrificing values such as community that had
not been given much attention in the rationale for high mobility. At
the same time, attention was being drawn to distributive issues in other
respects, particularly by the emergent new left but also within the

Social Democratic movement. Among other things, the distributive effects of the pro-investment bias in both the corporate tax structure and solidaristic wage policy began to be called into question, with far-reaching implications to which we shall return.

The political effects of the way in which the Rehn model was actually operating, if not the way in which it was intended to operate, made themselves felt in the 1966 local elections, in which the Social Democrats' share of the vote fell sharply to the lowest level since 1934. They were jolted into recognising that their capacity to gear capitalism to the labour movement's priorities was seriously deficient, and even that the way those priorities were defined tended to neglect needs and values important to those whose support they claimed. Moving in directions in which pressures had already begun to build within it, the movement responded in two ways.

The immediate response was the rapid inauguration of a series of measures heralded as a 'new industrial policy'. These included a state investment bank, an industrial ministry, a state enterprise holding company, research and development agencies, an expanded regional planning apparatus, and an agency for sectoral planning. The rationale for these measures was that they would increase the state's ability to influence the pace and composition of investment in the light of social needs, somewhat as in the postwar programme but on a much more modest scale than envisaged there. Still, the revival of concern with the investment process as such suggested that the limits of the second stage in the evolution of Sweden's Keynesian political economy were already being approached. In the short run, however, the most important impact of the Social Democrats' policy initiatives was again political. They involved enough of a shift towards microeconomic intervention to renew ideological polarisation but not enough to give much credibility to conservative charges of a revived socialist threat. Consequently, the mobilisation effects of the controversy over industrial policy were more like those of the one in the late 1950s over pensions than the one in the late 1940s over the postwar programme. This plus the Social Democrats' success in turning the Soviet invasion of Czechoslovakia to their advantage in the election campaign gave them their second parliamentary majority in 1968.

However, the new industrial policy did not add up to enough to do much to cope with the problems that were apparently inherent in the movement's economic strategy. These problems were again aggravated by the way it was implemented, for changes in the direction of demand management were again mistimed in 1969 and 1970. In addition,

reaction against various features of the strategy was growing both within
the unions and the wider public. There was an increasing frequency of
short, small wildcat strikes culminating in a wave of large wildcat
strikes in the winter of 1969-70. Meanwhile, criticism of Social
Democratic policy was building up in the political arena from both left
and right, with the Centre Party's attack on centralisation, bureaucratisation and environmental destruction striking increasingly responsive
chords.

The Social Democratic movement made a further effort to meet this
challenge with a stream of legislation on what was described as
'industrial democracy'. This second response had two main dimensions.
One was the provision of improved job security, implying substantial
reduction in mobility and making it necessary for management to take
existing workers' characteristics into account in designing jobs much
more than in the past. In other words, greater emphasis was thereby
placed on adapting work to the workers than the other way around.
The other dimension was a substantial enlargement of the unions'
voice in workplace and enterprise decisions — from work organisation
to corporate investment planning — that had previously been exclusive
managerial prerogatives. Both these features of the industrial
democracy reforms were addressed particularly to the insecurity and
stress associated with rapid structural change and to the related
weakening of rank and file support for the party and unions. In
addition, workplace union power was seen as an issue on which an
identity of interests could be established between LO and TCO unions
more easily than on wage issues. For that reason, it was also expected
that it would be an issue that would enhance the possibility of
mobilising electoral support in TCO, lending credibility to the Social
Democratic Party's claim to be the 'employees' party' rather than
merely the blue-collar workers' party.

As it turned out, industrial democracy did not prove to be a particularly effective mobilising issue, at least not sufficiently to prevent
declining electoral support in three successive elections culminating
in the loss of office in 1976. At the same time, there was another
problem inherent in the labour movement's economic strategy to which
neither the industrial democracy reforms nor the earlier industrial
policy initiatives provided a solution, and which suggested even more
strongly that the limits of the second stage were being approached.

On the Threshold of the Third Stage

The problem that seems to be insoluble within the limits of the second stage concerns the relationship between wages and profits and its consequences for investment and employment. As we saw, the Rehn model attached central importance to a squeeze on profits that would have a differential impact on firms with varying profitability as a result of the standard-rate wage policy. The least profitable firms would be forced to become more efficient or shut down while the more profitable a firm was, the more it would be able to expand. The resulting increase in employment in the more profitable firms was evidently expected largely to offset the reductions in employment in the firms hardest hit by the profits squeeze, with manpower policy facilitating and absorbing the costs of the transfer of labour from the declining to the expanding firms. However, the net effect of such structural change on the level of employment is bound to depend in part on the average level of profits resulting from the profits squeeze. As long as the firms whose expansion is expected to offset the contraction of other firms are private, capitalist firms, they are not likely to expand sufficiently for the offsetting effect to result unless they retain sufficient profits to induce and, at least partly, finance the required level of investment. Would the interaction of fiscal policy and solidaristic wage policy result in an average level of profits that left the more profitable firms with enough profits for that level of investment?

That could be the outcome of a standard-rate wage policy, for while the profits of the less profitable firms would be squeezed hard, perhaps fatally, by rates higher than they could pay, so to speak, the profits of more profitable firms would not be squeezed at all by rates that would in effect be less than they could pay. The pro-investment bias in solidaristic wage policy arises in just this way. But insofar as the wage policy operates in such a way that the effects of this bias have a magnitude of any significance, it implies an element of restraint in the wage policy in addition to that implied by the curtailment of inter-union wage rivalry. On the other hand, if this additional element of restraint is unacceptable or unworkable, and a solidaristic wage policy is nevertheless enforced, it implies a much harder squeeze, resulting in a considerably lower average level of profits. This could leave even the more profitable firms without sufficient profits to keep investment at the levels required to offset the reduction in employment in the less profitable firms, even more of which would be forced to shut down as a result of the harder squeeze.

As it was formulated, the Rehn model is not clear as to what is to be expected in this connection. It definitely anticipates that the profits remaining in the more profitable firms would not be sufficient fully to finance the required level of investment. But the increase in public sector savings, due to fiscal policy tight enough to produce surpluses much of the time, is expected to offset the decline in business savings, so that the remainder of the finance for the required level of investment would be assured. On the other hand, it is not clear how such public-sector savings would be channelled into industrial investment, most of which is evidently expected to continue to take place in the private sector. One issue in this connection is the form in which the savings would be channelled into investment, particularly whether it would take the form of loan or equity capital. Insofar as it is the latter, of course, it implies some growth in public ownership. Another issue is the effect of the profits squeeze on the willingness to invest, and hence on the extent to which the public sector's accumulation of savings would even be called upon to finance investment, in whatever form it was made available.

For a while, these questions were answered in practice in ways that postponed the necessity of squarely confronting the problems under-lying them. First, the effects of wage pressures on profits were eased by increasingly favourable tax treatment of profits. The investment reserve fund system and other features of corporate taxation sustained cash flow for successful firms. The more profits they had to invest the more they could take advantage of the tax breaks for investment. This pro-investment bias of the corporate tax structure probably had more impact than the pro-investment bias built into solidaristic wage policy because the latter tended to be partially offset by wage drift which varied with profitability. In any case, more internally generated funds were made available for investment, and the cost of capital and the required rate of return was made lower than would otherwise have been the case (Bergström *et al.*, 1975).

Second, the substantial growth of public-sector savings that occurred in the early years of the national pension fund did increase the supply of loan capital available to business. In part this occurred directly, either through a system whereby firms could borrow back payroll taxes they had paid in or by borrowing funds made available by the pension fund on the regular credit market. In large part, however, this seems to have occurred indirectly. Pension fund capital was used to meet the credit needs of sectors to which the government gave priority, primarily housing and local government. This left more of private capital, channelled through the commercial banking system, available to business.

However, there are limits to the availability of this private credit. The whole supply of credit has been subject to controls designed to make sure that the welfare state investments in housing and local government to which the government gave priority were financed. Moreover, in those periods referred to earlier when the government failed to make fiscal policy restrictive enough soon enough, it turned to its controls on the supply of credit to make up for its mistakes in fiscal policy. Given its allocative priorities and the controls to enforce them, the resulting credit crunches hit business borrowing especially hard (Lybeck, 1977).

Still, the amount of finance available has evidently not been as much of a constraint as the form in which it has been available. Since the savings accumulated in the public sector have been made available primarily in the form of loan rather than equity capital, their utilisation must increase debt-equity ratios in the absence of corresponding increases in equity capital, which has been the case. Insofar as this increases a firm's financial vulnerability, it is thought to inhibit relatively risky investments. This has been partly offset as interest rates lagged behind inflation so that the real interest costs were lowered. But insofar as the profits squeeze was sustained and nominal interest rates gradually rose, firms have apparently been increasingly reluctant to add to their debt burdens (Utma and Lydahl, 1977; Swedish government, 1978).

In fact, the profits squeeze was evidently sustained and even intensified, and the operation of the wage determination system, with its combination of central, industry and local negotiations, contributed to it.[7] The impact of wage pressures was uneven, fluctuating according to the pattern displayed in the mid-1960s described earlier. In this pattern, the first of two successive wage settlements results in a relaxation of the profits squeeze which is restored in the second. In the negotiations leading to each of the settlements, LO's demands reflect economic conditions and profit levels at the time, first underestimating and then overestimating economic conditions and profit levels during the periods in which the respective agreements are in effect. The underestimation is demonstrated by wage drift in excess of contractual increases in the first settlement, and the overestimation by wage drift lower than the contractual increases in the second settlement. This pattern was repeated again in the 1969-70 period and in the mid-1970s.

The successive relaxations and intensifications of the profits squeeze have not exhibited the symmetry that would result in the fluctuation of the relative shares of labour and capital around a constant trend. Instead, the net effect over the long term seems to have been a downward trend in the share of capital and in various measures of profitability.

These have reached record low levels as a combined result of the most recent pair of settlements following the described pattern, the first for 1974 and the second for 1975 and 1976, and the unexpectedly deep and prolonged recession in the international economy.

The cumulative effect of this trend seems to be that there has not been enough investment in the more profitable parts of the private sector to offset reductions in employment in the less profitable parts. Instead, the offsetting increase in employment has been provided by enlarging the public sector. This would have occurred anyway to some extent as a result of the Social Democrats' definite goal of expanding the welfare state. However, it is argued that the expansion of the public sector was accelerated each time the profits squeeze was intensified in order for the Social Democrats to fulfil their commitment to full employment as well. If this argument is right, then part of the expansion of the public sector essentially compensated for the net decline of employment in the private sector. While this is a way of maintaining full employment in the short run, the argument goes on, it fails to solve another problem which threatens full employment over the long run (Söderstrom and Viötti, 1977).

The problem arises from the substantial degree to which the Swedish economy is dependent on international trade. Between a quarter and a third of Sweden's GNP is accounted for by international trade. Recent and growing balance of payments deficits are interpreted as indicating that the international competitiveness of Swedish industry has declined. It is in Swedish industry, which is predominantly in the private sector, that most of the tradables are produced — goods that are exported or compete with imports. If the expansion of the public sector, in which most production continues to be of non-tradables, is accompanied by a sufficient change in the composition of demand to reduce imports, then the needed level of exports is obviously reduced. Thus, a reduction in Sweden's dependence on international trade would make entirely acceptable a decline in the tradables-producing sector resulting from the increased attrition of less competitive firms because of the intensified profits squeeze. However, to the extent that such a reduction in the degree to which Sweden's economy is integrated in the international economy cannot be brought about, the competitiveness of the tradables-producing sector has to be restored.

This presupposes the narrowing of the cost differential between Sweden and its trading partners that has been opened up by the system of wage determination, particularly the wage explosion that occurred as a result of the settlements for 1975 and 1976 (OECD, 1977). For this

to come about, there has to be some combination of slower wage increases and faster productivity increases. The latter depend on increased
investment, which will only be forthcoming in the private sector if
profit prospects are restored sufficiently to justify the investments, at
least from the firms' point of view, and to be able to finance the investment with what is regarded by the firms as a sufficient proportion of
equity capital, whether internal or external. Whichever way the equity
capital is generated, the extent to which it is generated at all depends
on the level of profits.

There is actually very wide agreement among participants in the
Swedish economic policy arena that some restoration of Swedish
industry's international competitiveness is necessary, and that this
depends on increased investment financed with an increased proportion
of equity capital.[8] However, there is fundamental disagreement over
the distributive terms on which this increased investment is to be
brought about. The LO's power in the labour market enabled it to bring
about the squeeze on profits; to relax it in order to permit investment
to increase has been ruled out as long as that investment takes place in
private firms so that the effect would be to increase the inequality of
wealth and also power. This is unacceptable on ideological grounds
generally. But it is particularly unacceptable on the ground that it
would make impossible the continued co-ordination of wage bargaining
on the basis of a solidaristic wage policy. The increase in drift would
diminish its effectiveness and, with it, its credibility. This would under-
mine its effectiveness as a means of avoiding inter-union wage rivalry
and thus of maintaining the cohesion on which the labour movement's
political dominance and therefore full employment depends. For LO,
then, and with some delay and reluctance the Social Democratic Party
as well, the conclusion is now that the only way out of the dilemma is
a change in the institutional framework within which investment takes
place that will make it possible to increase investment without
increasing economic inequality.

The change that LO has proposed is a partial collectivisation of
profits (Meidner, 1978). As adopted by the 1976 LO Congress, the
proposal is that some percentage of profits, say 20 per cent, of all
private firms above some specified size, be transferred in the form of
new, directed issues of shares to a system of 'wage earners' funds' set
up and administered by the unions. The portion of profits allocated to
the funds would constitute new equity capital, remaining at firms'
disposal for investment. But instead of accruing to private investors, the
new wealth thereby created would become the collective property of

all wage earners. Dividend income, like the shares, would not be distributed but used for a variety of services for all workers, such as education, and to provide the technical backing unions need to make the most of their enlarged voice in workplace and enterprise decisions. The voting rights as well as claims to wealth that go with share ownership would also accrue to the funds, so that in time they would gain controlling shares in the corporations.

In principle, LO's scheme for the collectivisation of profits short-circuits the link between profits and personal income of both private shareholders and workers. To the extent that the growth in equity resulting from reinvested profits accrues to the wage earners' funds instead of the original owners, the investment takes place without a corresponding increase in the private shareholders' wealth. Wage settlements that permit an increase in retained profits that are re-invested on this basis would therefore not imply a transfer to private shareholders of income that unions failed to extract for their members. In this way, wage patterns could be more easily insulated from profits — i.e. firms' ability to pay — as required by the solidaristic norm of equal pay for equal work, and as would also be required if increased investment is to be induced and partly financed by an increase in retained profits.

In the initial stages of the operation of such a scheme, it would of course only partially reduce private shareholders' gains from increased investment. But as an increasing proportion of total equity capital accumulated in the wage earners' funds, the effect would become stronger. Over the long run, in fact, the consequences of the scheme are clearly far reaching. It would mean the gradual but inexorable erosion of private-property institutions as the basis for organising economic activity. Throughout the industrial core of Sweden's economy, private property would be displaced by a form of social ownership, though not state ownership.

It was thereby only to be expected that LO's proposal should provoke intense resistance by the business community. Joined by the bourgeois parties, it mounted an ideological offensive against the scheme reminiscent of the anti-planning campaign prior to the 1948 election. This apparently contributed to the Social Democrats' defeat in the 1976 election — though the margin was miniscule and they were vulnerable on a great many issues, particularly nuclear energy. Although the wage earners' funds obviously presented an ideologically polarising issue, the Social Democrats did not try to make the most of its mobilising potential. Instead, they went on the defensive, trying to avoid any stand on the issue. They stressed that no decision would be reached until after the following election, once a commission it had appointed to look into it had reported. Their attempt to duck the issue may well have cost them more votes than they would have lost if they had declared their acceptance of LO's proposal in principle, even if not in detail (Martin, 1977). This is what they have since done.

The Social Democrats would really seem to have no alternative but to go along with some form of collectivisation of profits unless they are willing to subject their ties to LO to very severe strains, thereby jeopardising the most important political resources they have. LO's stake in some change of that sort would seem to be too strong to permit them to retreat on the issue. At the same time, the Social Democrats obviously have a stake in finding some formula for collective profit sharing sufficiently acceptable outside LO so as not to be an electoral liability and perhaps to be an asset. This essentially means a formula acceptable to the white-collar union federation, TCO. TCO has been so divided on the issue that it initially avoided taking any stand on it. But now it appears to be moving towards a position close to LO's, particularly as the latter has been modified in negotiations with the Social Democratic Party. The modification has included a reduction in the proportion of firms to be compulsorily brought under the scheme and a larger element of public-sector participation in accumulating and administering new sources of finance for investment.

Which way TCO decides to move on the issue is also crucial for the Liberals. The smallest party, the Liberals, are divided over their ideological orientation and also the strategy most likely to ensure their survival — one faction favouring continuing participation in the bourgeois coalition and the other leaning towards coalition with the Social Democrats. In either case, the Liberals need increased support within TCO. If the latter adopts a position close to that hammered out by LO and the Social Democrats, it would be difficult for two of the three bourgeois parties, the Liberals and Centre Party, to oppose it in view of their dependence on support within TCO. Each would more likely be split over the issue, with the balance within the Liberal Party tipping in favour of the faction more eager for a coalition with the Social Democrats.

Under such circumstances, it is difficult to see how the Social Democrats could fail to regain control of the state in the 1979 election, with or without the support of the Liberals. If this happens, it would establish the political conditions for the third stage in the evolution of Sweden's Keynesian political economy. The pattern of policy in that stage would be characterised by the socialisation of investment, as Keynes had anticipated, although in forms and for reasons somewhat different from those he adumbrated, in addition to the techniques characterising the first and second stages in Sweden. In particular, the form taken by the third stage would be a direct outgrowth and condition for continued operation of the pattern of policy character-ising the second stage in that country.

There is no certainty that this will happen, however. A common formula on which LO, TCO and the Social Democrats can agree will not necessarily be found. The Swedish business community has been carrying out a strenuous campaign in favour of individual profit sharing, which not only preserves the link between profits and personal income but also avoids establishment of any new institutions of social owner-ship (Sveriges Industriforbund, 1976). This is fundamentally different from the LO's approach and entirely unacceptable to it, while business continues to attack collective profit sharing as a threat to both freedom and efficiency. This could prevent TCO from arriving at any position in order to avoid internal conflict, and thereby shift the balance in the Liberal party towards the faction favouring preservation of the present alliance of the three bourgeois parties. The Social Democrats might then be reluctant to go along with LO's position, resulting in increased tension between them. Defeat in the next election would then be more likely.

However, even if the Social Democrats do get back into office without reaching agreement with LO on a pattern of policy permitting restoration of investment, failure to do so would make it difficult to cope with the problems of economic policy bound to confront it once in office. A decline in the cohesion of the Social Democratic labour movement would undoubtedly impair the effectiveness of economic policy. The result would probably be another election defeat for the Social Democrats, and this would be likely to lock the political economy into an even deeper stalemate. It would be impossible to move to the next stage of a Keynesian political economy at a time when the second-stage pattern of policy can no longer work. Further economic deterioration would probably be inevitable, with Sweden eventually succumbing to the 'British disease' (Dahmen, 1977).

A Concluding Note

We have suggested that a Keynesian political economy undergoes a process of evolution that has a definite logic, which we have tried to illustrate by tracing the development of the Swedish political economy during the long era of Social Democratic rule. This has involved a great deal of oversimplification of both the logic and the Swedish case. As for the former, we have neglected to spell out the alternative forms that the patterns of policy might take in the successive stages under different political conditions, and which they have taken in different countries. Moreover, we have glossed over the issue of how far other forms of intervention, particularly those designed to influence the composition of activity, can be assimilated within a framework that is still Keynesian, given Keynes's own inclination to assume that market mechanisms would take care of the composition of economic activity as long as its macroeconomic behaviour was correctly managed and, it should be added, the maldistribution of income was corrected. This issue is all the more important in view of the multiplicity of substantive goals and sectoral interests to which policy is actually geared, through techniques quite different from those ordinarily associated with Keynesian patterns of policy and by a wide variety of political formations. As far as the Swedish case is concerned, we have omitted a great deal that might have made its evolution more understandable and perhaps presented a some-what modified picture. In this connection, the most serious gap concerns the relation between Sweden's integration in the international economy and the basic long-term shifts taking place in the structure of that economy. This was only peripherally alluded to from time to time but is in fact a great deal more important for understanding the development of Sweden's political economy.

However, a more thorough analysis of at least the Swedish case would still make it difficult to avoid the conclusion that its evolution has reached a turning point, at which it is no longer possible to maintain full employment without institutional changes that would seriously en-croach on the capitalist character of its economy. Such a turning point may not be reached in countries with different configurations of power, especially where labour movements have less power in the political arena as well as the labour market. Under such political conditions, the difficulty of reconciling continuous full employment with the require-ments of capitalist investment may more easily be resolved in favour of the latter. If so, the Keynesian era would indeed have been brought to an end in those countries, not because there is no way of maintaining full employment consistently with the basic argument underlying Keynesian policy but because the political conditions for doing so are not present.

Notes

1. For a brief general discussion of the Swedish Social Democratic Party, see Scase, 1977.

2. On the German case, see Gates, 1974, and Woytinsky, 1961. For the British case, see Skidelsky, 1967, and Kavanagh, 1973.

3. An example from American economic policy in the early 1960s is provided in Martin, 1973:pp.48-54.

4. On the controversy over economic policy in the late 1940s, see Hancock, 1972:pp.208-14. On economic policy generally during the postwar quater-century, see Lindbeck, 1973.

5. The 1951 LO policy statement has been translated into English (LO:1953). See also the articles by G. Rehn and others in Turvey (ed.), 1952, and the discussion in Industrial Council . . ., 1969:pp.163-81.

6. What made the whole strategy acceptable to the LO was its confidence that if the Social Democrats did remain in power they would in fact maintain full employment. Thus, public sector savings would be the result of a literally 'full employment surplus'. In addition, the surplus would be in a total budget channelling a growing portion of national income into social expenditures and transfers, including manpower policy on the ambitious scale required to ensure alternative employment and cover the transition costs involved to workers in firms that shut down. LO's confidence was based on the record established by the Social Democrats since 1932, and was reinforced by the Social Democrats' subsequent performance in office. In contrast, British unions have had much less basis for confidence that British Labour governments would ensure full employment. While the Attlee government's performance in this respect undoubtedly offset the distrust created by the MacDonald government, the Wilson governments' record could hardly have reinforced the unions' confidence. For a more detailed comparison, see Martin, 1975:pp.22-4.

7. This discussion is based partly on sources cited and interviews by the author conducted in Sweden in 1975. Full documentation will be provided in my contribution to Lindberg, L.N., and Maier, C.S., *The Politics and Sociology of Global Inflation,* forthcoming.

8. An official expression of this view may be found in Swedish Government, 1971:pp.153-60. This is an English translation of the 1970 Long-Term Survey.

4 MARXISM, THE STATE AND THE URBAN QUESTION: CRITICAL NOTES ON TWO RECENT FRENCH THEORIES[1]

Michael Harloe

Since the late 1960s there has been a rapid growth of urban and regional studies with important contributions from economists, geographers, political scientists, sociologists and others (Anderson, J., 1975;Eversley, 1975). A prominent place has been taken by new Marxist analyses which have principally been developed in North America and Western Europe (although there are strong links between some of this work and theories of dependent development in the Third World).[2] In Britain two studies have been particularly influential, *Social Justice in the City* published in 1973 (Harvey and *La Question Urbaine,* published in French in 1972 and recently available in a revised English edition (*The Urban Question*)(Castells, 1977). The former is the work of the geographer, David Harvey, and charts his progression from a liberal formulation of urban analysis to a 'socialist' perspective. Harvey has since developed his work in a more clearly Marxist direction (1978; *see also* Harloe, 1977a). However, his central concern has not been the details of urban politics and state urban and regional policies, for he has preferred to concentrate on key economic processes of capital accumulation, laying particular stress on the role of finance capital.

On the other hand, both in *The Urban Question* and in his many other writings (1973; 1974; 1975; 1976a; 1976b; 1977), Manuel Castells places the study of urban politics and state intervention in the sphere of 'collective consumption' (a notion that will be further discussed below, but which mainly refers in practice to state provided urban facilities) at the centre of his analysis. Castells's powerful critique of previous liberal theories of urban sociology and politics is more compelling and less controversial than much of the theory which he wishes to replace them by. He is, in fact, only one of a number of French urban researchers who have been concerned with these topics in the past few years and many of the disagreements that exist are not confined to the limits of his specific subject matter, urban development. The fact remains, however, that Castells's bold attempt to develop a coherent Marxist approach to urban questions has been the most important intellectual source for much of the French work. His willingness to enter into critical discussion about his approach in Britain, America and elsewhere has been immensely valuable in stimulating a truly international debate in a field in which this has occurred all too rarely in the past. This paper takes a highly critical view of his theories of urban politics, the central theme of his work, but it is a critique which is founded on a clear recognition of the value and importance of Castells's pioneering effort.

Castells's work is heavily influenced by Poulantzas's theory of the political 'instance' and hence also by Althusserian 'structuralism'. There are important differences between this and the more orthodox Marxist treatment of politics, which tends to stress the economic base of society and the super-structural nature of the political system (i.e. the determination of the second by the first) more clearly than Poulantzas.

In particular, a vigorous debate has occurred between Poulantzas and various theorists of the French Communist Party (PCF) about the nature of the state and its relationship to the dominance of the advanced capitalist social formations by monopoly capital — a tendency recognised by both sides (Baran and Sweezey, 1966). Jean Lojkine is one of the leading participants in this debate and, in addition, just as Castells has applied Poulantzas's approach to the 'urban question', Lojkine has developed his own theories of urban development and politics, based on the PCF theory of state monopoly capitalism, which also employ the concept of 'collective consumption' (see especially his contribution in Pickvance, 1976).

A detailed comparison and critique of the two approaches, grounded in a consideration of the theory of monopoly capital, would go well beyond the bounds of this paper but Pickvance has recently analysed some of the divergences at length (pointing out that the differences between the two approaches are sometimes less than the protagonists seem to realise) (Pickvance, 1977). Both sides reject the idea that the state is 'above' social classes; rather it 'reflects' the class struggle. For Poulantzas, the state's role is primarily political. It consists of organising the political interests of the dominant class (i.e. the different fractions of capital under the hegemony of monopoly capital) and fragmenting the interests of the dominated classes. This 'political instance' has 'relative autonomy', i.e. it is not determined directly by the economic instance. As a consequence, state policies may involve courses of action which are opposed to the *economic* interests of the dominant class, in order to preserve their *political* power. Pickvance points out that Lojkine agrees that the state has the dual function

124 Marxism, the State and the Urban Question

of maintaining the cohesion of the social formation as a whole and directly enforcing the domination of the bourgeoisie. But Lojkine emphasises the *economic* intervention of the state, rather than political or ideological intervention, and considers that state intervention merely exacerbates contradictions.

A final point of difference is concerned with relationships between the state, dominant monopoly capital and the other fractions of capital. Poulantzas's discussion of this issue is complex but, briefly, he rejects the PCF view that the state and the monopolies are 'fused in a single mechanism'. The state's role in ensuring the continuance of capital's domination of the working class precludes the monopoly fraction from *determining* state policies solely in its own interests, even though the predominant feature is state action which tends to aid this fraction. Poulantzas underlines the importance of non-monopoly capital to the monopolies (an obvious example would be the role of small parts suppliers *vis-à-vis* the motor manufacturers) and the need to maintain a certain level of cohesion of the capitalist class as a whole (Poulantzas, 1975).[3] This aim would not be served if the state acted purely as a functionary for the dominant fraction. Nor could the state continue to be the instrument of political control over the working class and maintain its ideological 'neutrality' in this case, unless it relied on pure repression. Although Lojkine has tried to refute Poulantzas's claim that the theory of state monopoly capitalism ignores these vital distinctions between the state and the dominant fraction, by claiming that state action exacerbates contradictions and therefore 'reflects' the class struggle rather than simply functioning for monopoly capital, his studies of actual policies do emphasise the functionality of urban politics for monopoly capital, as we shall see. This enables him to support the PCF strategy of seeking an anti-monopoly alliance between medium and small capital and the working class. Poulantzas, on the other hand, regards the broad divisions between capital and labour as more fundamental to politics than the monopoly/ anti-monopoly split.

These comments can be no more than an outline of some important features of the approaches which underpin Castells's and Lojkine's urban theories. Both of them, despite their differences, emphasise the interrelationship of the state and monopoly capital in urban policy and the growing role of the latter in capitalist development, together with the possibilities which this situation offers for 'urban social movements', i.e. the organised opposition of oppressed groups which goes beyond a purely reformist perspective. Their substantive theories are complex and detailed, so this paper will simply highlight some of their main propositions and assess the extent to which these are adequate to the task of analysing political aspects of the 'urban question'. Their work is sometimes ambiguous. There often seems to be inconsistency between the stated theories and the way in which they are used in specific analyses. So the following discussion cannot be definitive, only attempting to make a limited number of points about the utility of broad concepts, theories and methodologies.

Manuel Castells

As mentioned above, Castells's work is heavily influenced by Althusser's 'structuralist' reading of Marx and Poulantzas's extension of such an approach to the analysis of the political instance (Althusser, 1970; Althusser and Balibar, 1970; Poulantzas, 1973).[4] According to this approach, the relationship between the economic and other 'instances or levels' (i.e. political and ideological elements) of the social formation consists of a complex but unified 'structural whole', in which the instances are distinct and relatively autonomous, co-existing within the complex structural unity and articulated with one another according to specific determinations fixed in the last instance by the level or instance of the economy. Each element can develop at different rates, and contradictions within and between elements are determined, not by a single factor such as economics, but by the complex effects of the structured whole. Althusser calls this 'overdetermination'. In any given historical period one instance will be dominant, hence autonomous, but only *relatively* so because of this structural determination. The structure determines the *places* and *functions* occupied and adopted by individuals, i.e. *practices*.

Now the fundamental relationship in Marxist analysis, that between capital and labour, is, at one and the same time, an economic, a political and an ideological relationship. The study of social formations (historical materialism) involves the study of these relations which form a complex and changing totality. This demands historically based accounts of social formations, or aspects of social formations, rather than abstracted theory. This is not to say that Marxism does not make use of abstractions from reality, but these cannot be thought of outside or above history or they become, like the theories of bourgeois economists that Marx criticised, empty and misleading (Marx, 1973: edition:pp.83-111). Tristram (1975) explains the dialectical relationship of theory to reality in Marx thus:

Marx's object of knowledge is an 'ideal average' of the capitalist mode of production, but it still has to be shown to be the 'ideal average' in real relations. Moreover Marx thinks that abstract theory must be shown to be valid or invalid by analysing the 'historical relations'. In fact Marx specifically warns against treating his theory as supra-historical. Such error can only result from failure to recognise that developments have to be studied within their historical context.

Althusser's reference to 'structures' and 'practices' is a *conceptual* distinction made in a philosophical (dialectical materialist) study. He is clear that *in actuality* these are not separable, i.e. it is people's actions that reveal the relations that exist between them (note the difference here between the Marxist approach and the view held, for example, by Weber that the analyst imposes his or her own concepts on the 'chaos' that is reality, (Althusser, 1970). However there is some danger that this conceptual distinction will be misapplied in the course of the study of aspects of actual social formations, and the resulting analyses consist of two parts, a formalistic, largely abstracted and ahistorical analysis of structures followed by the analysis of what people actually do, i.e. their practices or history, the former determining the latter. Some writers have, in fact, interpreted Althusser in this way.

Despite his repeated statements that structures and practices are not divisible in this way, Castells discusses the 'urban structure' and 'urban practices' separately in *The Urban Question.* He even suggests that 'any concrete situation is made up of systems of practices, defined by their position in the structure, but whose secondary effects express a relative autonomy, capable of redefining the situation beyond their structural charge'(1977:p.432). The inconsistency between his *theoretical* insistence on the inseparability of structures and practices and the way in which he actually uses them to provide distinct analyses of empirical material creates a good deal of the obvious tension and ambiguity in his work. He finds it extremely difficult to apply the methodology of his book, consisting of the attempt to outline an urban structure in order thereby to define the places and functions occupied by individuals, i.e. to analyse practices or the class struggle.[5] As a result he establishes a series of rather narrowly conceived propositions about the urban structure in a largely formalistic and *a priori* manner. And these, as we shall illustrate, can be extremely hard to relate to reality. However, his inadequate definition of the 'urban' serves to confine his discussion of urban practices to similarly restrictive

limits. This procedure, in application if not in intention, bears some
resemblance to the methods of earlier urban theories which Castells discusses in the first part of his book, in the sense that he seems to be
imposing a set of categories on the data. As he himself states, this has the
effect of generalising relationships which are in fact grounded in the
particular historical situation which these analysts were examining.
What results is ideology rather than theory, a particular 'moment' in
the relations between classes is misrepresented as a law which governs
human behaviour, i.e. something which men are subordinate to,
rather than something which they, through class struggle, can change.
A further consequence is that, as reality does change, such 'laws' —
which were probably only a partial and distorted abstraction from
reality in the first place — become less and less apposite to its understanding.

Castells's starting point is the analysis of space as 'an expression of
the social structure' and of its creation by elements of the economic,
political and ideological instances, by their combination and by the
social practices from which they proceed. His structural analysis is
then developed in depth, breaking down the three instances into a
series of sub-elements, at different levels, which form the overall
complexly articulated structure. The various empirical objects,
institutions and processes of the urban system can then be classified
according to this matrix. Thus the economic instance is divided into
production, consumption and exchange, and then production, for
example, into elements internal to the work process (e.g. factories and
raw materials), relations between the work process and the economic
instance as a whole (e.g. the industrial environment) and relations
between the work process and other instances (e.g. administration,
information). Further distinctions enable the position of the 'support
agents' to be specified. Thus housing, which is an element subsumed
under consumption, is further subdivided according to certain levels
(luxury houses, slums, etc.) and roles (lodger, owner, etc.).

Here there already seems to be an arbitrary imposition of concepts
on reality, for why should housing be subsumed under the element
consumption? At this first stage Castells is clear about just such a danger:
'there is no congruence between a theoretical element and an empirical
reality, which always contains everything at once'. However, he goes on,
'housing is economic, political and ideological, although its *essential
contribution* [my italics, M.H.] is placed on the level of reproduction of
labour power' [by which he means consumption] (1977:p.126). There is
no justification for this assertion but the requirement that Castells has

in practice for a structured reality imposes just such *a priori* choices, despite his theoretical disclaimers. In fact the importance of housing to a capitalist social formation at a given point in time may have more to do with stimulating production than the reproduction of the labour force (and the possible counter claim that this, in itself, will affect consumption is a mere tautology).

This approach leads to a method quite akin to the empiricist methodology which Castells wishes to reject, as may be seen in the series of analyses of the 'elements of the urban structure' which seem to be based on some arbitrary distinctions. For example, the section on 'the articulation of the economic system in space' (1977:pp.128-45) begins by breaking this down into production, consumption and exchange elements (P, C and E). The P element crisis consists of:

> the ensemble of spatial realisations derived from the social process of reproducing the means of production of the object of labour, C is the ensemble which derives from the reproduction of labour and E is derived from the transfers between P and C.

Castells then refers these conceptual distinctions to real spaces in a step which, as we shall see in the case of element C, he can never convincingly justify. The approach is illustrated by him, in the case of 'production space', by a classic piece of empiricist analysis of industrial location in the Paris region, in which he uses a series of statistics and descriptive concepts (indicators of technology and market position) to relate a typology of companies to a typology of locations. But this is a purely descriptive analysis which, if it is intended to define the 'places' which the 'agents' occupy in the class struggle over industrial location, only seems in fact to subordinate this to a series of factors, such as technology and market position, which are taken as the starting point for the examination. The separation of the conceptual distinction between structures and practices (which seems to Castells to require such a methodology) cannot be used to divide reality without distorting it.

The remarkable similarity between Castells's actual approach, as opposed to his intentions, and that of the bourgeois theorists he has criticised becomes even clearer when he subsequently discusses 'the theoretical delimitation of the urban'. The conclusion of his critique of bourgeois urban sociology was that it had no scientific, i.e theoretical object ('a certain conceptual cutting up of reality') or real object ('a specific field of observation') but was an ideological construction, for the reasons given above. However, his own theory, which we have argued falls into a similar methodological trap to that of his predecessors, leads him in turn to resurrect a distinctive definition of the 'urban' which is referrable to an element of his urban structure and to particular aspects of reality. (Note that the discussion is confused from the outset by prior reference to the structure, of which the 'urban' is a part, as the *urban* structure. Clearly Castells means, at the more general level, the *spatial* structure.)

His theoretical definition of the 'urban' is quickly achieved. Noting that he has so far laid out the basis for a field of study of the structure of space, he rejects this as 'common sense pragmatism' by reminding us that 'physical space is the deployment of matter as a whole' so the study of the structure of space is no more or less than a history of matter. Clearly, this argument is only sustained by forgetting the fact that it is a theory of the *social* structuring of space, such as he himself has just outlined, rather than a physical theory, that is required. His methodological desire for a specific relation between conceptual elements and segments of reality, noted above in the case of housing, then leads to the conclusion that 'the delimitation "urban" connotes a unit defined either in the ideological instance, or in the politico-juridical instance, or in the economic instance, (1977:pp.234-7). But, he claims, as neither urban ideologies nor politically defined boundaries adequately encompass commonly recognised urban phenomena, it follows that the 'urban' *must* refer to an economic unit. This attempt to redefine the Marxist study of the spatial expression of capitalist social development seems to be quite arbitrary. However Castells takes his definition yet one stage further.

The urban unit, the concept, has to define a unique reality, 'the city' in economic terms. But a part of production is concerned with reproducing the means of production and, in this case, 'the search for a specificity of the first [i.e. a spatial expression of the concept] leads us much more to what are called regional problems, (1977:p.236). So, by elimination (again): 'the "urban" seems to me to connote directly the processes relating to labour power'. The study of the urban thus becomes the study of the reproduction of labour power, i.e. consumption. Yet, in fact there is no obvious permanent relationship between the label (be it 'urban' or 'regional') which is applied to a given space in a given historically determined situation and either an instance — be it economic, political or ideological — or an element of an instance — be it production, consumption or exchange. To give 'urban' and 'region' a specific content, as Castells does in an ahistoric way, is simply

to impart a false and arbitrary distinction, as the examination of reality
soon makes clear.

When Marx referred to the distinction between the rural and the
urban, he was referring to a certain stage in the emergence of capitalism
when two different sets of social relations existed, the feudal mode
(rural) of exploitation, dominated by the capitalist (urban) mode. The
relations involved were economic, political and ideological. However,
in those advanced capitalist countries where the feudal mode has disappeared, this specific relationship between the 'urban' and the mode
of production has no contemporary relevance. Nor is there any reason
to resurrect a special content on the basis of an arbitrarily chosen
element lacking any historical reference — such as reproduction of
labour power. This is only feasible when the social relations which
define this reproduction differ in type in cities and in the countryside.

These difficulties affect Castells's discussion of urban politics.
'Urban' has the definition already mentioned and 'politics' is designated
as the system of power relations between classes. In practice politics
consists of the study of the state and its relationship to dominated
groups. The fact that class struggle is only analysed in this context itself
seems a rather arbitrary reduction, especially as Castells, following
Poulantzas, regards the state as a 'reflection' of this struggle. The
structure/practices distinction is again applied, so the study of urban
politics is broken down into two analytical fields, urban planning and
policy and urban social movements. And, although Castells is clear
that these are 'indissolubly linked', he then presents, on the one hand,
a series of structural analyses of various urban planning policies and,
on the other, analyses of practices, in the form of urban social
movements (1977:chs.13,14). Urban planning consists of state intervention in the field of consumption (reproduction of labour power)
with the aim of ensuring the continued domination of capital and,
hence, the reproduction of capitalism. Urban social movements are
organisations, formed by dominated groups to contest such consumption
issues, whose actions produce a qualitatively new effect on the social
structure (which means something other than the type of 'regulative'
adjustment involved when planners make 'concessions' in response to
pressure from protesting groups).

This language seems openly functionalist, for the ability to
distinguish a 'regulative' change from a 'qualitatively' new effect must
depend on the specification of some sort of state of system maintenance,
and therefore also of system disintegration. In contrast, the Marxist
conception of the capitalist social formation stresses that societies

develop and, at the same time, produce the conditions of their eventual destruction. If this is so, the main aim of analyses of urban struggles must surely be to examine a double effect, the extent to which the interests of capital *and* of labour are affected by such struggles. Naturally some struggles may result in outcomes which are more or less favourable to capital or to labour, but the attempt to divide urban social movements from mere reformist struggles seems misplaced *at the level of theory.* There is also a danger that Castells's particular 'structural' approach to the study of the state's urban policies as a way of defining the 'places' occupied in practice, will lead to the type of results seen above in the case of industrial location. And his claim that one can analyse urban politics from two perspectives, depending on whether 'the analysis bears on a modification of the relations between the instances of the logic of the social formation or the processes of its transformation' shows that he does indeed again operationalise the structures/practices distinction.

Castells's final step is to link the study of urban politics to 'collective consumption'. He claims that the urban units, the units of reproduction of labour power, are in fact *collective* units of reproduction of labour power, i.e. units which are structured by processes of *collective consumption.* The rationale for this last step is not clearly laid out at the point where it is first introduced but at the end of the book the argument, which Castells has subsequently developed, is set out thus (1977:pp.437-71; *see also* his contribution to Poulantzas (ed.), 1976):

> ... in advanced capitalist societies we are witnessing an increasing collectivisation of the conditions underlying the processes of reproduction of labour power.

He argues that the concentration of capital in advanced (monopoly) capitalism requires a concentration of the workforce in urban units (residential units, oriented to consumption practices) and so the workers' consumption becomes increasingly socialised. The analogy is with the socialisation of production, the extension of the division of labour and the co-operative organisation of the act of production (see the discussion of co-operation and the division of labour in Marx, 1974 edition: chs. XIII and XIV). Castells also seems to suggest that this development involves demands for means of consumption which require large-scale provision. But such provision, although necessary to capitalism, cannot or will not be provided by private enterprise. There are several reasons for this, e.g. because the provision requires co-ordination

between competing capitalists and subordination of sectional interests
or because profit rates in the particular industry concerned are low, as
in the case of housing for the poor. So state provision and intervention
become increasingly necessary. Therefore, as urban politics refers to
state intervention and urban social movements, collective consumption
is its specific subject matter. Moreover urban social movements are
growing in significance, because increasing state intervention causes
increasing politicisation of the issues involved and hence increasing
conflict occurs. Castells concludes that 'the state becomes through its
arrangement of space, the real manager of everyday life' (Harloe (ed.),
1976:p.64).

It is not difficult to appreciate the tendentiousness of much of this
chain of reasoning. Firstly, concentration of capital in present-day
capitalism does not necessarily involve both the concentration of
control and management of capital and the spatial concentration of the
labour force.[6] Castells simply projects on to present-day conditions a
state of affairs which existed in the early stages of industrialisation.
This obviously facilitates the analogy between socialisation of
consumption and production. However, rather than the simple process
of metropolitan agglomeration which he envisages, in reality capital
locates and relocates itself according to where profits can best be
achieved. This involves, as for example Warner has shown in his
historical studies of US urban development, 'the opposing characteristics of centralisation and decentralisation' (Warner, 1972:p.58),
both of which need to be considered in any concrete study. Secondly,
the parallel drawn with the socialisation of production (Castells (1977:
p.431) even says 'the urban unit is to the process of reproduction what
the company is to the process of production'), is never more than a
suggestive analogy whose content, on further inspection, is unclear.
What is the correlate for the division of labour in the productive act?
In other words, what is collective about collective consumption? From
the examples given by Castells and others, such as public housing,
public transport or public education, he certainly cannot be referring to
the act of consumption for this is both initiated and completed by the
individual. Pahl, in a recent critical examination of the many contexts
in which Castells uses the term, concludes that 'in much of Castells's
writing it is possible to substitute the phrase "state provision" for
"collective consumption" without materially altering the sense'. Not
too far, in fact, from Pahl's own earlier emphasis on urban sociology as
the study of the state management of urban consumer goods and
services (Pahl, 1978).[7] Castells has recently clarified this issue

by admitting that he is really referring to the nature of the production and management of these means of consumption (in Poulantzas (ed.), 1976:p.342). But even this seems to run together two definitions which should be considered separately. For example, British public housing is usually produced by private capital but is managed by the state. More generally, as Preteceille (1975;1977:pp.101-23) has effectively argued, the state intervenes in a wide-ranging manner in the means, relations and practices of consumption. And, just as significantly, it abstains from intervention in some cases as well.

Thirdly, must increasing state intervention lead to increasing politic-isation of issues? For Castells this seems to be unproblematic, because the state appears to have become, not just the 'reflection of the class struggle', but its actual manifestation. But if this is so, it means that relations between groups outside the sphere of state involvement are devoid of political significance (except of course insofar as these may be 'reflected' in state action). Furthermore is it *necessarily* true that increased state intervention results, *via* increased politicisation, in increased conflict? Even if capitalism is becoming an increasingly conflict-ridden mode of production, specific state activities may actually reduce or remove conflict.

To summarise, Castells's analysis of urban politics seems to make a number of arbitrary assumptions which are often rather one-sided abstractions from reality, as in the concentration/deconcentration example. The attempt to define the 'urban' in terms of consumption is unconvincing and the content of the urban analysis is further narrowed by his focus on collective consumption. Moreover the simple emphasis on the growth of state involvement (which is, of course, not specific to Marxist analysis), linked to a growing and necessary socialisation of consumption, is unsubstantiated. Nor is there any reason to confine consideration of the class struggle over urban issues to urban social movements.

In fact, what is conventionally called urban development can only be understood by reference to the social relations of production, circulation and consumption of goods and services. These social relations are class relations, i.e. relations between dominant and dominated groups, and they have contradictory effects which are expressed in economic, political and ideological terms. Moreover the expressions define the relationship; the two concepts cannot be separately referred to specific empirical data. So the *only* way to under-stand the relations is to study them as they actually occur, i.e. to study their history.

This involves not simply studying state intervention because, although this is, in the aggregate, increasing it is not totally pervasive, but also taking account of the various class interests which are expressed outside the sphere of state influence. In fact if we accept that state actions are both necessary yet insufficient to maintain capitalism, the really important task is to understand the nature, limits and effects of its interventions as they occur in the specific context being analysed. Such intervention may take a variety of forms and may increase or decline over time. All these are empirical questions, which is not to say that we cannot, tentatively at first, suggest some general features which are likely to condition this intervention. An illustration of this point is contained in a later section of this paper. Castells, however, advances a narrow and unhistorical concept of urban politics and, as we shall briefly illustrate, this leads him into difficulties when he presents specific examples for study.

Thus he analyses the British new towns policy (1977:pp.277-83) as, principally, 'a direct intervention by the state apparatus in consumption' even though he also mentions that the Royal Commission on the Distribution of the Industrial Population, the forerunner of the new towns policy, was concerned with industrial decentralisation. However, he dismisses the significance of this because the new towns, in practice, only absorbed a relatively small proportion of mobile industry. But then neither did the new towns solve the consumption problems of the urban masses (adequate houses, etc.)! It is really quite arbitrary to label new town development as state intervention in consumption but Castells is driven to do this by his definition of the urban.

Problems arising from this restricted definition characterise analysis of another example of urban planning — the recent policy of urban renewal in central Paris. As this concerns urban planning it must refer to reproduction of the labour force, in this case principally housing. Yet as Castells shows, the key to understanding why urban renewal occurred in Paris is the 'extended reproduction of the specialisation of productive spaces', office development, in fact, i.e. a regional phenomenon according to his previous classification. Castells resolves this difficulty by concluding that it is necessary to study 'the transformation of all the elements of the urban structure of the region'. It is unclear how this is possible, given his theoretical schema.

Turning to the study of urban social movements, Castells refers to several examples: firstly various groups who were being displaced by the policy of urban renewal in central Paris, and who organised in order to put pressure on the authorities for adequate rehousing; secondly

grass-roots movements for urban reform in Montreal; and thirdly
squatter settlements in Chile before and during the Popular Unity
government of Salvador Allende (1977:pp.304-22). But his evidence
shows that neither the Canadian nor the Parisian movements achieved
the qualitative changes that Castells uses as the basis of the definition
of an urban social movement, although he claims that in Chile some of
the squatter settlements, by linking up with the broader conflict
between labour and capital then occurring, did help to achieve such a
change. But it is unclear from the evidence he presents that this urban
movement really had any major effect; rather it looks as if the revolutionary nature of the squatter settlement *derived* from the fact that
they were dominated by Popular Unity. This is not to say that urban
issues *cannot* have a broader significance. Castells (1978) himself has
recently shown how urban struggles in Spain have brought forward
demands for democratic local government and this has particular
significance in a country which is emerging from a totalitarian regime.[8]
However, there seems no reason to accept his narrow definition of
urban politics as urban social movements, plus urban planning of course.

It is only fair to mention that Castells (in an afterword to the
English edition of *The Urban Question* (1977:p.445), has admitted the
'formalism' in this work but he still asserts that his concept of the urban
system is useful as a means of 'expressing the forms of articulation
between classes'. Moreover his repeated insistence on the usefulness of
a definition of the urban based on collective consumption still seems, to
this writer, to be unconvincing and still dominated by the search for
specific empirical referents for the various elements in his urban
structure (viz. 'an urban unit is not a unit in terms of production. On
the other hand, it possesses a certain specificity in terms of residence, in
terms of "everydayness" '.[9]) Furthermore, although he now recognises
that reproduction of labour power involves collective and individual
consumption, he continues: 'which of the two structures space?
The one that dominates the process as a whole will structure the other;
although both exist one must dominate and therefore structure the
other'. His answer is that collective consumption, the emerging form,
is dominant and therefore it structures individual consumption and
urban space as a whole. But even if state provision *is* dominant (surely
highly arguable) this is no argument for concluding that its study
reveals the structuring of urban space (if by this Castells means, as he
seems to, the actual patterns of activities and resources in specific
cases). Castells seems here to be implying that the dominant is also
determinant. Yet the examination of specific urban areas will direct

attention not just to collective consumption but also to the broader perspectives already outlined.

Castells believes that rising levels of consumption are politically, economically and ideologically necessary for the continuance of capitalism and for monopoly capital, the hegemonic fraction. Moreover there is increasing state intervention in this sector and hence growing conflict. This raises new possibilities for working-class action which, because of the special importance he places on consumption in advanced capitalism, gives strategic importance to consumption-oriented conflict.

Yet it seems quite unhelpful to place a special emphasis on consumption considered in isolation from production, for they are inseparable in the Marxist analysis of capitalism.[10] As Lojkine (1977: p.124) has noted, Castells's division seems to reproduce the way in which urban issues are normally presented by bourgeois ideology, as consumption issues remote from the struggle over production. We shall suggest below that several aspects of Castells's theories may well have been unduly influenced by the particular situation in France at the time when his work was done. But this also seems to be the case with some of Lojkine's work, to which we now turn.

Jean Lojkine

Lojkine is highly critical of Castells's work, not just of the theory of the state he shares with Poulantzas, but of his methodology and the various restrictive and unnecessary limitations he places on the content of urban studies. For Lojkine the examination of production and consumption are inseparable. He also insists that an analysis of the class struggle and class interests must be central to such considerations, rather than something which can be approached via Castells's type of structural methodology. He would almost certainly agree with much of Mingione's (1977:pp.25,26) recent criticism of the Poulantzas/Castells approach to the analysis of political institutions and his outline of what he regards as the correct Marxist method.[11] Mingione writes that the key to the analysis of political institutions is an understanding of the relationship between base and superstructure. Class relations are fundamental to society and these are based on, at one and the same time, production and power relations. Power relations cannot be considered independently from the organisation of production. Class confrontation and struggle and the social relations of production form the basis or structure of society, but political organisation and institutions (social relations of power 'in the strict and formal sense') are part of the superstructure. There is a complex dialectical relationship between

structure and superstructure; altimately superstructural phenomena are
explained by structural ones, but they also influence structural events.
Normally this influence reinforces structural relations but occasionally,
for reasons originating in the structure itself, it may operate in the
opposite sense. For example, the proletariat, although dominated and
exploited, can acquire political power, and use it against the bourgeoisie,
which is unable to maintain a political consensus. Poulantzas would
disagree with this definition of structure because he denies the dialectical
unity within the structure of economic relations (conditions of capital
accumulation), power relations (conditions of class struggle) and
ideological relations (conditions of class consciousness on both sides).
(Indeed, as we have seen, each of these sets of relations becomes a
'structure' in Poulantzas/Castells.) Mingione concludes that the Marxist
study of a state or state policy demands a class analysis which is
historically and dialectically oriented and which surveys conditions of
capital accumulation, of class struggle and class consciousness.

Lojkine's recent major study, *Le Marxisme, L'Etat et la Question
Urbaine* (1977) besides repeating his earlier criticisms of Castells already
mentioned, does emphasise the need for historical and comparative
studies of urban development, in order to distinguish broader trends
from more specific features. He particularly draws attention to the
existence in France, since feudal times, of a highly centralised and
powerful state apparatus, in contrast to the situation in many other
capitalist countries. He is also at pains to deny that the 'fusion' of the
state and monopoly capital means that there is a monolithic power bloc,
and he lays great stress on the need for a careful analysis of the various
class interests involved when discussing urban policy. Indeed he
criticises Castells's accounts of urban renewal in Paris for failing to do
this and for 'exporting' class struggle and contradictions from his
structural analysis to the separate consideration of practices.

Lojkine, like Castells, bases his analysis of urban development on a
more general survey of advanced capitalism. The socialisation of
production has reached an advanced stage. This has precipitated an
acute crisis for the whole capitalist system. The concomitant growth
of monopoly capital has altered the pattern of class struggle, because
these big firms have expropriated many small and medium concerns.
Lojkine explicitly states that this is a more important division, at the
present stage, than the capital/labour division. Furthermore, the new
skill requirements of the monopolies, which involve the deskilling of
the bulk of the salaried staff and the acquisition of new skills by a
minority, have produced, on the one hand, a new working class and,

on the other, a new stratum tied to advanced capital. These conclusions have led Lojkine (and the PCF) to believe in the possibility of establishing an anti-monopoly front. His book seeks to suggest that struggles around urban issues are central to such a strategy. An important requirement is to show the close connection between the aims of state policy and those of the monopolies, by historical analysis rather than theorising. This relationship does not, he insists, reduce the state to a simple agent of the economic infrastructure. For example, he quotes research which showed that there are divisions in the French state between the dominant Ministry of Finance, representing the interests of the monopolies, and other ministries which tend to promote the interests of various groups of non-monopoly capitalists and others. (1977:pp.120, 121).

Lojkine's argument that urban development is especially important in the current situation is based on an extension of Marx's suggestion that there are certain 'general conditions of production', unproductive in themselves, i.e. not creating surplus value, but nevertheless essential to the operation of the productive process. According to Lojkine, Marx referred to transport and communication but he suggests that the means of collective consumption and the spatial concentration of the means of production and reproduction (reproduction of capital and labour force *via* individual and collective consumption) of the capitalist social formation must now be added to this list. Modern cities are typified by the growing concentration of the means of collective consumption. And this in turn gives rise to further needs and a particular type of agglomeration of capital and labour which itself becomes more and more necessary for capitalist development. We shall not discuss the details of Lojkine's arguments for this extension of the 'general conditions of production' but he makes two important points about the means of collective consumption (by which he means public housing, transport, etc.) which help to explain why the state has to make provision. Firstly, the means of collective consumption are unlike normal commodities whose values are relatively simple and specific, making it easy to offer them for sale. For facilities such as a school or a hospital have complex and diffuse uses whose value is difficult to measure in terms of an individualised need. Therefore, it is difficult to incorporate them in the normal process of commodity exchange. Secondly, the means of collective consumption tend to last a long time, requiring long-term investment which provides only a low rate of profit. It seems rather doubtful whether Lojkine is correct in assuming that these are general characteristics of facilities such as schools and hospitals, given the existence and even, in some countries, the growth of private 'collective consumption'. At best it seems a rather one-sided explanation of the situation, which is further weakened by his later remark that some schools, roads, etc., can be profitable.

According to Lojkine, the new type of urban development that is occurring gives rise to three categories of problems, all of which derive from the technical necessity for socialisation, which is manifested in the extension of the general conditions of production. These are, firstly, on the one hand, the need for planned co-ordination and, on the other, the need for, and the problem of, anarchic capitalist competition which limits this co-ordination. Second is the obstacle to urban development caused by individual land ownership, which, he suggests, is declining due to its appropriation by the financial monopolies. Third is the problem of financing unproductive and unprofitable means of collective consumption. None of these problems can be solved by individual capital, hence the necessity for state intervention. However, he stresses, this is not to imply that state action in these cases simply reflects monopoly capital's requirements for these problems to be solved. There are 'secondary' contradictions, most notably caused by certain units of the local state, which represent the interests of the dominated groups, and which therefore oppose the local or central interests of the monopoly state. Here Lojkine is thinking of the Communist and left-wing local administrations in France, which have grown in number in the past few years.

Therefore, urban politics is concerned with these problems and hence with organising the production and circulation of 'built forms' and the use of land. Lojkine, as we have seen, argues that state intervention in these matters exacerbates the contradictions which it aims to solve and deepens the basic monopoly/non-monopoly division. But to establish this he wants to show that urban politics is dominated by the interests of monopoly capital and that any 'concessions' to the dominated groups are marginal. Here Lojkine's method becomes highly dubious, for he ignores his own strictures on the need for careful historical analysis specific to the country in question (in his case France). Such an analysis would, in order to establish his wide ranging set of hypotheses, have to encompass a fairly comprehensive study of urban politics. But instead he only selects four examples of urban policy, where 'concessions' were made, for detailed analysis. Furthermore, the principles of such selection are not stated so we have no way of telling whether they are representative of the general situation or not. In each of these cases, concerned with property compensation, the autonomy of local government, hypermarket development and urban renewal, he claims to prove that the 'concessions' made to dominated fractions of capital or of labour were a sham. In fact these policies actually *advanced* the interests of the monopolies.

If Lojkine really believes these examples are representative and 'concessions' arising from the pressure of dominated groups have no real effect, he is clearly — for all his denials — suggesting that the state is merely a tool of monopoly capital, even though this may be masked by the bogus 'concessions'. In Marxist terms such an identity implies that society is on the verge of revolutionary changes or, alternatively, that there is massive repression either by physical means or by 'repressive tolerance'. Neither of these seems evident at the moment to the outside observer of the French situation.

Lojkine also seems to ignore his earlier concern about the need for care when extending analyses which draw on one country's experience to other places. He argues that the domination of state urban policies by monopoly capital is widespread but provides little convincing evidence for this. For example, after discussing the way in which, in France, local government (which is often controlled by non-monopoly groups) is increasingly under the power of central government and hence of monopoly capital, he extends this to Britain by reference to the changes in the 1972 Local Government Act and the establishment of Regional Economic Planning Boards. This is a very modest base on which to rest such a broad conclusion and, even though one accepts (on the basis of better evidence than he produces) that central control is increasing in Britain, this leaves the question open about whose interests this development serves.

Similarly flimsy arguments are used elsewhere in Lojkine's book to establish the generality of his conclusions. He stresses the severe limits to the power of left-wing local administrations to achieve progressive policies, given the dominance of central government. Using several examples, he argues that the increasing domination of central government by monopoly capital has led to a cut-back in funds for new urban facilities in the municipalities. This has particularly affected left-wing local authorities of course. And he does present some evidence which *suggests* that this has occurred in France. But, quite insupportably, he then extends this conclusion to Britain, by arguing (1977:p.310) that *nationally* UK central government contributions to local government covered 36.9 per cent of their budget in 1963/4 but that in 1974, only 10 per cent of the *GLC* budget came from central government! In fact, of course, the rate support grant now covers about 60 per cent of local expenditure.[12]

Clearly, Lojkine thinks that the state is, in *effect*, monolithic. It is not just dominated by the interests of monopoly capital but it has the power to *determine* the outcome of its actions so that they are in the interests of this fraction. In consequence, any consideration of class struggle, which is not almost foredoomed to failure, is excluded from the examination of state policies. Thus, as in Castells's book, but for different reasons, the study of urban social movements — taking up less than 30 pages in a 360-page book — is rather marginal to the main thrust of his study, which always emphasises the dominance and functionality of state monopoly capitalism. For Lojkine, a social movement is defined by the capacity of a dominated group to differentiate itself from the role and functions whose acceptance ensures its subordination in the system. This only seems to mean that they are groups which, being conscious of a disjunction between their interests and those of the dominant group, take some action to gain their own ends. However, Lojkine seems to be in difficulties with this definition, although he does not appear to recognise this, simply because of his earlier dismissal of the reality of 'concessions' to dominated groups. If this *is* so, how can urban social movements exist?

Despite this apparent inconsistency, Lojkine argues that the present pattern of urban development and the associated state intervention are the most advanced expression of the monopolistic socialisation of production which is now occurring. So urban struggles that arise in this situation, which focus on the three problem areas mentioned above, are of major importance. However, as with Castells, the argument for the strategic importance of urban struggles does not seem to rest on an analysis which establishes the importance of the very many protests against aspects of urban development which do occur. Indeed he appears to think that these achieve nothing. Rather, it derives from a theoretical explanation of the centrality of urban issues in the present stage of capitalism and from the proposition of a type of urban movement which *would* have the ability to effect a qualitative change (to borrow Castells's term) in this situation. The examples Lojkine gives of such movements are very restricted, consisting of a general strike which occurred in Turin in 1969 in protest against the rising cost of living; industrial action in 1974 by workers seeking to prevent the closure of the Rateau firm by its multinational parent company because of its wish to relocate the plant more profitably; and a new PCF urban programme, announced in 1975, which proposed urban policies to counteract the spatial segregation in the Paris region which was resulting from the actions of monopoly capital.

Critical Aspects of the Two Theories

Lojkine's and Castells's attempts to define the content of the Marxist analysis of urban politics are valuable because they raise many of the issues which such an analysis must confront. But, at crucial points, they employ faulty evidence and arguments. They both seek to establish that urban development is dominated by monopoly capital and that the contradictions that arise have wide reaching implications. This, they argue, is because urban development of a certain type is ever more centrally necessary for monopoly capital and because a point has been reached where the further evolution of capitalism is seriously in doubt. In this crisis certain types of urban protest movements can play a vital role. However, on inspection, these appear to exist more in theory than in practice. So, although the potential for significant class struggle exists within the urban scene, its *actual occurrence* is, as yet, rather limited.

Much of this argument seems to be based on a wish to convince the reader of the role of urban social movements and urban contradictions as a potentially important area for revolutionary political activity, but the suggestion that such conclusions follow from the arguments advanced is unconvincing. Both writers stress the limited or non-existent effects of the bulk of urban protest, although Castells sees some possibility for raised consciousness occurring. Such protests merely result in regulative action or even, according to Lojkine, action which involves no compromise by monopoly capital at all. This amounts to a division of urban politics into an element based on 'ineffective' class struggle, encompassing the majority of urban political issues, and a far smaller element based on 'effective' class struggle (from the point of view of dominated groups and their interests).

This is accompanied by an analysis of state intervention which stresses its functionality for monopoly capital. However, such a one-sided emphasis on functionality seems to remove meaningful class struggle to the periphery of urban politics; other conflicts exist of course but these merely affect the form rather than the substance of what occurs. This tends to contradict, rather than to support, the importance of urban struggles which both Castells and Lojkine are trying to establish.

So both theories tend to treat most of urban politics as merely functional. This may be compared with the alternative approach, outlined by Mingione, which stresses the dialectical relationship between structure and superstructure and that dominated groups can, despite their exploitation, exercise political power. Castells and Lojkine seem to pay little real regard to the effects of opposing interests, except with respect to what seems a rather limited form, urban social movements. This is despite their recognition, at points in their texts, that the analysis of state policies has to demonstrate the *tendency* of action in favour of the dominant group (for they both accept theories of the state which contain a distinction between the state and monopoly capital). In addition, Castells, reflecting the concerns of Poulantzas's theories, concentrates on discussing the regulative political role of the state in consumption issues, underemphasising the economic interests involved. For example, as Lojkine himself has noted, Castells's study of urban renwal in Paris only focuses on its role in developing the city as an office centre, without reference to the other economic interests concerned. In contrast, Lojkine concentrates on the regulative role of state policies based on an analysis of the economic interests served (*see* the discussion in Pickvance, 1977).

Apart from stressing the dialectical nature of the Marxist analysis of the state, Mingione also emphasises the need for an analysis which combines economic, political and ideological considerations. Such an analysis would require far greater historical specificity than Castells, or even Lojkine, achieves. Both of them try to establish a special theoretical content to their studies. This involves them in the formulation of general propositions about the role of urban development in current capitalism. If such propositions exist, beyond the most general level, one would expect that the best way to establish them would be *via* a careful comparative analysis, along the lines that Lojkine initially proposes or, at least, a fairly comprehensive analysis of French urban development which would then suggest directions for comparative studies.[13]

Rather than doing this, one is strongly under the impression that Castells and Lojkine have abstracted elements which are specific to French experience, or even specific to certain political strategies of the French left, and incorporated them, at an unjustifiable level of generality, in their theories. A definitive discussion of this possibility cannot be attempted here but one or two possible examples will be given. Some of these are very clear, for instance the way in which Lojkine tries to show that recent reductions in central government subsidy to local government (a specific development in French politics) is a more general trend. Another example is Castells's (1977: p.464) reference to a new petty bourgeois revolt based on an 'environmentalist' counterculture. This seems to be a popular political issue in France, provoked no doubt by the rapid economic development in recent years (Ardagh,

1977:pp.243-51). But, despite particular protests such as the anti-nuclear and anti-motorway campaigns it would surely not merit such an important role in an analysis of British urban politics.

More importantly, the emphasis both theories place on the state, its closeness to the interests of monopoly capital, its central control, and their de-emphasis of opposition, are surely influenced by:

(a) the historic centralisation of the French state (which Lojkine mentions but fails to take fully into account later on) and the weakness of local government.[14]

(b) the close links between civil servants and advanced sections of capital in carrying out the economic planning strategies of the last 20 years. In particular the Sixth Plan was specifically aimed at modernising French industry and building up its ability to meet foreign competition. As part of this policy, decisions about urban investment were closely tied to decisions about industrial expansion.[15] Also it is generally recognised that, under the Pompidou regime, there was a close link between urban development interests and the government.[16] Much of this occurred just when Castells and Lojkine were doing a good deal of their original work.

(c) The long period of domination of central government, and of direct or indirect control of local government, by the Gaullists and the exclusion of the left, especially the PCF.[17]

Other influences can be suggested. For example, in 1963 the French government decided to expand Paris and develop it as a tertiary centre. The subsequent urban renewal involved the removal of the working class.[18] Has this over-influenced more general references in Castells to the functionality of the metropolitan areas for monopoly capital and similar references in Lojkine to the new segregation of space between metropolitan areas occupied by the monopolies and peripheral towns which house the working class and the lower orders of capital? One cannot help feeling that if Castells and Lojkine had been living in London, their analyses might have been rather different.[19] Lojkine's stress on the destruction of small and medium capital, and hence, the possibility of an anti-monopoly alliance (apart from ignoring the question of whether dominated labour and ex-petty capitalists are likely to perceive common interests,[20] seems to be heavily influenced by a particular feature of France, because it was an economy which was largely based on such smaller producers 20 years ago but has since been rapidly 'rationalised'. Moreover there has been some quite significant political resistance to these changes from small business. Of course small business has declined in Britain too, but has it done so at

the same rate and with the same political consequences, and was it ever
as significant in the postwar British economy as in France?[21] Time and
again the need for either more detailed historical comparisons, or more
qualified conclusions, is apparent.

The connection of political strategy and analysis in Lojkine's case
has already been discussed, but did the aftermath of the 1968 struggles
in France, with the return to a lower level of militancy in industrial
relations, combining with the rather plentiful supply of urban research
funds, also lead radical sociologists towards an interest in urban politics
in order to explore its possibilities for political mobilisation? Pickvance
(1976:pp.1, 2; and in Harloe (ed.), 1978) has suggested that this may,
initially at least, have been so. This would also help to explain the lack
of a comprehensive consideration of the politics of urban policy and
the rather narrow focus on urban social movements. Pickvance (1976)
has added that with the growth of left-wing local administrations in
France, interests are broadening out. However, it remains to be seen
whether a theoretical framework which seems to have incorporated so
much of the content of a particular historical moment and political
strategy can be of real value in this new work (see the critiques of
earlier studies contained in Pickvance, 1977; Dunleavy, 1977a, 1977b).

The State and Urban 'Management' — Some British Examples

An effective analysis of state urban policies cannot view them in
functional terms but must recognise that their domination by the
interests of capitalism is tendential. Because the state 'reflects' the
class struggle, state policies are unlikely unequivocally to serve the
interests of one or other element in this struggle. State policies are
likely to be contradictory, being in more conventional terms, a
'compromise' between opposing economic and political interests.
But these 'compromises' often fail to provide a satisfactory resolution
of the problem concerned because this would involve the complete
subordination of some of these interests in favour of others. Two
consequences of this problem are the use of ideology to 'rationalise'
policy proposals and the fact that state actions often appear to solve
one problem, only to create another. The study of such aspects of
specific policies focuses attention on the general problems of state
management.

Claus Offe (1975a:pp.125-44) has discussed this problem of policy
formation. He has suggested some important considerations whose
usefulness, he stresses, can only be assessed as they are applied to
specific cases but which do seem to be based on more general features

of the capitalist state than many of those which Lojkine and Castells incorporate and which, at the same time, do focus on some aspects of the problematic nature of state 'management', rather than accepting somewhat uncritically an ability as well as a need to intervene. It is hoped that the following brief account will suggest the value of Offe's discussion when applied to a recent study of the problems of local state management.

Offe says that the state has a mandate to create and sustain the conditions of accumulation. In fact it is dependent on the continuance of such accumulation, for example, via taxation. However, it can only maintain this role by appearing to pursue the general interests of society as a whole, legitimating itself by concealing the real nature and consequences of its policies. Offe argues that, in earlier stages of capitalism, the state mainly created and maintained the conditions of accumulation in an authoritative manner. In this situation power in and over the state apparatus can determine the allocation of resources because these are already under state control. However, in the later stages of capitalist development, the state becomes increasingly deeply involved in productive activity, making investments in constant and variable capital which no individual capitalist would find profitable but which are nevertheless necessary. Offe suggests that they are unprofitable because they are too costly, too risky or involve external-ities, or all three, and explains why this situation canot be solved without state intervention. He uses health policy as an example of the shift in state activities. In the nineteenth century the state was mainly concerned with laws that made certain behaviour mandatory (e.g. public health rules) or laws which made certain claims legal (e.g. claims by private bodies or individuals for state financial assistance). But today such regulation exists together with a growing involvement in productive activities, such as public hospitals, state directed medical research, etc. So far this outline bears a resemblance to Lojkine's discussion of the general conditions of production and Castells's reference to the state's role in urban policies.

But Offe then considers the mode of state operation in this situation. He suggests that bureaucratic methods are able to cope with allocative activities which, after the initial policy decisions, tend to be routinised. But the success of intervention in productive activity tends to be measured by its output — an activity is 'adequate' if it leads to certain results. The routine application of given inputs, without an ability to adjust them flexibly, within limits at least, to achieve the desired results, is largely ineffective because of its rigidity (as numerous critics of bureaucracy have pointed out).

A typical reaction is to move towards 'rational' management and planning. But this requires a coherent set of goals which is possible, for example, for a firm which derives its production goals from an analysis of market conditions. However, the state apparatus is confronted by contradictory needs, interests and demands and this makes 'rational' action difficult, except in special situations where, for example, there are clear cut, uncontroversial and operational goals, a stable environment and/or a short production cycle and no physical constraints.

A third approach, 'participation' allows policy to be determined by decentralised processes of political conflict and consensus. There are clearly limits to this approach, for the permanent interference of conflict, at every stage of policy formation, would reduce not increase the possibility of relatively coherent policies. It might involve accepting objectives at variance with fundamental constraints imposed by the nature of the mode of production. Alternatively conflict could be exacerbated when these objectives were not realised in practice.

Offe concludes that these three management strategies correspond to the major doctrines of administrative organisation and reorganisation which are actually implemented and often coexist, only to create or magnify the types of problems he has raised. Cynthia Cockburn (1977) has considered such issues in a recent study of local government management in a London borough. Her results tend to confirm the importance of a study of the 'management' factor to the analysis of urban politics and the usefulness of Offe's work. She describes the evolution of local government from simple administration to an enhanced role in the postwar period. Thus the Royal Commission on Local Government referred to the fact that the government now has to 'assume far more direct responsibility for the economy' and stated that this required new methods of management. The innovation proposed was corporate management – methods of planning and rational decision-making first developed in private industry. Cockburn describes how this was implemented in her study area and how its apparent usefulness did indeed arise from the increasing involvement of the state in the conditions of reproduction of capital and labour and the need to find more efficient ways of managing this intervention. She then refers to the problems that arose for corporate management because it faced a 'turbulent' environment. She illustrates these problems by references to particular aspects of local housing administration, where a series of policies responsive, in varying degrees, to conflicting demands created a morass of difficulties and as a result increased tension between the council and the electorate and within its own structure. In response to these problems, the council began to encourage more public participation, in an attempt to improve its flow of market information, by setting up neighbourhood councils. But some of these councils soon began to demand the right to make regular inputs into policy formation. And the specific demands raised created more difficulties for the local authority. An example was the use, by a neighbourhood council, of legislation to force the authority to do housing repairs. If this had occurred on a large scale, it would have put the authority in serious financial difficulties.

This brief example suggests that the analysis of urban policies must contain a recognition of the problematic nature of urban management 'in itself', given the general nature of the state's role in advanced capitalism. It is an issue which is largely ignored by Castells and Lojkine.

Finally, we will now illustrate some of the points raised about the nature and content of urban policies and hence about the consideration of class interests. Again it may be possible to suggest some more general propositions, of a rather fragmentary nature, which relate to the way in which the state 'deals' with these interests and which may prove useful in the analysis of actual policies.

J. Hirsch (1976) has remarked that it is necessary to demonstrate *how* the state operates in a manner which tends to reproduce capitalist relations including, importantly, the problem of the compliance of the governed. He has put forward a number of considerations which may be helpful.

He first outlines the reasons why the domination exerted by capital over labour in the workplace cannot be directly exercised outside the firm, thus resulting in a state which is relatively autonomous. In consequence there are complex and varied relations between the state and the various class interests, so these require detailed specification, according to the issues involved. He then notes, as do also Castells, Lojkine and Offe, the involvement of the state in the 'general conditions of production' — for example, the provision of infrastructure and a qualified workforce.

Discussing the issue of compliance, Hirsch refers to the limitations of domination by means of purely physical repression and therefore to the importance of ideology in the establishment of legitimacy. This ideology takes its general form from the way in which the basic economic relationship is presented as an 'equivalent exchange' between free and equal individuals, the state being represented as a neutral arbiter, intervening in the public interest. The policy 'content' to which this ideology refers concerns the 'general conditions of production', including the reproduction of the labour force. The nature of the contents depends on the class struggle. The form policies take aims to mask the true effects of what is being done because these involve the reproduction of an unequal relationship. This is achieved by means of ideological conceptions such as those already referred to. Maintaining the general conditions of production is not a simple process because of unequal development and the consequential existence of different fractions of capital and labour, whose economically based interests find political expression.

How then does the state react to these political demands in ways which attempt to ensure continued reproduction of the social formation? Hirsch suggests that the state apparatus operates a process of structural selectivity, which is patterned by the considerations already discussed. This aims to prevent disruption of the basic economic and political relationship between capital and labour. He lists several ways in which this process structures state policies; clearly these are tendencies rather than functional imperatives. Firstly, the state will usually be more concerned to support productive activity rather than to carry it out directly. This hypothesis is not intended to exclude intervention in the 'general conditions of production' or, for example, the takeover of 'lame ducks', but rather to reflect the limits to the functionality of state appropriation of the private production of surplus value in a capitalist economy. Secondly, this constraint implies that the resources available to the state are structurally limited to the extent by which taxation is restrained by the need to maintain accumulation. Another consequence is that state resources will vary according to changes in the level of economic activity. Thirdly, the selective effect of the repressive and ideological aspects of the state's activities must be considered. Fourthly, the issues which are treated are presented in a way which obscures the class nature of the policies proposed, fragmenting and interpreting the problems in a way which tends to ensure that they do not have radical effects. Fifthly, Hirsch argues that the civil service will often have an interest in maintaining overall stability. Although he does not mention it, this is not a static concept, but implies an interest in obtaining new means of control over destabilising possibilities. Finally he suggests that the state will be characterised by a reactive approach, responding to problems posed by the consequences of various developments that threaten stability, tending to deal with visible symptoms rather than underlying causes.

Some of these general suggestions seem to be helpful in understanding aspects of a recent major development in British housing policy — the government's Housing Policy Review which was set out in a Green Paper (HM Government, 1977a) and three technical appendices published in the summer of 1977. An outline of the various and often conflicting interests involved in housing and their relationships to housing policy would be a major task which cannot be attempted here. But the result of the historical development of these factors in the context of the evolution of the British economy and political system is a set of arrangements for housing production which is largely based on private enterprise. There is a greater degree of state involvement in distribution, both via financial arrangements (subsidies) and ownership and management (public housing). Political and economic interests in favour of expanded owner occupation are strong, for example, because of the additional profits which flow from the private rather than the public control of residential development, because of the processes of housing exchange (estate agents, solicitors, etc.) and because of the desire to foster a 'property-owning democracy' (CDP collective, 1976). Moreover, individual ownership offers real benefits to the owner occupier, for example, relative freedom from bureaucratic intervention and possession of a capital asset. So there is political support for owner occupation among substantial sectors of the working class as well as among the bourgeoisie.

By the mid-seventies a severe crisis seemed to be engulfing housing finance and therefore state intervention in the field as a whole. Inflation contributed strongly to a sharply increasing level of public expenditure on housing. This could not continue if overall government expenditure was to be kept within the limits that were likely to be necessary, given the difficult economic position, particularly as a substantial proportion of the expenditure that was available would have to go towards industrial investment and the relief of unemployment in a chronically stagnant economy. Official consideration of housing finance reform was principally motivated, at the time when it occurred, by this situation, as well as by the fact that the rising cost of housing posed problems of price and accessibility for individuals in both the main tenures.

Housing finance is chiefly concerned with subsidies to owner occupiers via the tax system, and subsidies to those in the council sector to meet building costs and to reduce individual rents. Clearly, there are various ways in which outlays could be reduced, or at least brought under control: for example, by bringing the production of housing or the management of its exchange into social ownership,[22] hence reducing its cost by the elimination or diminution of profits. Under certain, rather extreme, political circumstances this might happen and the cost reductions could benefit owners and council tenants. But such a policy would hardly benefit private finance or building capital. These interests would, on the contrary, welcome the expansion of owner occupation and a decline in state provision, while probably wishing to maintain a system of subsidies which would support high levels of private housing consumption. (This is not to say that private finance and building capital does not benefit from council housing; it does, but a reduction in the socialised element of housing provision to the minimal level, which would be implied by a service solely for the very poor, would be beneficial to these interests.)

Typically therefore the housing system is presented in ways which tend to enlist popular political support for owner occupation and against council housing. One way in which this has occurred arises because the owner occupier subsidy is *indirect*; it is a tax foregone, not a revenue distributed, so it does not appear as official 'public expenditure' (indeed some, including the Treasury, have denied it is a subsidy at all). The whole force of the blame for higher taxes on 'state handouts' and, at a more rarefied level of attempts to restrain government expenditure in the interests of accumulation, therefore falls on expenditure which mainly supports council housing. The Housing Policy Review has proposed changes in this sector, related to subsidies and the planning of investment, which will provide the means to keep such expenditure under firmer control in future (Harloe, 1977 b and c). Indeed it seems to mark the acceptance by a Labour government of a housing policy which allows, encourages and increasingly helps to finance the expansion of owner occupation *without* any substantial increase in the social control of this sector, while gradually reducing the role of the socialised sector to one of complementarity, of provision for those unfit or unable to buy.

However, this reform must be presented in ways which do not reveal the possibility that they will do little to reduce the problems of access to housing, its cost to the individual consumer or even perhaps the level of public resources spent on housing as a whole. So the policy is presented in the Green Paper in a way which obscures these problems. This is not to say that the politicians and civil servants who drew up the document were wholly conscious of doing this; obviously methods of thought and presentation are largely conditioned by dominant economic, political and ideological relations. But some more conscious 'arrangement' of the argument does occur. For example, the new method of central control of local government housing investment is double edged. It frees local government from certain rigidities of central control (especially the predetermined allocation of finance between various heads) but it also imposes stronger and more quickly operable *strategic* control. The Green Paper emphasises the freedom and flexibility of the new system which, it claims, will enable a more rational allocation of finance in line with housing need, and it de-emphasises the enhanced degree of control involved (which is in fact negative control, a power to reduce what local housing authorities do, but not a power to compel them to do more).

The Green Paper hardly concerns itself with the production of housing and, in contrast to its treatment of the public sector, deals with the private sector institutions, notably building societies, circumspectly. Indeed it is interesting to note that the policy review was aided by the advice of a group of outside experts which included representatives of a wide range of public and private agencies, but the question of the finance of owner occupation was dealt with by a special group which mainly consisted of DoE and Treasury officials and representatives of the building societies and financial capital. The impact, or lack of impact, of the Green Paper's proposals on the questions of individual cost and access and on the level of total public resources involved is avoided by omission of any projections of the effect of the suggested changes on demand, supply, costs and resources. This also, of course, obscures the distributional effects of the new policies.

General aims for housing policy, embodied in concepts such as equality and flexibility, are operationalised in proposals which, by selective interpretation and suppression of some of their implications, appear in the Green Paper in a form calculated to appeal to what is sensible and is in the 'general interest'. Words such as 'choice', which are current favourites in the language of housing policy, have a latitude of meaning which greatly aids this process. Thus, the Green Paper wants a housing system which permits choice. The strategy proposed is based on increasing owner occupation, with public housing playing a complementary role for the poor. But such a system allowing meaningful choice might involve arrangements which would enable an individual, during his or her lifetime, to move easily between the two main sectors, as and when the particular use values that attach to them are most appropriate to personal needs.[23] This is not considered in the Green Paper which regards choice as a static concept based on a clear and permanent division between those who would be owners and those who, despite the rhetoric, are mainly forced to become council tenants. This policy does reflect the political support and 'choice' for owner occupation (British Market Research Bureau, 1977), but this is a constrained choice founded on the specific economic, political and even ideological arrangements (e.g. stigmatisation of public housing and its tenants) which support the commodification of housing. It has no necessary relationship to a choice based on use values.

Conclusion

Many of the general conclusions about the scope and nature of state policies which Hirsch outlines seem to be useful analytical aids, although any proper account and estimate of their worth would require a clearer and more complete analysis of the Green Paper and housing policy than presented here and their application to a wide range of state policies in different advanced capitalist economies. However, the discussion of the Green Paper does seem to reveal elements of the 'structural selectivity' to which Hirsch refers. Examples include the avoidance of actions to reduce the parts of the housing system which are privately profitable; the limitation of public finance (which is itself an argument employed against 'nationalisation' of housing, municipalisation of rented accommodation, the takeover of builders and of land, etc.) and the increased pressure on this when further accumulation is threatened; the interest in stability and control; and the fragmented and ideologically coloured treatment and presentation of problems, in ways which both invite and sustain certain conceptions of political interest and the state's role as representative of the public interest (or interests). In addition, although there is not space to discuss the issues here, there would appear to be a number of further contradictions which will arise from the new housing policies being proposed.[24] This does suggest that the state has reacted to the symptoms of problems rather than their real causes.

Likewise the general usefulness of Offe's conclusions about the problem of management of policy-making itself, which must also be part of the study of urban politics, cannot be determined on the basis of the account presented here. However it is hoped that the illustrations which have been given will indicate ways in which such analyses might be of use in understanding urban policies without giving rise to some of the problems that Lojkine's and Castells's approaches generate, such as the wish to maintain a special theoretical 'urban' content, the over-generalisation of specific social relations, and an analysis of political outcomes based on functionality rather than on contradictory tendencies.

Notes

1. I am grateful for helpful comments on an earlier draft by Doreen Massey, Chris Paris and Ray Pahl.

2. For example, Castells has edited the collection *Estructura de Clases y Política Urbana en América Latina* (1974). Mellor (1977) has discussed the possible application of Gunder Frank's theory of underdevelopment to British regions.

3. The debate between Poulantzas and Lojkine is dominated by the current argument over left-wing political strategies in France and elsewhere. Interesting material relevant to the wider debate may be found in Hunt, A. (ed.), 1977, and Ross, 1977.

4. In fact there are probably substantial differences between Althusser's approach and Poulantzas's work which cannot be discussed here. For a further discussion of this approach and critical references see the introduction to Harloe, 1976.

5. For example, introducing his study of the US urban crisis ' . . . the urban process is produced through the inter-action between the elements of urban structure and the variations of urban politics. We would like to show the empirical influences of the whole theoretical discussion through the analysis of a concrete historical process: the development of the urban crisis in the United States. It should be clear . . . that this analysis, does not use systematically and explicitly the whole conceptual apparatus that we have presented . . . We are not yet in a position to present a systematic account of a whole urban process in a form which could follow exactly the terms of our definition' (1976a:p.379).

6. See for example the discussion in Mellor, 1977:ch.2. Castells's insistence on spatial concentration seems especially ironic at a time when one of the principal preoccupations of British urban policy is the decline of big cities as expressed in the White Paper, *Policy For The Inner Cities* (HM Government, 1977b). Note also this White Paper's acceptance of the crucial importance of the economic base to urban growth and decline, unlike Castells's consumption-based analyses. Also Prais (1976:p.62) has recently shown that in Britain, while total output is increasingly concentrated in big firms, the numbers of plants owned by each big firm rose by 230 per cent between 1958-72 and average employment in each plant fell from 750 to 430.

7. I am grateful to Ray Pahl for showing me this paper and pointing out the similarity with his earlier work noted in the text.

8. An interesting account of squatter settlements in Chile in the Allende period, partly critical of Castells's work, is contained in Leeds, A. and E., 1976.

9. For discussion of the point see Harloe (ed.), 1976:pp.21,22.

10. See the discussion of consumption and production in Marx (1973 edition: pp.90-94).

11. Note however that Mingione goes on to argue, as we assert below, that Lojkine's own approach introduces the very schematism that he himself criticises in Castells and Poulantzas, and that he 'substantially under-values the dialectical class dimension and the role of the French working class in his [account] of state intervention and policies in urban development' (1977,p.29).

12. As a part of the recent reduction in public expenditure, the British government has established the percentage at about 60 per cent, but the historical trend is clearly for an increasing proportion of local expenditure to be met centrally.

13. Castells has recently, for the first time, sketched out an historical analysis of postwar French urban politics. But whether more detailed studies will lead to a modification of his urban theories remains to be seen. In an afterword to the English version of *The Urban Question*, written in 1975, he does little more than

elaborate some of the more controversial details of his original thesis (see Poulantzas (ed.), 1976:pp.187-204; and Castells, 1977:pp.437-71).

14. The influence of this historical factor is commented on by many analysts of the modern French state and society; see, for example, Ardagh, 1977, and (in a comparative perspective) Schonfield, 1965; Denton *et al.*, 1968; Hayward and Watson, 1975.

15. On the relations between civil servants and big industry see the works cited above, also d'Arcy and Jobert (1975:p.305) in particular refer to the explicit link between urban investment and the focus on developing advanced industry, the main priority of the Sixth French Plan (1970-75) viz '. . . it must be emphasised that, taking into account the priority given to industrialisation by the Sixth Plan, the Towns Commission placed much greater emphasis on investment in infrastructure which was necessary for industry, such as transport and tele-communications, while the preceding plans had stressed the necessity for developing public spending destined directly for the benefit of the inhabitants'.

16. When discussing property development in Paris in the late 1960s and early 1970s, Ardagh (1977:pp.298, 301, 663) refers to the positive climate towards such development, from the government and 'the well-known links between President Pompidou and the big banks'.

17. Note also the weakness of French unions. For example many employers refused to bargain collectively before 1968; by the end of the 1960s only about 22 per cent of the workforce was unionised (42 per cent in Britain) and the movement was not unified (Hayward, 1975).

18. The Fifth Plan (1966-70) aimed 'to modernise the Paris region rather than halt its development. The Plan accepts the fact that the growth of the national economy must involve at least a moderate expansion of industry and employment in the Paris region' (Denton *et al.*, 1968:p.324). Note also the direct control by central government, until recently, over the Paris government. Also, Ardagh (1977: p.304) remarks on the policy of developing Paris as an office centre with some new housing and adds 'with land costs so high, the new housing is mostly expensive and middle class, while the former slum dwellers have been evicted to new houses in the outer suburbs. Thus inner Paris has become increasingly a bourgeois "ghetto" − to the fury of the Left.'

19. Thus in London housing politics have revolved round the successful resistance of the outer boroughs to providing substantial rehousing for working-class inner Londoners. For an account see Young and Kramer, 1978; and Harloe *et al.*, 1974.

20. Thus Watson (1975:p.471) notes the support of small business in France for moves to control trade union activity. Runciman's (1966) findings on relative deprivation might also tend to suggest that failed capitalists would be highly unlikely to feel much affinity for the working class they were joining.

21. Ardagh (1977:p.24) refers to two economies 'uneasily coexisting' in France; a modern one of big firms and state enterprises, much of it implanted since the war and below 'an old creaking infrastructure based on artisanship, low turnover with high profits, and the ideal of the small family business'. He suggests that this situation has only really rapidly altered since the 1950s. He also quotes (p.62) the fact that in 1964 there were 64 firms in the world with a turnover of over $1000m including 49 American, five German, four British, and none French, and over 50 per cent of French workers were in firms with less than 200 employees. Evidence presented by Prais suggests a far greater preponderance of large firms in Britain than in France and a far less significant sector of small business. Thus, in 1963, 2.1 per cent of total manufacturing employment in the UK was in firms employing under ten persons. The corresponding figure for France was 10.8 per cent (Prais, 1976:ch.6 and table 6.4, p.160).

22. The CDP report mentioned above (1976) contains an extensive discussion of the role of private capital and its returns in housing.

23. It might be argued of course that if choice were totally based on use values all real distinctions between the sectors would disappear; but this would be a somewhat Utopian situation.

24. For example, an increasingly stigmatised minority council sector which will encourage problems of social disorder and social tensions, and a possible conflict between the sharply increasing amount of private sector resources that will be required for a housing strategy based predominantly on owner occupation and the national economic priority of increasing investment in productive industry.

5 THE CITY, INDUSTRY AND THE STATE

Frank Longstreth

Much recent material attempting to analyse the state in advanced capitalist societies from a Marxist perspective has tried to formulate 'systemic constraints' on state activity beyond the rather contingent relations of political forces, i.e. to go beyond the usual concerns of political science. Similarly, such Marxist 'political scientists' as Miliband or Poulantzas, who posit a 'relatively autonomous' field of politics and call for a specific analysis of the political level, have been criticised for their inability to locate the 'systemic constraints' imposed upon the state by its relation to the process of accumulation (Holloway and Picciotto, 1977:p.82). Their critics, however, often fall into the trap of making a reductionist link between state activity and capitalist accumulation, assuming that the requirements of the latter, the 'logic of capital', can be 'read off' unambiguously as specific state policies (Bullock and Yaffe, 1975). One recent article, which attempts to relate the changing forms of state activity to their changing function in the process of accumulation, does manage to avoid the 'fundament-alist' error of economic reductionism, but nonetheless has difficulties conceptualising the relation between these systemic limitations and the actual production of economic policy (Holloway and Picciotto, 1977). The authors realise that the requirements of the accumulation process are only fulfilled in the political system (or the economic system for that matter) through a process of class struggle. They conclude that 'if social and political development cannot simply be derived logically from the formal analysis of capital, this does not mean that the formal analysis is irrelevant: for it explains not only the inevitability of class struggle, it provides also the point of reference and the framework for that struggle, (Holloway and Picciotto, 1977:p.94). They emphasise the necessity of including both moments, formal analysis and historical analysis of class conflict, in studies of state activities and politics within capitalist societies. This formulation, while infinitely preferable to the 'capital logic' approach, remains at a very high level of abstraction. It is difficult to perceive how it could be applied to the analysis of concrete political conflicts, particularly insofar as one wishes to distinguish between types of regime, national traditions, etc.

The core difficulty for Marxism remains the logical impossibility of reducing state activities to economic imperatives. In the political realm politics is always in command. In other words policy outputs are in the immediate sense set by the power relations instituted within the state apparatus, by *politics,* once one recognises that this term does not simply refer to the parliamentary arena but must include the entire state system, especially the administrative apparatus. If the formal analysis of the process of accumulation can indicate the necessary inputs into the economic system for the continued reproduction of capitalist relations and in this sense indicate the locus of class conflict, it none-theless remains the case that the implementation of those requirements *via* the mediation of the state can only be accomplished politically, i.e. through the mobilisation and institution of the power resources of any particular group or class. Such resources can vary from the capacity to administer violence, to access to finance, the ability directly or indirectly to influence the pace of economic activity (strikes, investment crises, depletion of exchange reserves), the ability to mobilise electoral support, control of the media, etc. The mobilisation and organisation of such political forces and resources remains the key to understanding politics and policy outputs. The question is how far it is possible to treat politics thus understood in a theoretical fashion.

A related problem for Marxist studies of the state is what connection if any is presumed to exist between the political forces which constitute the immediately visible world of the state and the class structure. The traditional relation between the two has been the concept of interest, i.e. the idea that political groups coalesced around distinct sets of interests corresponding to the underlying class divisions in a society. This concept has been much abused in recent years as failing to dis-tinguish between Marxist theories and those of 'bourgeois pluralism'. One position is that the different strategies are no more than that: distinct political strategies based on the fact that knowledge of the requirements of accumulation is inevitably incomplete or ideologically shrouded and thus bearing no direct relation to specific classes or class fractions. One 'anti-instrumentalist' formulation takes this position to a rather unusual conclusion for a theory claiming in some sense Marxist derivations:

> . . . the state in no way favours specific interests or enters into an alliance with specific classes; rather it protects and sanctions institutions and social *relations* which in turn are institutional pre-conditions for the class domination of capital. The state is not the 'servant' or 'instrument' *of one* class in contrast to another, but its

structure and activity exists in the carrying through and long-term guarantee of rules which in turn institutionalise the specific class relations of a capitalist society. The state defends not the particular interests of class, but rather the *general* interests of all members of a *capitalist class society* (original emphasis) (Offe and Ronge, 1976).

State activities in this formulation assume a particular form dependent on four 'functional determinations': (1) the private nature of production; (2) the dependence on the tax system and the consequent indirect reliance on private accumulation; (3) the consequent existence of the process of accumulation as the central point of reference, the precondition for state power; and (4) the necessity for democratic legitimation. Politics then constitute the generality of strategies that attempt to secure the harmony of these structural determinations. The most general strategy informing state activity is then the production of those conditions under which each citizen is embraced by exchange relations. The central problem for the state is securing capitalist development against its own self-destructive tendencies, which would otherwise interrupt exchange relations. Thus the most general strategy bears no immediate relation to any particular class interest, but rather simply aims to produce and reproduce the commodity form. The various alternatives generated in the political system can be depicted as simply different routes to the fulfilment of this general strategy with no necessary relationship to any class or class fraction.

While this formulation goes somewhat further in its 'structuralism' than others it typifies much modern Marxist state theory in that the state is dealt with only at the highest level of abstraction, in this case as the guarantor of the commodity form. Such theories tell one very little about the specific class forces or the observable political conflict of a given society at a particular period in time.

I will contend in the following that while such abstract approaches might be useful in providing a general approach to the analysis of the state, they must be complemented by analyses which are more 'instrumental' not in the sense that the state is depicted as a neutral instrument in the hands of a cohesive dominant class but insofar as they see it as a system penetrated and structured by particular class relations which may vary from society to society and over periods of time. Moreover, the state can be, and in the case of Britain has been, dominated by a particular fraction of the dominant class, a *ceta dirigente,* which by no means exercises power consistently in the *general* interest of the dominant class taken as a whole.

More particularly, in the case of Britain a traditional power bloc has predominated over the determination of economic policy since the beginning of the present century. Many of the political struggles over the course of this century can be interpreted as attempts either to overturn or modify the domination of this 'establishment' in the state system. Yet, despite two world wars, numerous changes of government, the disintegration of the Empire, and the institution of social democracy and Keynesian political economy as the dominant force in Parliament, this power bloc has maintained its position largely intact through pragmatic adaptation to changing circumstances in the world economy and the national class struggle.

The Historical Importance of the City of London

Divisions within the dominant class can obviously be based on different factors, by no means all of them economic. However, in the case of Britain the classic division in the period of capitalist ascendency was that between landed and commercial interests, epitomised in the struggle over the Corn Laws. Tariffs and commercial policy have often been a disuniting factor since such policies often have differential effects on different sectors, industries or firms. Similarly, questions about the proper exchange rate for the currency, the need for deflation or inflation at various conjunctures, the desirable role of state intervention through regional or investment policy, in short the entire range of economic policies, can elicit different responses from different fractions of capital depending on their position, the perceived effects of various policy options, and their ideological orientations. Capitalists meet as 'hostile brothers' in the political system as they do in the market place, capable of combining to meet an external threat to bourgeois class relations, but more characteristically divided among themselves – if not by party then by definable interest groups or class fractions. Their cohesion is by no means automatic even over fairly fundamental issues and must often be reinforced by various social mechanisms, e.g. membership in clubs, attendance of the same schools, kinship ties, interlocking directorships, special policy-making groups, etc.

In Britain since the declining importance of the landed interest the dominant class has existed predominantly as two fractions, the City or banking capital (including here generally the financial sector) and industry or productive capital. On the political level the City has exercised a dominant position in the determination of economic policy, which is to say that its perceived interests have generally, although not exclusively, been the guiding thread for economic policy even when faced with opposition from the political agents of other groups within the dominant class or those of the subordinate classes. This is not to say that the aforementioned changes have left the exercise of power just as it was at the turn of the century, nor that changes of government have no effect, but rather that such changes have been accommodated without changing the basic articulation of interests within the dominant power bloc.

The City's position of dominance has been institutionalised within the state system largely through two media. First, directly through the Bank of England and its relation to the Treasury, thus securing a direct voice in the formulation of economic policy. The nationalisation of the Bank of England in 1945 did not change its basic mode of operation (it remained *de facto* self-governing), but merely formalised a gradual process of placing ultimate legal control over monetary policy in the hands of the government. Secondly, and more importantly, the political position of the City has been reinforced by the maintenance of its key role in the British economy, a function tied up with first the British Empire and then the maintenance in the world after World War II of a dollar-discriminating club, the Sterling Area. The continuance of an international role for sterling up until the mid-1960s not only helped revive the City's position as a market for world finance after 1945 but reinforced its ideological hold over British industry and welded a new economic relationship insofar as the latter developed in a multi-national direction. The consequent delicate balance of payments situation served as a means of checking and reorienting government policy through periodic exchange crises. These have at times backfired in that their effects have engendered criticism of the City's role, especially in 1931 and 1959, but generally they have reinforced finance capital's dominant position. Only since the late 1960s following the 1967 devaluation, the jettisoning of sterling's international function, and the breakdown of the Bretton Woods agreements, have the rules of the game changed substantially. However, to anticipate my conclusions somewhat, the City's role in the international economy has crystallised as an international financial entrepot (rather than being concerned solely with the export of British capital as in the earlier periods); while its political position was buttressed by the increasing intervention of the International Monetary Fund in the determination of economic policy.

The City has, in other words, largely set the parameters of economic policy and its interests have generally predominated since the late nineteenth century. Its dominance has been so complete that its position has often been taken as the quintessence of responsible financial policy. There have been challenges in the past — Keynesianism in the 1930s and 1940s and the planning movement in the 1960s — but these have only secured a degree of modification in the formulation and orientation of economic policy. What is surprising is the political weakness of the opposition, both within the ranks of capital and on the part of the labour movement, given the steady decline of the position of Britain *vis-a-vis* other national capitals and the evident disadvantages at various moments of the City's preferred option of credit restriction in the face of problems with the external balance. Nonetheless, conflict has materialised in various forms at various times, and in what follows I will attempt to sketch their main outlines and their resolutions historically and in the recent past. Industrial capital has not mutely accepted City hegemony, nor has it been totally integrated into the latter's *Weltanschauung*. However, the articulation of distinct interests has been very circumscribed, mainly in the past by the commitment to the imperial system and the consequent acceptance of the pivotal role of finance in that system.

The first significant expression of industrialists' discontent with financial dominance was Joseph Chamberlain's Tariff Reform campaign at the turn of the century. Chamberlain, a screw manufacturer and former mayor of Birmingham, was responding to the new needs of Midlands manufacturing, in particular their declining position with respect to German and American manufacturers. His Tariff Reform League, organised 'for the defence and development of the British Empire', included prominent industrialists apart from the woollen and cotton trades, yet not one important banker. In Semmel's (1960:pp. 101-3) account this social or preference imperialism was oriented towards winning working-class support for a 'producers' alliance', i.e. a Bismarckian programme of imperial tariff and social reform.

Semmel argues as well that a second current of imperialist strategy emerged in the decade before World War I. Liberal or 'cosmopolitan' imperialism under the leadership of Rosebery and with a Liberal following including Grey, Asquith and Haldane supported the principles of imperialism *and* free trade. Liberal imperialists also favoured social improvement in education and housing, as well as temperance, in the interest of national efficiency, as 'a condition of national fitness equal to the demands of our Empire — administrative, parliamentary, commercial, educational, moral, naval and military fitness' (1960:p.63). However, free trade imperialists opposed the protectionist measures of the Tariff Reformers, preferring instead direct taxes, especially a land tax, as the means of financing the necessary reforms. Not surprisingly, they had close links with the City, in effect constituting the political wing of high finance. The City regarded protection as anathema, viewing the system of free trade based on the gold standard as the precondition of its own and hence British prosperity. As Sir Halford MacKinder, a leading theorist of liberal imperialism who later converted to a neo-mercantilist position, expressed the nature of the controversy:

> This gives the real key to the struggle between our free trade policy and the protection of other countries — we are essentially the people with capital, and those who have the capital always share the proceeds of the activity of brains and muscles of other countries. (Semmel, 1960: p.168).

The debate between the neo-mercantilist Tariff Reformers and free trade imperialists explicitly recognised a conflict of interest between the two fractions of British capital. Free traders like MacKinder even expressed publicly the view that 'the City of London may continue to increase whil the industry, at any rate, of Britian, becomes *relatively* less', believing that the growth of finance would more than compensate for industrial decline (Semmel, 1960: p.62). Neo-mercantilists like Austen Chamberlain deplored these tendencies, insisting instead that the growth of the 'productive sector' was the only cure for rising unemployment and the basis for national power. In terms of bourgeois support, then, the free traders could count on finance plus those sections of industrial capital which did not as yet feel the threat of foreign competition and depended on international trade, e.g. ship-building and cotton. Preference imperialists had as their base of support the engineering manufacturers of the Midlands and received some additional aid from imperial developers in the white Dominions. However, if neo-mercantilism had a major weakness it was its inability to convince the enfranchised sections of the working class that preference would not mean a drop in their living standards through the proposed tariff on food. Labour leaders continued to support free trade and the 'cheap loaf' and consequently deprived the manufacturers of a necessary source of electoral support (Semmel, 1960: chs. 7 and 10). In the end, of course, the tariff campaign was defeated and free trade was ensconced as the central principle of foreign economic relations until the collapse of world commerce in the 1930s.

Conflict between industrial and banking capital flared again in the interwar period, though the issues raised varied considerably from the simple opposition of free trade *versus* preference. The era was marked by the personality of Montagu Norman, who reigned over the Bank of England throughout the period and was at the focus of many conflicts. An understanding of the role of the City in the formation of state economic policy is impossible without a fairly close consideration of his aims and activities. In general one may say that City hegemony was expressed, first, in the return to the gold standard and, second, in the specific relations between the state and the financial system, i.e. the rules governing public borrowing and expenditure. In both cases practices appropriate to an earlier era of British domination of the world market were perpetuated into an age when conditions had vastly altered.

The return to the gold standard in 1925 is rightly seen in the literature of this period as the focal point of the controversy. There is little doubt about the aims of the City and the Bank of England in the decade following World War I:

> The men of 1919 believed that the best monetary system was that of 1913; a world gold standard centered on London, with the Bank of England controlling the system by manipulation of Bank Rate, and acting as the watchdog of financial practice. (Sayer, 1976:p.11).

The Cunliffe Committee on Currency and Foreign Exchanges after the war had recommended as early as April 1918 a return to the gold standard at the prewar parity as soon as possible. The Committee in fact does not seem to have considered any alternative (Clay: 1957).

With regard to internal policy the Bank wanted to get prices down quickly from their inflated war levels. Likewise, the vast growth of Treasury Bills during the war meant that the Bank rate had little effect on the short rates in the money market. This debacle was itself a result of the *way* in which the war had been financed, i.e. on the terms set by finance with the Bank of England acting as a private intermediary. As a consequence the excess of expenditure over revenue had been financed through borrowing, vastly increasing the size of the floating debt. The reduction of the latter was, thus, a main aim of the Bank and the Treasury during this period, but of the three possible means for achieving this end — running a budget surplus, funding (conversion to long-term debt), or a capital levy (for example, on war profiteers) — the Bank favoured the first. Its fear of inflation because of the lack of control over the money supply also led it to support a high Bank rate, though the government held back for a time for fear of unemployment and the consequent likelihood of social unrest (Howson, 1975:p.11).

The government's policies were constrained by the fact that the Bank acted as the sort of institution it was, a private bank following 'sound financial principles' as articulated by banking capital.[1] In any case from 15 December 1919, the government had an avowed policy of returning to gold at the prewar parity at the earliest favourable moment. By April of the same year the Bank rate had been raised to 7 per cent, falling somewhat thereafter and then rising again in preparation for the return to gold. Deflationary policies fitted the national and international goals and ideological axioms of the dominant agents in the policy-making process. The Bank advocated them as a necessary step for the restoration of the prewar international financial system and the Treasury out of an equal commitment to the reduction of the war debt through budget surpluses.

Norman's position in the campaign for the restoration of the gold standard was crucial. As Strange argues, his perspective demonstrated the inherent schizophrenia of a 'top currency' state, namely the conflict of interest between the needs of international finance and national productive capital (Strange, 1971:p.51). A 'top currency' in this case is simply the one primarily used in international transactions. There is no question that Norman put the international financial system at the head of his list of priorities, supporting the City's attempt to re-establish its central financial role. As Clay points out in his apologia for the 'Norman yoke', the Governor of the Bank of England viewed devaluation (returning to gold at a lower exchange rate) solely in negative terms. He felt that its positive effects would be eliminated by the rise in price of necessary imports and by the reduction of income from overseas investment, shipping, and other invisibles, all of which were denominated in sterling:

> To these obvious advantages in working for the prewar rate, Norman would add the less definable but not less real advantages of restoring and maintaining the country's international position — the advantages of possessing a world currency, which made payments to other countries easy because they were always willing to hold balances in it, and facilitated the entrepot trade and international services which contributed a large part of the country's overseas earnings. (Clay, 1957:p.160).

Furthermore,

the Bank and the City would naturally [have attached] great importance to the loss of prestige which devaluation would have involved,
and the Treasury officials do not seem to have differed. (Clay, 1957:
p.155)

To make a long story short, he led the move back to gold as soon as the
two major destabilising features, the war debt and German reparations,
were resolved to his satifaction, even if the latter problem returned
with a vengeance a few years later.

The trappings at least of the prewar gilded age of British finance
were resurrected on the occasion of Churchill's Budget speech at the
end of April in 1925. The position of the City, the Bank, and the
Treasury was, as indicated above, fairly straightforward. Banking capital
and its agents viewed the move as an expression of London's rightful
place in the world financial system, as the only basis for the revival
of British capitalism and for the impostion of a world monetary order.
In this aim they were tacitly supported by all governments concerned,
including Labour and its Chancellor, Philip Snowden, who proved one
of the most steadfast adherents of Bank and Treasury orthodoxy for
the entire interwar era. The return to gold and the preliminary efforts
of the early 1920s had revived the Bank's pre-eminent position in the
policy-making process after its relative eclipse during World War I. Its
freedom from any sort of political direction was secured by the
complete acceptance of its view of financial matters, that these were
best left to the 'automatic' regulation of the gold standard and
international capital flows.

Yet there was some opposition to this plan of action on the part of
industrialists. This opposition, however, either lacked coherence, in that
it attacked mainly the *effects* of the Bank's policies and not their pre-
suppositions, or it came after the fact as a response to deteriorating
conditions rather than as a prepared set of alternative policies.
Industrialists were, even in their most contestative moods, only
agnostic on the question of gold. They believed in the competence of
the City and the Bank on the questions of monetary policy, and they
do not seem to have been fully aware of the latter's effect on either
international trade or domestic activity. If anything they viewed the
appreciation of the value of the pound as a sign of the revival of British
economic power. According to one historian (Brown, W.A., 1970:p.51) the
only manifestations of industrial dissatisfaction with City hegemony
were, first, 'a rather vague feeling that the interests of the City,
particularly the speculative part of the City community, were best

served by a fluctuating exchange, while the best interests of industry
were best served by a stable exchange', and, second, an 'attitude of
nervousness and apprehension on the part of industry over a possible
hardening of money rates and credit contraction in connection with
a return to gold'.

The central organisation of industrial capital, the Federation of
British Industry (FBI), was only in its formative years at the time and
manifested the diverse views of its membership in its inconsistent
positions. Nonetheless, its leadership did display open apprehension at
the course of events, even if such statements were politically ineffectual.
W. Peter Rylands, the President of the FBI in 1921, sponsored an FBI
memorandum in September of that year to the government which
emphasised that,

> So far as trade . . . is concerned, it is important to remember that
> stability is of far greater importance than the re-establishment of
> any pre-war ratio with gold or any other standard of value. From
> this point of view, deflation can be as potent a source of instability
> as inflation. (Hume, 1970:p.141).

At the annual general meeting he argued that a stable exchange rate at
around the then current value of four dollars to the pound would best
serve the interests of manufacture.

The currency issue remained a major item on the agenda of the
FBI's managing committee, but, according to Hume (pp.141-2), from
July 1924 onwards the emphasis shifted considerably as they dropped
their objections to the goal of re-establishing gold at the prewar parity.
Yet, even as late as 24 July an FBI communique to the government and
the Bank of England explicitly brought forth their justifiable fears that
an increase in the Bank rate would be the chosen instrument to deflate
British prices the necessary 10 per cent against American prices. It
complained that:

> . . . any attempt to raise the real value of the pound sterling by 10
> per cent by a process of arbitrary credit restriction would, in the
> present state of credit, and in view of the present trend of trade and
> prices in this country, involve the most serious consequences to
> industry. (Brown, W.A., 1970:p.52)

Industry's reception of the government announcement of the return
to gold was not exactly exuberant either. The President of the FBI, Col.

Willey, stated in terms reflecting their ambivalent position:

> From the long point of view the decision is to be welcomed, but the immediate effect may create difficulties. At the present moment the pound is overvalued in relation to the dollar — i.e. in relation to gold . . . It is to be assumed that the announcement made today, together with the powers given to the Bank of England, will rapidly bring the pound to parity with the dollar and will, for a time at least, increase the present difficulties of our export trade, which is already suffering from a greater rise in the value of the pound than is justified by the relative level of sterling and gold prices. (Hume, 1970:p.144).

Similarly, Sir Alfred Mond, a leading industrialist, gave a somewhat prescient last-minute plea in Parliament against an over-hasty return to gold:

> Now, apparently, we are to be harnessed to the money rate in New York, our trade to be further depressed whenever there is a flurry on Wall St., because some people seem to think we must be hanged on a cross of gold. I hope that doctrine will be repudiated. I can think of nothing more dangerous to the harassed and already depressed state of trade of this country than that we should hitch ourselves on to the American money market, and take it as the guide and lodestone of British finance, (Brown, W.A., 1970:p.55)

However, the first consideration, the desire for exchange stability in any form, was probably uppermost in the minds of less farsighted industrialists. W.A. Brown's contention (p.56) that the 'majority of manufacturers were not particularly interested in the question of gold and monetary policy', and that 'they did not clearly relate it to their own practical problems', is perfectly believable. Their lack of concern or understanding in conjunction with the prestige that the City and the Bank still exercised within the dominant class induced most of them to follow the lead of finance in the hope that restoring the symbols of the old order would put things right in reality. There seems to have been little direct questioning of the structure of the already decomposing international financial system, the City's presumed place of honour in that system or the right of banking capital and its agents to set the aims of monetary policy.

Big industrial capital was probably more concerned at this time with

the 'real' problems affecting them most directly at the point of
production, namely the complete reorganisation of the structure of
ownership that occurred in British manufacturing over this decade. An
alternative ideology for industrialists was expressed mainly in the
movement for 'rationalisation' or 'planning' which coincided with the
restoration of gold. As articulated by its most coherent advocate,
Lyndall Urwick, rationalisation included two main elements, 'financial
combination of business' and the application of 'scientific methods of
management to existing units of control'. Rationalisation provided an
alternative to both free-market competition and the socialism of the
labour movement. It seemed to be the answer to the problems of over-
capacity and flagging demand in the traditional export industries as
well as the means to create a more stable relationship with labour after
unprecedented levels of confrontation immediately after the war and
during the General Strike. One could hardly believe it to be coincidental
that one of the central opponents of the return to gold from within the
ranks of industry, Sir Alfred Mond, was also a leading figure in the
merger and rationalisation movements. He participated in the
Amalgamated Anthracite and International Nickel combinations and the
setting up of ICI, as well as acting as a principal figure in the Mond-
Turner talks between industry and organised labour, in which rationalisation was offered as the key to improving the social welfare of the
working class (Hannah, 1972:pp.28-44).

Indeed, the Mond-Turner conferences must be seen as a crucial
moment in the political struggle of the time and a harbinger of future
developments. For they not only amounted to an arrangement between
union leadership and management allowing rationalisation and
implicitly higher unemployment to continue in the short run in return
for the maintenance of wages of those still at work. They were also the
first attempt since the collapse of the Tariff Reform movement at
welding a corporatist 'producers' alliance' against banking capital's
control of the state. As Pollard recounts (1970:p.151):

> In the section on the 'Gold Reserve and its relation to industry,' the
> interim report, adopted by the full conference of 4 July, 1928,
> demanded the assurance that in the future 'industry will not be
> arrested by the lack of credit facilities (due to the shortage of gold)
> as soon as increased production becomes effective'. The conference
> therefore resolved 'that under the special conditions in which the
> gold standard operates at the present time, we are not convinced
> that it is either practicable or desirable that the credit policy of the

country should be determined more or less automatically by gold
movements as in prewar days.'

Yet, despite the undoubted questioning of past practices, industrial
opposition never crystallised as a coherent political force. 'Keynesian'
ideas were evidently current before they were set down in *The General
Theory*, but it required a general reorientation of the structure of the
British economy to put them into practice. Industrialists do not seem
to have challenged the priority of an international role for sterling,
or the necessity of a gold standard (apart from the question of parity),
or the idea that the City should play a central role in the world economy.
Even the most 'progressive' industrialists concentrated on the concerns
which seemed to them more basic, namely amalgamation, rationalisation and scientific management, as the appropriate response to a
deflationary situation.

In the end the gold standard was brought down by the internal
contradictions of its operation not by any political act, that is, it was
the oscillation of capital flows to and from New York and then eventual
withering away that forced Britain off gold in the first of many runs on
the pound. The immediate consequence of the financial crisis was the
ignominious disintegration of Ramsay MacDonald's Labour government.
The history of that government illustrates the disarray of the potential
political opposition as well as the complete ideological domination of
banking capital over the state system, epitomised in the inflexible
orthodoxy of Labour's Chancellor of the Exchequer, Philip Snowden.
Its collapse capped a two-year period of almost total incapacity and
demonstrated the political clout of the banks in very concrete terms.
On 23 August 1931 the Deputy Governor of the Bank of England
cabled Morgan's in New York on the possibility of a joint Franco-
American credit to support the pound. Morgan's replied that they
could only back 90-day Treasury bills but not more until the fiscal
programme of the already shaky government was settled:

Are we right in assuming [the telegram read] that the programme
under consideration will have the sincere approval and support of
the Bank of England and the City generally and thus go a long way
towards restoring internal confidence in Great Britain? Of course
our ability to do anything depends on the response of public
opinion particularly in Great Britain to the Government's
announcement of the programme. (Clay, 1957:p.392).

The programme demanded was, of course, the imposition of 'fiscal responsibility', i.e. the reduction of the Budget deficit forecast at £120m by the May Committee Report a few weeks earlier. That Report had simply confirmed the fears of foreign bankers as to the weakness of sterling, and its majority proposals for £96m worth of cuts in public expenditure, including a 20 per cent slice off the unemployment benefit, was the essence of their notion of 'internal confidence'. Given the hostility of the unions and the left wing of the Labour Party to such measures, their imposition necessitated the splitting of the Party and the dissolution of the government.

The position of finance did, however, suffer a major blow with the toppling of the gold standard, even if the bankers managed to bring down the Labour government as well and thus debilitate any political opposition from taking radical measures. If concerted political opposition was impossible at this point, the collapse of the bankers' strategy for British regeneration and the prospect of a major world depression and continuing stagnation of British exports at least afforded the opportunity for some rethinking. The Macmillan Committee in particular opened up one avenue for consideration. Its report urged a closer association between industry and the banks, in effect the 'German solution' of a full-blown finance capitalism to 'meet in the gate' the more financially powerful overseas competitors, carry through the process of rationalisation and reduce destructive competition (cited in Pollard, 1969:p.233). However, the provisions of that report were never carried out, and the banks' industrial holdings dropped off with the process of recovery, reflecting the fact that they had only grown in the first place because of the inability of financially pressed companies to pay off their overdrafts or loans during the slump and not as a result of a consciously developed change of policy (Pollard, 1969:p.234).

If the left was in disarray following the fall of the MacDonald government, the right was never in a position to mount a serious challenge to the prevailing political order. Mosley represented the frustrations of 'progressive' Conservatism in that epoch, drifting gradually towards more extreme positions as he came to appreciate the obduracy of the dominant power bloc. His movement was, in effect, the perverted continuation of the social imperialism of an earlier generation of industrialists, supporting imperial autarchy, social reforms to construct a 'land fit for heroes', conversion from a bankers' to a producers' economy, protectionism, public control of credit, the suppression of class struggle through the state, and an imperial development bank. His disdain for finance capital and the traditional racism of his imperialist ideology biased his following towards reacting to the crisis with a more extreme version of the imperial vision: a British fascism. However, whether owing to the lack of a serious threat from the left or to the effect of the Empire in cushioning the impact of the slump on the middle class, fascism never attracted substantial support from either the dominant or middle classes, and the Mosleyites were reduced to a rather ludicrous imitation of their Continental counterparts (Skidelsky, 1967; Semmel, 1960:ch. XVI).

Yet, if radical solutions were precluded, the fall of the gold standard dealt a fairly severe blow to free traders and to banking capital. The Import Duties Act of February 1932, and the Ottawa Conference later that year finally ushered in an imperial tariff policy. However, while this might be depicted in some sense as a 'victory' for the industrialist position, it paradoxically laid the basis for the re-emergence of banking capital's economic and political dominance at a later date. Going off gold was without a doubt a major blow for the City and its political spokesmen. Norman himself regarded it as a personal defeat and his health suffered correspondingly. The Bank and the Treasury were forced to control international capital flows much more closely than before under a general policy of imperial discrimination.

At the same time the emergence of the sterling area in association with the institution of imperial preference created the conditions for the City's revival in a future period of capitalist expansion. Essentially, once Britain had gone off gold, several dominions were in need of substantial loans to prevent default. Financial backing was quickly given to stabilise their various currencies against the pound, thus maintaining a single monetary area. While the arrangement remained a fairly loose one for the duration of the thirties, under the impact of the war the relations were tightened considerably, a form which continued into the postwar period (Strange, 1971:p.55).

The thirties thus constituted a decade in which the political power of banking capital was definitely diminished, although there is a tendency to overestimate the changes involved, particularly on the part of Keynesian historians. The *ancien regime* was finished, although it took World War II to put the nails in the coffin. Yet, there remained the possibility of re-establishing City dominance under altered conditions, a possibility later seized. Given the depth of the crisis and the political upheavals of other advanced capitalist nations, one can only be struck by the paltriness of the changes introduced by the governments of that decade. Even with regard to imperial preference what was remarkable was not so much its adoption, but, as Pollard rightly complains, '. . . its delay until 1931 in the face of the protectionism of all the other leading industrial states' (Pollard 1969:p.192). The fact that industry's aspirations could be contained by a few alterations in the imperial system meant that the City remained in a position to use those relations as a springboard for its own recovery in the 1950s.

Development Since World War II

World War II was, of course, the catalyst for major changes in the way in which economic policy was formulated. The mode of financing the war differed considerably from that of World War I, corresponding to the more complete mobilisation and the subordination of policy to strategic war aims. With the installation of Keynes in the Treasury along with other economists following the failure of the March 1941 war loan of only £300m and the military disasters of that summer, the government relied much more on taxation for its rising budget. Although home borrowing still had to cover almost half the increase in expenditure, as a proportion of the total it fell steadily over the course of the war years, and the government was more insistent that borrowing take place on its terms rather than those of the financial sector (Pollard, 1969:p.328).

In other respects as well the role of industrialists and the ideology of industrial capital were enhanced by the war effort and the Labour government which followed. The whole 'sponsorship' network between industries and the appropriate state departments emerged at this time, institutionalised under Attlee as 'democratic planning'. With regard to the mobilisation of resources, increased state co-ordination meant that traditional policies were abandoned at least for the duration of the war and the period of severe exchange problems which followed, i.e. the government employed various direct controls when needed.

International financial transactions were likewise affected by the war, but new forms of control over the flow of capital were undermined by the reconstruction of imperial relations under the new if less stable guise of the sterling area. Import and financial controls were gradually imposed over a whole range of transactions with food importing taken over entirely by the state. The Treasury assumed directorship of all dealings in gold and foreign exchange, limiting the powers of the Bank still further than they had been in the thirties. However, payments within the newly constituted sterling area were left uncontrolled. In fact the creation of the latter under the political pressures of war reversed the previous trend towards a looser currency area. Although voluntary in principle the sterling area amounted to a near monetary union and laid the foundations which, in the words of Strange (1971: p.56), 'made possible the post-war development of a dollar-discriminating club and a banker-customer relationship between Britain (with depleted reserves behind her) and her sterling area associates'.

In this alliance the members held their exchange rates in line with sterling and pooled their reserves in London under British control. For the countries of the Empire this helped secure the viability of Britain both as a military power and as their chief trading partner, a mixed blessing from their point of view. For Britain a fairly severe price was paid for maintaining this form of the relationship, namely increasing indebtedness to primarily sterling area countries, the so-called sterling balances. The degree of debt grew at a rate of about £600m a year during the second half of the war, allowing Britain to run a substantial trade deficit and still wage war but leaving a tremendous burden by the end, completely overturning the traditional position of London as a net world lender.

Until October 1943 these increased debts were balanced by the inflow of dollars from the Lend-Lease Agreement with the USA. But, after that time the US stopped supplying industrial goods *gratis*, allowing the gradual depletion of British reserves to a level of around £250m by the end of the war with liabilities some fifteen times greater, i.e. a sum close to the total overseas investment at the start of the conflict. American and British policy thus meant that the sterling balances kept rising while reserves either remained the same or fell off. At the end of hostilities it seemed as though the American administration might drive a hard bargain over the resolution of British liabilities. They first argued that the sterling balances should essentially be written off as the Empire's contribution to the war effort. However:

> The British delegation in Washington, which included Lord Keynes, reacted to the suggestion with incomprehension. Britain saw herself as banker to an association of countries whose support Britain still needed politically as much as sterling needed their financial confidence. They took the opposite view that it was not for the banker to default. (Strange, 1971:p.60; see also Pollard, 1969: p.334, and Gardner, 1969).

In the end the Americans more or less accepted the British position in return for the establishment of at least the general outlines of a multilateral regime for world trade. The US became the financial guarantor of the sterling area, tacitly accepting the importance of reconstituting an international role for sterling even if limited to roughly the boundaries of the Empire. For they never forced the reduction of British liabilities through requisition or confiscation. In this way the US promoted and continued to finance an international association which discriminated against American products, largely out of political considerations and the need to reconstruct the world financial system after the disintegration of the thirties. The war had generated the conditions for establishing a new financial unity among sterling-holding countries, but this was only made possible in the postwar period through the 1946 Loan Agreement and later Marshall Aid. The Americans thus propped up sterling's international role and contributed to concealing the disintegration of the basis of that role until the mid-1960s. Britain maintained an international currency, but only at the price of an extremely sensitive balance of payments position, given the ratio of liabilities to reserves.

The 1950s saw the return of Conservative predominance in Parliament: governments which proved unlikely to question the leadership of the City and the Bank of England on questions of economic policy. Nigel Harris (1972:Part III) has already documented the re-emergence of a free-market ideology within the Tory Party after the war, but one could add to his analysis that their rediscovered liberalism well accorded with the needs of banking capital. From 1951 when London reopened as an international market in foreign exchange to 1957 and the attempt at sterling convertibility, the story is essentially one of successive removals of the restrictions on financial activity in order to restore sterling and London to their former positions in international finance. The increased use of sterling in international transactions was reinforced by its role in the discriminating sterling area, all of which sustained the illusion that it was possible to resurrect the old system. However, as Strange (1971:ch.2) points out, all this was dependent on a few contingent factors: (1) the necessity of American tolerance of and support for an association which discriminated against dollar imports; (2) a continuous massive outflow of capital into the Commonwealth (which had negative effects on the balance of payments during those years); and (3) the capacity and willingness of the dependent countries to earn dollars and exchange the surplus for larger sterling balances in London, all of which allowed the system to continue on the basis of reserves that were low even by British standards.

The policies of successive Tory governments, resorting to a 'free-market' economy and international role for sterling, and the discrimin-

atory system of Commonwealth preference, were thus mutually
reinforcing. They managed to delay the recognition of the decline of
sterling from its top currency position, and no doubt contributed to
the complacency of British exporters who could still rely on protected
markets and only very gradually began to compete in the industrialised
capitalist regions of the world. The cost to the British economy was
high:

> It was the acceptance of difficulties with the balance of payments
> that made it far more difficult to manage the domestic economy
> than it was to manage the other European economies and much more
> difficult than it had been to manage the British economy in the days
> when sterling was Top Currency and London the unchallenged
> financial hub of the world. (Strange, 1971:p.71).

Over the course of the 1960s the function of both the pound and the
City changed substantially. In general terms sterling lost its international
role at the same time that the City regained its international prominence
as a financial entrepot. Four developments were intertwined in this
process of financial restructuring, all of which had a negative impact on
the balance of payments. In the first place there was substantial investment overseas especially into the sterling area. As an international
investor Britain was second only to the United States and far ahead of
the nearest competitor. In the late fifties and early sixties this investment amounted to a substantial burden on the external account,
although by the end of the decade repatriated income was balancing
capital outflow.[2]

Secondly, the disintegration of the remnants of the Empire had
manifold repercussions. The gradual decay in sterling's reserve role
among the sterling area countries could not be staved off any longer,
and by the end of the 1960s the latter had diversified into other
currencies. Particularly after devaluation in 1967 the pressure to drop
sterling as a reserve currency became insurmountable. The realisation
that it was possible to separate the reserve role of the pound from its
transactions role in world trade or even jettison both no doubt reduced
alarm and despondency in financial circles, as is clear in the following
passage from *The Banker* (1967:p.1031):

> A decline of the reserve role of sterling need not be too damaging to
> its use as a world trading currency. Britain remains a great trading
> country, and it will continue to be convenient to transact a great

deal of world commerce in sterling. Similarly, the attractions of the
City of London as a financial centre will survive the devaluation of
sterling. Its remarkable success in Euro-currency business in recent
years is evidence, if it still be needed, of its enterprise and adaptability.
The pound will still be used as a leading world currency for trade
and finance.

Thirdly, the dissolution of the Empire was also expressed politically
through increased government spending abroad for military and
economic purposes. While this might seem paradoxical, the point is
simply that the period of transition to 'home rule' for the former
colonies necessitated increased military and political involvement to
secure regimes friendly to British and Western interests. The burden of
the state's overseas payments has been frequently noted in the past,
but what is less commonly recognised is the reinforcing tendencies of
foreign political involvement and the international role of the pound.
The fourth development was the revival of London as the main
international financial centre of Europe, increasing the volatility of
short-term capital flows and preparing the way for the eventual divorce
of the fortunes of the City from those of the pound. London emerged
in the sixties no longer an instrument for funnelling British capital to
the Empire but primarily as an international financial entrepot. The
City prospered as never before, but its international transactions were
increasingly denominated in currencies other than sterling. In fact the
most spectacular growth area was in the Eurodollar and Eurobond
markets, i.e. markets in short and long-term credit denominated in
dollars and often held by foreigners (Strange, 1971:p.205; and Inter-
Bank Research Organisation, 1973).
In the sixties economic policies of successive governments were
constrained by the priority given to these developments, i.e. maintaining the City's position as an 'offshore island' and supporting the
pound until the financial sector realised that it could survive
devaluation. This, however, is not to say that no political conflict
existed over economic policies, which in fact recalled the disputes of
earlier decades.
In particular opposition was expressed against the overwhelming
priority given to the balance of payments and the exchange rate of the
pound by the Treasury. A strategy of growth and indicative planning,
the *economie concertee,* was counterposed to the 'stop-go' policies
which were seen as dominant in the state administration and debilitating
for home-based industrial capital. The frustrations of British industry at

its decling world position on the eve of the resurrection of capitalist
planning, some 30 years after its first appearance and 15 after the brief
experiment in World War II and the first years of the Attlee government,
come out quite clearly in the following passage from Sir Norman
Kipping, the then Director-General of the FBI (1972:p.90):

> So throughout 1955-7 we groped our way again and again through
> crises. Our reaction to plateaux, pauses, freezes and squeezes was
> that they might on occasion be a means to an end, but they were
> not a policy or an end in themselves. The fact is that we were out
> of touch with economic policy-making, and the government was out
> of touch with us. For outside advice, it relied mainly on private
> consultation with men of its own choosing, more of whom, I suspect,
> were men of the City than of industry. As tools of economic
> management, the government relied on orthodox monetary and fiscal
> methods.

The revolt against orthodoxy began at Brighton in November 1960
at a conference organised by Hugh Weeks, the then president of the
FBI's economic policy section, and a few other disgruntled industrialists
on the topic of 'The Next Five Years'. A group at the conference
concerned with 'Economic Growth in Britain' produced a report heavily
critical of the short-term management of economic policy. It called for
'a more conscious attempt to assess plans and demands in particular
industries for five or even ten years ahead'. (Leruez, 1972:pt.2, ch. 1;
see also Brittan, 1971:p.241).

The conference apparently considered two sorts of models of
capitalist planning. The first, indigenous, example was that of the Iron
and Steel Board, set up in the early 1950s under Churchill to oversee
the industry after it had been denationalised. This body had acted
much like a cartel except that it had not simply stabilised production
but promoted five-year plans, having nearly reached the end of the
second by the date of the conference. The second model, ultimately
the chosen instrument, was that of French *planification indicative*,
particularly appropriate given the simultaneous initiative to join
the EEC.

The influential National Institute for Economic and Social Research
organised a second conference some five months later to take a closer
look at the framework of the 'concerted economy' across the Channel.
Staff from the *Commissariat du Plan* and French businessmen attended
both to explain the French system and to reassure British industrialists

that indicative planning involved no more than the name implied, i.e. that the *Commissariat* did not have the powers of unilateral intervention but served, rather, as a meeting place for the 'voluntary collusion between senior civil servants and senior managers of big business'. (Shonfield, 1965:p.128).

Industrial opinion was moving rapidly towards a pro-planning, anti-Treasury position. Following another exchange crisis in July 1961, and the usual bout of deflationary measures, the Macmillan government finally responded to the increasing pressure for some kind of planning body. As far as industrial capital was concerned the form of the agency desired was straightforward. In the terms of one account:

> . . .it was simply a matter of industry's using its influence to get the kind of planning agreements it considered desirable. Its representatives made a strong case for an almost total transfer of the French model, particularly its use of 'indicative planning' by a council of government officials, industrialists and trade unionists, supported by a strong development office of experts. What the FBI did not want was a continuation of the Treasury's monopoly of planning. (Christoph, 1965:p.77).

By mid-winter the fledgling planning agency had emerged tentatively from its Whitehall shell. The National Economic Development Council incorporated essentially the industrialists' programme, a tripartite body designed to hammer out a consensus for a high-growth economy. The technocratic branch of the new apparatus, the National Economic Development Office, included a staff of 75 and was to draw up indicative plans for various sectors of the economy in consultation with NEDC members. It was hardly coincidental that the first Director-General of the NEDC had previously pioneered corporate planning in the private sector as the head of the Iron and Steel Board, namely Sir Robert Shone (Shonfield, 1965:p.96).

Thus, by mid-1962 the planning apparatus had taken the shape it more or less preserved through its several transformations up to the present. Constituted by an advisory council of business, labour and state appointees and served by a staff of economists, it retained its independence from the Treasury and brought 'both sides of industry' more directly into the policy-making process than ever before. Industrialists might well have been pleased at this point since Neddy was essentially the materialisation of the proposals put forward by the Beaver Committee of the FBI (Kipping, 1972:pp.92-4). A concerted economy in industry's mould seemed to be the emerging reform programme of the sixties.

The main difference with the French system that had so captured the imagination of industry's leaders consisted in the inclusion of some figures from the trade unions. In France the unions had refused to participate whereas in Britain they were only initially reluctant. From the point of view of industrial capital and the government the inclusion of some form of TUC representation in the planning programme was dictated by the need to impose some form of wage control, for the latter was presupposed by the whole strategy of *planification indicative*. The first NEDC forecast, *Growth of the United Kingdom Economy to 1966*, assumed, for example, that consumption would rise at a rate below that of GNP; that is, it presumed an incomes policy even if it did not stipulate one outright for fear of antagonising the unions before the ball even got rolling. Unless one was willing to turn to increased suppression, some form of co-operation with union leaders was necessary to discipline working-class demands under conditions of full employment if one wished to avoid the classic deflationary policies. 'Corporatism with a human face' involved in other words the implementation of the social contract first proposed in the Mond-Turner talks of the 1920s; rationalisation and planning including a national productivity agreement and hence restriction of wages growth to that of productivity increases. The unions were to collaborate with the state and big industrial capital through the NEDC and thus ensure the acceptability of the concerted economy to the working class, a vision of self-regulating capitalist accumulation which remained the Holy Grail of the Conservative and subsequent governments.

If the planning movement was initiated under the Conservatives, it was left to Labour to carry through in securing the new regime. The Tories failed in an immediate sense because they could not get union agreement on a voluntary incomes policy and were unwilling as yet to impose a statutory one; not that the latter would have proved any easier. Nor do I wish to imply that had they secured union co-operation they would have removed the only obstacle to a programmed crisis-free process of development. The experience of Labour has demonstrated that TUC co-operation by no means concludes class conflict in capitalist society, but simply changes the form of its expression, although at the same time it helps to win at least a greater degree of manoeuvrability for the government. In any case the Conservatives were hardly very convincing that their conversion to planning was much more than an exercise in public relations.

The Labour government of Harold Wilson was to prove no more successful, despite its ability to win union acquiescence on an incomes policy and the initially strong reformist thrust of Labour's programme. State economic planning was not scuttled by working-class militancy, at least in the short run. Rather, the initial barrier proved to be the inadequacy of the planning apparatus in controlling the effects of the boom, which led right back to the old constraint of increasing imports and an exchange crisis, followed by the usual medicine of deflation. When faced with the alternatives of deflation or devaluation the government hesitated but eventually followed the orthodox prescriptions. In the end economic planning amounted to no more than the ideological exhortation needed to establish an incomes policy. As one protagonist of Labour's policy put it:

> The unions will not co-operate in what they and their members recognise as wage restraint, but if it can be wrapped up as a 'planned-growth-of-wages,' they may be prepared to help the government. (Denton, 1964)

What the Wilson government did manage to accomplish was to bring most of the planning machinery within Whitehall as part of the new Department of Economic Affairs under George Brown. Labour was shifting the emphasis towards a slightly more *etatist* version of corporatist policy-making, with the DEA as the institutional voice of industrial capital within the state apparatus and not on its fringes, at the same time as maintaining the NEDC as a consensual vehicle for concluding a 'producers' alliance.' Although there may have been doubt on the part of industrialists about their inclusion in the game plan of a 'socialist' government, George Brown, for one, has emphasised (1972:p.94) that, 'At the initial stage, and for quite some time afterwards, the relationship between leading industrialists and the Labour Government was exceedingly close and good'.

Just as the Tories had set up the NEDC as a 'pressure group for growth', so under Labour the DEA was to function in creative tension with the Treasury in the formulation of economic policy. It was to be 'the spokesman for industry, when industrial needs conflicted with other objectives of policy' (Brittan, 1971:p.312; Leruez, 1972:pt. 3, ch.1). This meant in fact that the whole scheme was compromised from the start. The scope of authority of both bureaux naturally overlapped considerably, since both were supposed to deal with the basic parameters of economic policy from different perspectives. This contradiction was nominally resolved through an administrative concordat which divided the responsibility for policy-making between them: the DEA would concentrate on the long-term and physical resources while the Treasury would look to the short term and handle financial matters (Brittan, 1971:p.312). This, however, begged the question of just how short-term management and long-term programming were to be related, particularly given the all-too-likely event that they demanded opposing policies. Or, alternatively, the formulation presumed that priorities would be settled by political struggle within the state bureaucracy and the Cabinet, a struggle on the chosen terrain of the dominant power bloc. As Brown unhappily discovered (1972:p.92):

> Once the heady first days had gone and the novelty had worn off, the Treasury began to reassert itself, and with its absolutely superb mastery of the government machine gradually either filched things back or — more to the point — made it rather difficult for us to effect the grand design we had in mind so that a coherent and continuous economic policy could emerge.

When the 'grand design' did appear, at least in its printed form as the 1965 National Plan, it was to say the least not very impressive. Even before it was published the imposition of deflationary measures had already shown the government's hand to more perceptive observers, namely that short-term considerations and support for the existing rate of exchange of the pound were still the paramount features of economic policy. To put it simply, the National Plan lacked teeth. In the words of one sympathiser, 'Far from being directive, or even indicative, it was merely subjunctive' (Beckerman, 1972:p.172). There were too many 'ifs' and no means of subordinating short-term management to the plan's objectives.

One of the most important 'ifs' was the balance of payments, and, when the crunch came, the defence of sterling took precedence over the strategy for economic growth. The pursuit of the latter would have necessitated devaluation much earlier than took place and perhaps exchange and import controls or at least skilful manoeuvring to borrow from other central banks or the IMF for the duration of the exchange crisis on terms which did not include the usual deflation. Fear of the loss of electoral support may explain the failure to devalue in the early period of the government, when it had to face another battle at the polls. However, the failure to devalue *after* Labour was returned in 1966 with a sizeable majority in the Commons gives the lie to that excuse. Neither will it do to assert blandly, as have Graham and Beckerman, that the failure to devalue in July 1966, '. . . is one of the major political puzzles of the 1960s' (Brown, 1972:p.22). This puzzle has an uncanny familiarity to it, as it is imprinted with policy priorities of finance.

Indeed, the Prime Minister gave a fairly clear indication of his views on the subject of devaluation shortly after the publication of the National Plan. He argued that devaluation would have been 'totally wrong' since 'there are many people overseas, including governments, marketing boards, central banks, and others, who left their money in the form of sterling balances, on the assumption that the value of sterling would be maintained. To have let them down would have been not only a betrayal of trust, it would have shaken their faith about holding any further money in the form of sterling' (cited in Miliband, 1972:p.362). Maintaining the exchange rate was in other words still the top priority in deference to the City and its international support in the IMF and the United States.

Financial spokesmen were not ignorant of this unexpected support from Labour. One of the clearest expressions of gratitude came in the 'Commentary' columns of *The Banker* in October 1967 (p.827). After listing all the 'bitter pills' that the City had been forced to swallow under Wilson, e.g. corporation tax, curbs on overseas investment, special deposits, dividend freeze, etc., the article went on to note that the relationship between Labour and the City had nonetheless been 'relatively harmonious'. It explained that:

> . . .the main reason for the City's acquiescent mood is that, contrary to expectations, the government has endorsed the City's order of priorities. It has put sterling first. Many of the unpopular measures — such as the restraints on overseas investments — have been made necessary in order to achieve an overriding objective which the City also holds: the need to strengthen sterling. Furthermore, the Government has endorsed not only the City's priorities, but also, to a considerable extent, its remedies. It is true that it postponed deflation for as long as it could — thus aggravating the situation further. But, at the pinch, in July, 1966, it was prepared to be as ruthless in curbing demand as any Tory Government, and to sacrifice the National Plan and many other dear schemes besides in the attempt to cut imports by deflation.

Conclusions

In conclusion, the City maintained its position of political dominance
through the 1960s despite widespread economic changes and the return
of a reformist Labour government after 13 years 'in the wilderness,'
one which was, moreover, committed to industrial regeneration. The
continued supremacy of the traditional power bloc can hardly be
depitced as supportive of the process of accumulation, at least
domestically, as the policies of rigid adherence to the given rate of
exchange and consequent deflationary measures undoubtedly undermined the competitive position of domestic industry as against foreign
capitalist units of production. It would appear impossible to derive
such conclusions from the 'logic of capital' approach to the state, yet
such 'illogic' defines the peculiarity of the British state. This 'illogic'
is displayed in the rigidity of the particular power bloc institutionalised
within the state apparatus, a dominant political-economic fraction
which has outlived its 'world-historical role' by some decades and has
only managed to pursue a defensive strategy of preserving the vestiges
of its past grandeur in the face of vast changes in the political economy
of the capitalist world system. The persistent experience of British
decline from the late nineteenth century, with the partial exception of
the interwar period, did not instigate any major change of orientation or
shift of balance in the politically dominant forces, even as late as the
1960s. They were content in the postwar era with shoring up the old
defences, attempting to resurrect the City's once key position in the
world economy by establishing once more a liberal international regime
as modified by the retained imperial system of economic linkage, now
in the form of the Sterling Area. Only after the economic dissolution of
this system owing to the changing patterns of world trade was a
concerted effort made in the late sixties and early seventies to redirect
the energies of British capital, this time under the unfavourable
conditions of world slump.

City dominance over the policy-making process involved several
aspects of the structuration of power within the state. Most immediately
and visibly the ability of finance to precipitate financial crises on the
foreign exchanges forced the Labour government to heed the advice of
its spokesmen when formulating economic policy. Labour was faced
with such a crisis almost immediately upon forming a government in
1964, and the initial response to this, the decision not to devalue, set
the parameters for Labour's policy, or the lack of it, over the next six
years. Exchange crises necessitate immediate action, whereas more
general conditions of accumulation rarely impose themselves upon the

state with such urgency (the period of extreme liquidity squeeze in 1974 due to the price freeze and rapid wage increases constituting one important exception). Richard Crossman, the former Labour minister, is among those who noted his experience of government as one of reacting to rather than initiating events(1976:50,51). This is a personal confirmation of the significance of these crises in setting the limits to a reformist administration, reinforcing the position of finance in most cases, especially when an increase in international debt brings about the intervention of the International Monetary Fund (Hirsch, F., 1965 and Beckerman, 1972). The Wilson government failed to seize the initiative over the question of exchange rates, and as a consequence its programme of an 'industrial coup d'etat' after the example of Napoleon III was severely hamstrung from the start. Successive runs on sterling after 1964 simply reinforced the direction of overall economic policy, in the main a reaffirmation of deflation as an 'instrument' of economic control.

In institutional terms the position of finance has been preserved through its penetration of key state bureaucracies, its ability to control important levers of power. The Bank of England is the linchpin of this presence, its traditional autonomy confirmed rather than eliminated by the Nationalisation Act of 1945 (Hirsch, F., 1965:ch.6). The Bank's position of authority is the locus of financial interests in the state. In its self-description it mediates between the City and the government. The Bank's view was probably best expressed by its Governor before the Select Committee on Nationalised Industries (1970:pp.273,274). Noting that the Bank was 'an arm of Government in the City,' Sir Leslie O'Brien also thought it was fair 'to claim that the Bank has an understanding of the legitimate interests and needs of City institutions.'

'I am not, then,' he concluded, 'the representative of the City but I do represent City interests where I think it is right and proper to do so . . . I am a discriminating advocate.' One might add that it has also supported a fairly consistent set of priorities from advocacy of the removal of exchange controls in the fifties to the monetary targetry of the present, a set consistent with the interests of finance. The City has thus been in the privileged position of having its 'discriminating advocate' at the heart of the state apparatus where economic policy is formulated. Industrial capital has had no such direct means of representation and many of the reforms of the 1960s in the area of industrial policy can be seen as an attempt to redress the balance — to secure industrialists' advice and consent on the various economic strategies.

While ultimate legal control rests with the government, the Bank's influence on economic policy is far from insignificant. In the first place, 'Somebody from the Bank of England is on nearly every economic committee in the Treasury. Therefore, there is a view of the Bank of England expressed there' (Select Committee, 1970:p.5). In the second place, Hirsch noted in 1965 (ch.6) that in the 20 years since nationalisation the government had issued not one directive to the Bank although it was explicitly empowered to do so. Had a Chancellor attempted such actions he would almost certainly have been faced with the Governor's ultimate weapon of 'moral suasion', resignation. Given that reformist Labour governments work within this institutional arrangement, they must amend their policies so as to take account of the views of those in key positions of political power, and the Bank of England is certainly one of the most resourceful institutions in the state system.

In historical terms it was the particular pattern of capitalist development in Britain which served as the basis for City domination in the political realm. From 1870 the growth of foreign investment was funnelled through the London capital markets, which as a result developed almost entirely upon the foreign trade. In a world order based on free trade and the gold standard the City was the focus of economic power and prestige and developed an outlook which corresponded with its international position, as Susan Strange has argued. The British strategy of portfolio investment abroad as a response (and contributing factor) to domestic industrial decline had a long-lasting impact on the political as well as the economic system (Gilpin 1975: ch.3). In the twentieth century British capital under the traditional leadership of high finance perpetrated a series of defensive manoeuvres in an ultimately disastrous attempt to preserve markets and British hegemony through the imperial system and the free export of capital. In political terms this pattern of development meant the coincidence of interests between imperialists and the City, an alliance which persisted up through the sixties. In fact it only collapsed once the pattern of trade and investment had shifted so much to the advanced capitalist world that the special relationships instituted in the Sterling Area no longer made any sense and came to be perceived by all as a liability rather than an asset.

In a recent essay Stephen Blank (1977:p.705) has referred to this political alliance as the overseas or sterling lobby and has argued that it was the influence of this pressure group rather than simply City dominance that explains the policy priorities of the postwar era. While his point about the extent of political allies is taken, it none the less remains true that financial interests had the greatest stake in the old system and constituted the basis of that lobby in the economy and class structure. Only after their realisation that the City could carve a new niche in the advanced capitalist world as an international financial entrepot, with or without an international British currency, did economic strategy shift fundamentally.

At the same time we can agree with Blank (1977) that 'if the sterling lobby or the Treasury dominated policy making, it was because there was no serious opposition to the policies they put forward, not because the Treasury, the City or the Bank forced their views upon the policy makers.' The picture of banking capital forcing through certain measures in the teeth of strident opposition is indeed a false one. At the same time there was, at least by the early sixties, *some* opposition coming mainly from the ranks of industrial capital and centred on the alternative programme of economic planning on a modified French model. What is surprising perhaps is that this opposition from within the ranks of capital was so muted and tentative. Organised labour offered more consistent criticism but was unable to exert much influence on the main lines of economic policy (see also Panitch, 1976).

The answer to this puzzle lies again in the pattern of capitalist development established in Britain which weakened industrial capital to the same extent that it strengthened finance. As one index of this feebleness one could point to the inability of British industry to form on its own initiative a single peak organisation to secure its political and industrial aims. Both the initial formation of the Federation of British Industry in 1916 and its amalgamation with the other major organisations to constitute the CBI in 1965 occurred only with state support or sponsorship, the latter of course under Labour (Blank, 1973:p.14; Grant and Marsh, 1977:p.19). Contrast this with the continuous presence of the Bank of England at the centre of the policy-making process. At the same time British industry remained wedded to the idea of an imperial system up through the 1950s, in part because it derived real benefits in the form of protected markets and outlets for investment. Especially with the increasing predominance of the multinational enterprise in the British economy the interests of industrial capital cannot be easily identified with those of the nation state, nor their priorities equated with the national economic growth targets so dear to state planners. In 1971 for example while the USA accounted for the lion's share of foreign direct investment (52 per cent of the total), the UK was an easy second in this league (14.5 per cent), far ahead of France (5.8 per cent), West Germany (4.4 per cent), or Japan (2.7 per cent) (Gilpin, 1975:

introduction). The fact that the industrial sector is completely
dominated by multinationals implies that it shares various immediate
interests with finance, namely the desire to keep open the option of
capital export, and has good reason to follow the City's lead in
matters of industrial policy even if the consequence is erosion of the
home base to some degree.

Additionally, the only political option offered in the past decade
and a half was some form of increased state direction which has various
pitfalls even if it promised advantages for domestic industry. One can
postulate that capitalists will always be fearful of state economic
planning except under conditions in which they can ensure its insulation
from working-class demands, as in Japan for example and to a lesser
extent in France. While the revision of Labour's socialism in the fifties
and the development of tripartite modes of representation attempted
to secure just those reassuring limits to autonomous working-class
pressure, incorporating labour as a 'responsible partner' in a national
effort, the very fact that they were necessary probably increased the
insecurity of industrialists on the whole question of greater state intervention in the economy. By the 1970s the turn in the Labour Party
towards greater state direction through the NEB and planning
agreements raised the threat of an actual programme of transition to
socialism and repulsed even those 'progressive industrialists' who had
backed earlier measures. In the end the latter were appeased as Benn's
wings were trimmed and the planning agreements system was reduced
to little more than the 'concerted economy' initiated in the sixties,
but the point is that state capitalist strategies entail risks that disturb
the fainthearted of the dominant class.

Since the early sixties Labour has pursued essentially this policy of
greater state intervention into the process of domestic capital formation
and the determination of wages, a programme with the corollary of
instituting new forms of representation of the forces of labour and
industrial capital, the so-called 'new corporatism'. Yet, this programme
of a 'producers' alliance' has foundered, ultimately, I would argue
because it does not attempt to transform the underlying class divisions
of a capitalist society but simply attempts to find a common ground in
nationalist terms. But even the more limited reformist impact of Labour
administrations has been blunted because of their inability to challenge
the underlying logic of economic policy once they have accepted the
institutional constraints of the British state as the setting for their
activities. There is no doubt that the position of industrial capital has
been strengthened in the past 15 years; the continuing role of the NEDC

and the CBI and such limited experiments as the Industrial Reorganisation Corporation (IRC), and National Enterprise Board (NEB) and
planning agreements all testify to that. Yet, one is inevitably struck by
the paltriness of the changes in the face of an almost continuous crisis
and the existence of popular support for substantial change at various
points, especially 1964-6. In the present period the apparent victory
for the advocates of monetary targets is yet another example of the
power of finance in the determination of economic policy. The increasing authority of monetarist myths has been correctly interpreted
as indicative of both the enhanced autonomy of the Bank of England
and the resurrection of an ideological equivalent to the gold standard,
a fixed point of reference which represents 'a self-imposed constraint,
or discipline, on the authorities', as the present Governor of the Bank,
Gordon Richardson, put it in his inaugural Mais Lecture.[3]

If national political institutions prove incapable of enforcing these
measures of credit restriction they are amply reinforced by the international agencies of finance, mainly the IMF. The latter has played
an increasing part in the determination of economic policy in Britain as
well as in other troubled nations of the advanced capitalist world since
the middle years of the last decade. While the IMF is no doubt utilised
in part by governments as a convenient whipping boy, forcing the
implementation of policies with which they are in basic agreement, it
has at the same time remained very consistent in the sorts of remedies
it prescribes when its lending services are required, namely
liberalisation of exchange and import controls, maintaining a free flow
of goods and capital, deflation, and when necessary for third world
countries, devaluation (Payer, 1974:chs.1-3). This last measure is of
course much more problematic and less favoured in the case of a central
international currency such as the pound, but we might add monetary
target practice as the latest weapon in the arsenal of this watchdog of
the liberal international regime. Similarly, the repeated moves towards
developing a European 'unit of account' point towards the centralisation of monetary policy under institutions both more directly
responsive to the views of international finance and more capable of
excluding the 'inflationary' demands of the European labour movement.
This project of placing monetary policy under the unhindered control
of some autonomously constructed agency of the central banks of the
advanced capitalist world has been attempted at various times since
initially proposed by Montagu Norman in the 1920s. So far it has
foundered on national political differences, the Bretton Woods system
being the closest achievement but even in this limited form it has only

been possible during the period of unchallenged American hegemony. The present moves by Europeanists like Roy Jenkins should be interpreted against this background of relative failure, for such international programmes are inherently highly unstable.

At the same time these conditions and present trends hardly bode well for Labour's ideology of 'one nation' and its underlying political-economic strategy, a corporatist 'producers' alliance'. If monetary targets in Mr Richardson's words 'provide the framework of stability within which other policy objectives can be more easily achieved', it does not take much thought to discern that the 'framework' will be accorded greater priority than the 'other objectives' (*The Times,* 10 Feb.1978). The legitimacy of the Labour Party as the party of the working class is liable to further erosion as successive governments renew the demand for deferred gratification, discipline and restraint, adhere to monetary orthodoxy and can only offer in return budgetary crumbs, growing unemployment and urban decay.

Notes

1. For many points in the following argument I am indebted to Jim Tomlinson.

2. The following draws heavily from Strange (1971:ch.4).

3. *The Times,* 10 February 1978; see also *The Guardian* same date, and the *Sunday Times,* 12 February 1978 for further analyses.

6 CAPITALISM, THE STATE AND INDUSTRIAL RELATIONS[1]

Dominic Strinati

It may be the case that the state has been neglected, at least until recently, as an explicit topic of sociological inquiry (Poggi, 1977). But to say this is to ignore a large amount of sociological writing relevant to a conception of the state as a social phenomenon, and to pre-empt the more fundamental bases of discussion; for to regard the state as an independent object of sociological analysis depends upon premises which construe the state as such an object, and thus upon a theorisation of its independence from other social institutions; and in terms of the debate which has arisen over the role of the capitalist state this is precisely what is at issue. Rather, what is required is an elaboration of theoretical principles which allow for an understanding of the state: the examination of theoretical and empirical issues in order to decipher the structural constraints acting upon, and the role played by, the capitalist state.

This is the general problem to which this paper is addressed, with its more specific reference being the development of state intervention in industrial relations in Britain in the 1960s and 1970s. In endeavouring to elucidate the social-structural factors associated with the role of the capitalist state it will be oriented towards the following questions: What causes state intervention in industrial relations?; and what determines the form and content of such intervention? These questions will be dealt with in relation to the concrete example chosen for illustrative purposes, but they have a more general theoretical relevance which requires that the conceptual means for the asking of these questions and the arguments that can be advanced as answers be established: that is, it is necessary first of all to provide the theorisation appropriate to and adequate for the analysis of the relationship between the capitalist state and industrial relations.[2]

The Theoretical Analysis of the Capitalist State

The main thesis of this paper is as follows: state intervention in industrial relations derives from the systemic relationship within capitalism between the state and the economy as distinct institutional structures within which the state provides certain indispensable conditions for the maintenance and continuity of capital accumulation, such that just as capitalism entails distinct modes of economic production, so it entails

191

distinct modes of state intervention. However, while this determines whether state intervention will occur at all, the *nature* of the form and content of this intervention is shaped by class interests and struggles, by political conflicts, by the operations, practices, rules and structures of the state and its apparatuses and by political organisations. Like state intervention *vis-a-vis* capital accumulation these state apparatuses and political organisations mediate, integrate and even constitute class interests and are thus not reducible to economic or class interests. Class conflicts and political struggles (the level of social integration) as such are not determinative of state intervention; this derives from the level of system integration and system problems, the relationship between the state and capital accumulation.[3] Such problems as may hinder the accumulation process are engendered in the form of the articulation of economic and political class interests and conflicts which inhere in and derive from the accumulation process and the state. Given this, the actual nature, the form and content, taken by state intervention is determined by these interests and struggles as they are organised and constituted by the role of the state. It can also be suggested, although this is a point that will not be pursued here, that the consequences of state intervention tend to 'overdetermine' rather than resolve the causes leading to intervention (Habermas, 1976).

Central to this theoretical framework is the general, descriptive concept of system contradiction which is intended to encapsulate the relationship between the state and economy and the political contradiction characteristic of capitalism (Offe, 1977; Parkin, F., 1972). Capitalism is predicated upon and distinguished by the institutional separation of polity and economy such that the structural forms and modes of procedure and characteristic operations of the one are not determined by nor interfered with by the other (Poulantzas, 1973; Giddens, 1973; Holloway and Picciotto, 1977). The capital relation requires the autonomisation of politics and the state from the economic representation of this relation so that, in ideal typical terms, capitalist economic processes can secure their own reproduction without the assistance of the state. The state is excluded from production, from actually engaging in production activities and intervening in the economy and industry which for the ideal operation of capitalism have their own internal mechanisms to ensure their continuity without state involvement (Jewkes, 1977). However, historically forms of the capitalist state have always had direct implications for such putatively autonomous economic processes which are, in the light of an adequate theorisation of the conditions of capitalism and scrutiny of the historical development of capitalist societies, in fact dependent upon specific modes of state intervention, if we interpret intervention very widely as the role performed by the state in relation to non-state areas of social structure. Hence, the extreme ideal typification of bourgeois economic, political and ideological practices (the autonomy of the economy and its insulation from the state) is subverted by the conditions of existence that the state actually provides for the economy, a feature historically evident in the development of capitalism. Empirically, the principle of separation is breached by the state, not merely in times of crises, but in structuring the very conditions on which the capitalist economy depends. This implies that ideologically the capital relation represents the separation of the state and economy as the means of ensuring its stability and continuity but politically this requires in contradiction the transgression of this principle of separation and the intervention of the state. This system contradiction characterising the role of the capitalist state and class interests relating to the use of the state will be manifest later on in this paper when the relationship between capital, labour and state intervention in Britain is discussed, in particular as it is expressed in the articulation of class and political interests.[4]

The concept of system contradiction as applied to the role of the capitalist state is as such only descriptive and requires further theorisation which will also provide further conceptual grounds for approaching the problems that this paper has posed.[5] We may define the state, following Jessop (1977a), as an institutional system of political domination, embodying both modes of political representation and means of intervention in capital accumulation and class conflicts, having definite effects in these respects, but which is not *essentially* capitalist. The state is a capitalist state in so far as its structural connections with the capitalist economy and its own internal structures and modes of operation serve to secure, in however a contradictory fashion, the conditions of existence of capital accumulation and, thus, control of class struggle — since accumulation is class struggle. The capitalist state is such a state not because it is *determined* by the capitalist economy but because it objectively organises structures indispensable for the functioning of the capitalist economy: the circuit of capital, the production, realisation and appropriation of surplus value, generalised commodity production and exchange, the reproduction and restructuring of capital and labour power, the conditions that allow the circuit of capital to exist.

It is not possible however to determine ahistorically the role that the state will play. The specificity of the structures of the state can only be grasped in the context of the concrete, historical phases of the development of capitalism, the development of the state-economy relation and of class struggles within capitalist social formations. The general concepts regarding capital accumulation and the state that can be formulated, while necessary in that any empirical research must be theoretically informed and structured, are not exhaustive or determinative of the conjunctural conditions in which this relationship may be realised.[6]

A major contention in our argument is that in analysing the role of the state explanatory priority, logically if not empirically, must given to the systemic, institutional relationship between state and economy rather than the direct and overt expressions of class interests and conflicts, that is to system contradictions rather than social conflicts, since the former constitutes the social matrix within which the latter must be located. The system relationship between state and economy provides the context for class formation and class conflicts (Lockwood, 1964). This is not to say that class conflict cannot influence state intervention nor that it can have no impact upon the alignment of or changes in the state-economy relationship, but it is to argue that such impact as it may have upon the state is dependent upon the possibilities for this to be so, as created by systemic, institutional relationships.

To further theorise the state-economy relation under capitalism and to begin to effect a concrete analysis along the lines already indicated, it is important to note that the state and economy cannot be seen as undifferentiated totalities. The economy is composed of distinct structures and processes and the state consists of, to varying degrees, distinct apparatuses, which may be differentially related to each other in terms of the specific function performed. It is not the state as a whole, as it were, which performs functions for capital accumulation but specific state apparatuses charged with differing and specific functions. This problematises the state-economy relationship in so far as it raises the question of determining the relationship of specific state apparatuses to the specific structures and processes entailed in the capitalist economy (Johnson, 1977). In particular, the tendency to totalise conceptions of state and economy leads to a neglect of a crucial issue, especially as far as this paper is concerned: the construction of required but unavailable state apparatuses or the reorganisation of already existing ones. This is precisely what is often entailed in analysing state intervention, namely determining the particular, conjunctural problems faced by capital accumulation which require the intervention of the state, the specific state apparatuses involved in the implementation of such intervention and/or the construction of other state apparatuses appropriate for intervention.

It follows from this point that in order to assess the structural relationship between the economy and modes of state intervention as policy outputs emanating from the state system, the mediatory and organisational role played by institutions, mainly state apparatuses, linking and managing this relationship becomes of crucial importance (Offe, 1974 and 1976; Bourdieu, 1977). The state-economy relation as expressed in modes of state intervention is necessarily structured and made possible by institutional forces that integrate and produce such modes of intervention. The nature and influence of these forces, be they economic, quasi-economic or political, state apparatuses or whatever, need to be examined in any explanation of state intervention since they are the mechanisms which make intervention possible.

This is of especial relevance to the much discussed notion of the autonomy, relative or otherwise, of the state, for it is in the context of the institutional linkage between economy and the state and the state's management of the economy that the autonomy of the state and its various apparatuses is realised. Structuring the nexus of connections between capital accumulation and the class struggle on the one hand, and specific forms of state action on the other, provides the social foundations for the autonomy of institutions organising these connections due to the structurally strategic significance of such a mediatory position. The structuring of state apparatuses and the construction of modes of state intervention are not reducible to the determinations exercised by the economy and class interests. Rather it is the case that classes and class interests themselves necessitate the construction of representative organisations which may or may not be effective and they also require their constitution at the level of the political by specifically political organisations and state apparatuses: political class interests only exist as political forces if they are by one means or another actually constituted, not merely expressed or organised, by political organisations and state apparatuses. The formulation and establishment of modes of state intervention is thus a consequence of the role of state apparatuses and political organisations, even if enacted in the face of class struggles and in response to problems confronting capital accumulation. This is bound up with the stress placed upon the need to bear in mind what is termed the specific effectivity and the structural selectivity of state and political forms (Offe, 1974). The claim being proposed here is that the institutional structures of the state and the polity in the process of intervention exercise their own specific and determinative influence and have direct effects upon class struggle and capital accumulation. Even though the state 'responds' to these processes, this response is organised and generated by the state and it is necessarily processed through determinant structural channels by means of definite procedural norms which have a constraining impact upon the form taken by state intervention.[7]

It must also be asserted that, for the purposes of this paper, industrial relations are not conceived of as hermetically sealed and self-sufficient entities but as a central element in the social structure of capitalism, and in particular as one of the ways in which class struggles are expressed in capitalist societies. Industrial relations are conceptualised as a particular aspect of the class structure of capitalism manifest in the structure of industrial enterprises while industrial conflict is similarly conceptualised, being seen as an identifiable expression of class conflict. Thus, industrial relations are not *sui generis* systems but can only be understood when viewed within the wider framework of the capitalist class structure and class struggles.[8]

The main objective of this paper is to examine the social-structural factors associated with, determining, and affected by, the inception and nature of interventions in industrial relations by the capitalist state. The general conceptual means that will inform this analysis have been set out above and the following discussion will extend and illustrate these contentions. But before proceeding to considerations of a more directly concrete character, given the concern of this paper with changes in the mode of state intervention, it is necessary to provide some historical background by means of a conceptual schematisation of the changing forms and nature of state intervention.

The Changing Nature of State Intervention

Conceptualising changing modes of state intervention in connection with the changing nature of capitalism and the economy is essential for analyses of the contemporary role of the capitalist state, for state actions like incomes policies and industrial relations reform legislation are tokens of a more all inclusive change in the role of the state. This transition has been marked in the British social formation by the change from *laissez-faire* to 'interventionist' forms of state involvement in the economy and industrial relations. Therefore to understand and illustrate the structural determination and nature of state intervention requires its historical and social-structural location in the phases of capitalist development and a conception of the structural factors that are combined in the overall configuration of state intervention. To clarify conceptually the object of analysis and particular aspects of that object (the role of the capitalist state) in these terms, an initial and preliminary theorisation of the relationship between the development of the structure of the capital relation, the capitalist economy and modes of state intervention is set out in Figure 6.1. Our immediate concern with these formulations is not so much with the overall long-term process of transition but with its relevance for contemporary capitalism in Britain. However, it is not intended to represent certain phases and structures as totally or completely transcending prior structures and phases. They may be retained either in the operation of the state though subsumed under subsequent forms, or as the political and ideological objectives regarding the role of the state adopted and supported by certain class and political interests; and as such they remain relevant for our analysis.

We shall now briefly define the conceptualisations employed in the schematic depiction of the development of capitalism and modes of state intervention.[9] We shall not discuss directly the stage of primitive accumulation since this is certainly peripheral to our immediate interest. Nor shall we confront explicitly the nature of the changes in the economy, the economic dimension of the capital relation (but see Holloway and Picciotto, 1977; Mandel, 1975; Mattick, 1971), especially since quite often attempts to deal with these problems which start from an extensive analysis of the economic dimension of the capital relation by intent or by default either leave a purely residual role for the state or see it as being reducible to economic relations. Neither will the constant factors employed in the theorisation (class struggles and the re-structuring of state apparatuses) be dealt with until they are specifically identified concretely in respect of state intervention in industrial relations in the contemporary British social formation.

Let us therefore turn to the relevant conceptualisation of the state-economy relation, political representation, and forms of state control of industrial relations. The notions of *laissez-faire* and interventionism as applied to the role of the state are intended to designate the overall complex of factors mentioned. But they are also designed to convey the distinction between (i) forms of state intervention whereby the state provides the limited but essential external conditions for capital accumulation and economic processes but does not directly intervene in such processes, rather orienting its action to preclude such a possibility, *laissez-faire*, and (ii) forms of state intervention whereby the state directly intervenes in capital reproduction, becomes internally involved in the economy, and orients its action to secure such interventionism. The conceptual distinction is thus intended to

Figure 6.1: The Development of Capitalism and Modes of State Intervention

| Economy | State-Economy Relation | | | | Polity and State | |
Structure and Problems	General Form of State Intervention	Method of State Intervention	State Strategies (Goals)	Functions of State Re: Economy	Political Representation	Forms of State Control of Industrial Relations
Primitive Accumulation	'Military'	Force	Inception of Capitalism	Creative	Exclusionist	Coercion
Competitive Capitalism. (absolute surplus value extraction, business cycle, unemployment)	Laissez-faire	Allocation (politics)	Inaction	Facilitative	Liberalism or Paternalism	
Monopoly Capitalism. (relative surplus value extraction, profitability crises, lack of accumulation, inflation)	Interventionist	Production (policies)	Protective-welfare. Administrative re-commodification	Supportive Directive	Pluralism or Corporatism	

Capital Accumulation — Class Struggles

Class Struggles — Re-structuring State Apparatuses

denote a qualitative difference in the relation of the state to the economy: between optimising as far as possible the autonomisation of the economy to resolve its own crises and conflicts and secure its reproduction with minimal but nonetheless indispensable assitance from the state, and, conversely, politicising the economy by the direct intrusion of the state into the process of the economic reproduction of the capital relation.

This formulation can be extended and supplemented and made more secure if we consider in turn the other conceptions advanced. The distinction between allocation and production, or allocative and productive state functions (taken directly from Offe, 1975a), refers to the methods by means of which the state intervenes in the economy, and, by extension, in industrial relations. In Offe's terms, allocation conceptualises intervention whereby the state allocates resources (e.g. taxes, repressive force) which it already controls, as realised by the state's capacity authoritatively (e.g. by constitutional norms) to allocate such resources in securing the conditions for capital accumulation. Furthermore decisions over allocations are reached as a result of politics, of direct political struggles between competing interests; and it is also important to note that Keynesian economic policies, the management of aggregate demand through state-owned resources like taxation and expenditure, exemplify state allocative functions. However, also occasioned by the changing nature of capital accumulation is the need for productive inputs which the accumulation process, given its essentially competitive structure of relations between discrete capital units, is incapable of providing (Offe, 1975a; also Altvater, 1973). Hence, allocation is supplemented by and subordinated to productive state functions whereby the state actually produces inputs for capital accumulation to ensure its continuity. In this case, politics as the struggle of competing interests is no longer adequate for these functions and the state has to 'produce' its own policy decision-making rules and organisational forms appropriate to such productive functions.[10] Consequently, 'production' as a state function increases the significance and importance of the need to reorganise and construct state apparatuses for the purpose of intervention in that with productive state functions the means or mechanisms for state intervention also have to be produced.

Turning to the next set of distinctions (taken from Offe and Ronge, 1976), those concerning the strategies adopted by the state towards capital accumulation, three general strategies can be delineated in respect of the state's relation to the maintenance of generalised commodity production, the universalisation of the commodity form, and the reproduction and re-structuring of capital. First, the state can chose inaction, it can choose to do nothing and orient policy to secure the minimisation of its intervention. This, however, is undermined by the failure of the putative self-correcting mechanisms of the economy to work to regenerate commodity forms and accumulation. Secondly, the state can be protective, providing subsidies and so allowing de-commodified forms to survive under artificial conditions created by the state until they can be returned to the accumulation process. Since this tends to produce fiscal crises the increasingly dominant strategy adopted by the capitalist state is that of administrative re-commodification by which the state creates the 'conditions under which values can function as commodities' (Offe and Ronge, 1976:p.143). These contentions are highly relevant to state intervention in industrial relations in that state action to control strikes by one means or another is intervention to prevent labour from renouncing its commodity status and the form and details that may mark such administrative re-commodification are thus crucial for any concrete analysis. In particular, it may be hinted at here that this, as well as the development of productive state functions and a directive role for the state, is intimately bound up with the institution of corporatism as a mode of political representation.

The types of strategies distinguished above are clearly connected with the functional effects of state intervention in terms of its relation to the economy, that is, the effects of the functions performed by the state on the economy (Winkler, J.T., 1976b). Firstly, state functions in this sense can be facilitative, that is allow economic processes to take place but strictly delimit the role of the state in these processes. Secondly, state functions can be supportive by protecting and buttressing the economy. Thirdly, state functions can be directive, subjecting the economy to state direction by its intervention into decision-making processes affecting the reproduction of economic structures.

Quite clearly, the conceptual distinctions outlined above are connected in that they collectively define the general forms of capitalist state within the British social formation that have been identified. It may therefore be suggested that allocative means, inactive strategies, and facilitative functions are characteristic of the *laissez-faire* state.[11] Conversely, productive means, administrative re-commodification, and directive functions are characteristic of the interventionist state, with protective strategies and supportive functions being transitional between the two forms of state intervention.[12] These constitute what may be termed the modes of intervention of the capitalist state, i.e. what is entailed in the theorisation of *laissez-faire* and interventionism. They also represent a process of transition although this need not necessarily imply the complete supersession of one mode by another, but if it is so conceived as a process of transition it is one structured by class and political struggles. It is a suggestion of this paper that the role of the capitalist state in the contemporary British social formation is marked by such struggles grouped around attempts to establish and secure or reverse the institution of the interventionist role of the state. It therefore becomes necessary to identify as we shall begin to do below the forces and interests involved in these struggles in order to move towards a clearer understanding of the role of the capitalist state, taking the area of industrial relations to illustrate the nature of such struggles and this role. But to do this it is also necessary to consider modes of political representation and forms of state control of industrial relations.

State Intervention, Political Representation and the Control of Industrial Relations

Almost inevitably, to raise the issue of the nature of state intervention in Britain in the latter half of the twentieth century is to raise the question of whether this will be marked by the inception of corporatism. And a survey of this issue provides the opportunity for clarifying the relationship between state intervention, political representation and the control of industrial relations in the British social formation arising from the role of state intervention in capital accumulation and class struggles.

A consideration of the dimensions entailed in the structure of corporatism will allow for its distinction from other modes of political representation and control of industrial relations. But much of the discussion of corporatism is seriously deficient in failing to locate analysis within the context of a theorisation of the capitalist state or of the changing nature of its role.[13] The consequence of this is to leave unexplained one of the central institutional forces involved in the inception of corporatism; the capacity of the capitalist state to initiate or accommodate corporatism is assumed and thus unexplicated. Therefore, the conception of corporatism developed here needs to be seen in the light of the formulations established above, especially since we wish to argue that corporatism is a particular mode of political representation and a particular form of state control of industrial relations. Attempts to institute corporatism are connected with the development of the interventionist capitalist state.[14] And, as such, it is not merely a question of the class interests to which corporatism corresponds but rather a question of the state's role *vis-à-vis* capital accumulation, and of corporatism as an effective means of securing this role in maintaining accumulation. It is the state's organisation of the conditions for capital accumulation as it is affected by class and political struggles which constitutes the context for the elaboration of modes of intervention, political representation and control of industrial relations, including corporatism. Corporatism is thus generated by and represents a response to the development of capitalism, of the capitalist economy and capitalist state, i.e. of advanced monopoly capitalism and the interventionist state (Panitch, 1977; Crouch, 1977; Schmitter, 1974; Brenner, 1969; Beer 1965; Winkler, J.T., 1976a). The role of the capitalist state entails, on the one hand, the restructuring of capital, the production of inputs for accumulation, the maintenance of commodity forms, and the control of class struggle, and, on the other hand, the construction of organisational means of intervention and modes of political representation to facilitate such intervention. Corporatism is therefore a potential institutional arrangement organised by the state and class and political interests to provide the political conditions for economic intervention. The state not only produces inputs for capital accumulation but also the organisational means and modes of political representation to sanction, legitimate and hence make this possible, corporatism being a potential form of political representation corresponding to the means and purposes of intervention of the 'interventionist' state. It is in this sense that we may agree with Panitch (1977:p.66) that corporatism is a mode of political representation 'within advanced capitalism which integrates organised socio-economic producer groups through a system of representation and co-operative mutual interaction at the leadership level, and mobilisation and social control at the mass level'.[15] A number of points need to be established as a consequence of the use of this definition and its relevance to state control of industrial relations.

In the first place, corporatism as a mode of political representation is clearly inimical to parliamentarianism, requiring the large-scale hierarchical organisation and political incorporation of socio-economic groups authoritatively sanctioned by the state rather than the more fragmented diversity of interest groups and political parties autonomous from state control (Schmitter, 1974:p.96). To note this is to address a problem not always confronted in the literature; namely, if corporatism is emerging,what forms of political representation and state control of industrial relations will it need to replace? We have already noted a contrast between corporatism and parliamentary liberalism in terms of political representation consistent with the development of the transition between *laissez-faire* and interventionist forms of the capitalist state. Hence, much of the reality of twentieth-century (especially middle and late) politics in Britain can be viewed as a process of conflicts surrounding the transition between *laissez-faire* and liberalism on the one hand, and interventionism and corporatism on the other, even though such a process is uneven and reversible and corporatism itself is potentially unstable (Schmitter, 1974:pp.111-12; Panitch, 1976 and 1977; Crouch, 1977).

However, as it stands this is too simplified a conception, for while pluralism denotes group autonomy from the state it is clearly possible for this to co-exist with the emergence of interventionist forms of state action. The growth of monopoly capitalism and the interventionist state necessarily involve the re-structuring of modes of intervention and political representation. But it is arguable that the limitations thereby imposed do not preclude the adoption of one or another of a confined range of alternatives nor indeed of totally contradictory political structures. Structural determination is not the same as structural determinism. It is possible to argue that parliamentary pluralism is structurally symmetrical with *laissez-faire*, allocative state functions, and *political* struggles between classes and political interests as the 'liberal' moments of capital accumulation and the state (Holloway and Picciotto, 1977:pp.88-91). Parliamentary democracy, for example, allows for the political institutionalisation of class struggles and the integration of working class and bourgeois political organisations in parliamentary conflict. However, the overall complex of factors involved in the transition from competitive to monopoly capitalism (Mandel, 1975; Mattick, 1971; Harris, 1972) includes ideological changes such as the rise of collectivism and its strained co-existence with individualism (Harris, 1972:p.36; Crouch, 1977) and processes of political restructuration, away from parliamentary pluralism and towards corporatism. For Schmitter (1974:pp.107-8), this 'can be traced primarily to the imperative necessity for a stable, bourgeois-dominant regime, due to processes of concentration of ownership, competition between national economies, expansion of the role of public policy and rationalisation of decision-making within the state to associate or incorporate subordinate classes and status groups more closely within the political process'. In view of the establishment of hierarchically structured and controlled organisations representing 'particular capitals' and 'particular labours', as well as those seeking to represent capital or labour in general, and the political institutionalisation of working-class interests and organisations, the state endeavours, for the purposes of intervention, to develop state apparatuses divorced and insulated from popular democratic and working-class struggles. Consequently, there develop trends towards the centralisation of power within the state in the hands of the executive (Mandel, 1975:p.482; O'Connor, 1973; Hirsch, J., 1973) and the corporatisation of political representation in order to incorporate the representative organisations of capital and labour and thus to by-pass class struggles. The political representation of the leadership levels in such organisations and state sanctioning of their formation and/or control structures[16] thus becomes the mode of political representation structurally connected with the role of the interventionist state.

Now, because corporatism is necessary it does not mean that it will be established, since its institution is a matter of struggle and of the role played by the state. However, the above argument does not yet provide a sufficiently precise distinction between modes of political representation and forms of state control of industrial relations constituted as potential alternatives in the British social formation. Bound up with corporatism as a mode of political representation are the following characteristics: the institutional incorporation of the leaderships of capital and labour organisations within state apparatuses and state administration; the state's sanctioning of the control structures of such organisations, in particular organisations of labour, to buttress their structural effectiveness as means of social control over their membership; and the restructuring or construction of state apparatuses insulated from parliamentarianism and popular-democratic struggles[17] formed as 'para-state agencies' (Winkler, J.T., 1977; Schmitter, 1974; Hirsch, J., 1973).

Such state apparatuses are particularly significant in the process of instituting corporatism, functioning both as a representation of, and the means to, the establishment of corporatism, and operating in the structural context between political representation on the one hand, including the contradiction between tripartism and parliamentarianism, and, on the other, the means of state interventionism. Thus, as will be argued below, a state institution, such as ACAS (the Advisory, Conciliation and Arbitration Service) and also the CIR (Commission on Industrial Relations) from which it developed, can be seen in this light, as state apparatuses constructed to effect the control of industrial relations so as to maintain capital accumulation. But no matter how central this is to corporatism, still a relatively separate question is that of the principles which inform such state control. We will therefore consider these before returning below, to the construction and operations of this form of state apparatus.

These principles are given by the other features, identified with corporatism above, namely leadership integration and state sanctioning of the control structures of capital and labour organisations. Quite apart from opposition to state apparatuses insulated from parliament, liberalism would thus also imply opposition to state incorporation and state regulation as intervention in the internal affairs of what are properly seen as private organisations. Thus, for example, while countenancing the authoritative allocation of legal resources legitimately belonging to the state it would reject the direct corporatisation of private organisations including the intervention of the state in the internal control structures of such organisations since this would represent, ideologically, a denial of organisational autonomy.

These distinctions between liberalism and corporatism as modes of political representation can be developed with respect to forms of state control of industrial relations as well as to other modes of political representation. Liberalism and corporatism connote a differentiation between autonomy and regulation which are structurally related to *laissez-faire* and interventionist forms of the role of the capitalist state. If we can combine these features this will provide us with a social map of the alternative ways of effecting state control of industrial relations. Such a map of alternative forms of state control of industrial relations, formulated in the context of definite means of state intervention and definite modes of political representation as discussed above, will allow us to locate the class interests and political forces associated with and committed to these varying forms and, thereby, the nature of the struggles surrounding attempts to institute corporatism. Leaving to separate analysis para-state apparatuses, the features of concern here centre on, firstly, the external conditions of control of industrial relations provided by the role of the state — the extent to which this is imbued with the complex of structural factors defining *laissez-faire* or interventionism and involves the incorporation of organisational leaderships into state apparatuses. And, secondly, the internal conditions of control of industrial relations, control by means of the role of trade unions or labour collectivities which connects with different modes of political representation in terms of the distinction between autonomy and heteronomy (Weber, 1964:p.148). This can concern, collectively or separately, (1) the extent to which the state sanctions the internal control structure of trade unions to ensure leadership control of the rank and file; (2) the extent to which state support is provided for collective bargaining structures and union incorporation into such structures in industrial enterprises; (3) internally generated, employer sponsored organisations of labour internally contained within particular enterprises and therefore separated from other types of labour organisation; (4) the legally coercive denial of the right of union organisation by the state or the informal denial of such a right by a particular capital unit. While this may seem to be a somewhat extensive list, it nonetheless hinges upon the clear-cut distinction between the regulation of trade unions by one means or another or their being allowed to perform, and their taking upon themselves, an autonomous role. The structural contents which may and do inform this distinction will be described below, but what is important for our present purpose is that synthesising the elements that have emerged in our discussion so far provides us with the means of both differentiating the types of role the state can play in industrial relations and assessing the relationship between these types and the articulation of class interests and political objectives regarding the form to be taken by state intervention in industrial relations. This is the rationale of Figure 6.2 and although these general conceptions of the role of the capitalist state in industrial relations should by now be clear we can briefly define the respective concepts identified and indicate some illustrative examples.

Figure 6.2: The Capitalist State and Industrial Relations: Competing Structures and Strategies

| | | Internal Control of Industrial Relations: The Role of Labour Collectivities | |
		Autonomous	Heteronomous
External control of industrial relations: the role of the state	Laissez-faire	Liberalism	Paternalism
	Interventionism	Pluralism	Corporatism

1. Liberalism

This represents the structural connection of *laissez-faire* as the means of intervention and pluralism as the mode of political representation as the external and internal conditions for the control of industrial relations. It thus represents the minimisation of direct state intervention in industrial relations except in exceptional circumstances and by means of the allocation of already existing authoritative powers, such as the courts or military, relying thus, in large part, on the initiatives of capital to invoke the powers of the state against labour, and not involving any means of continuously or systematically regulating the role of trade unions. This, it can be argued, was characteristic of Victorian capitalism in Britain from 1871 onwards after the 1871 Trade Union Act legally recognised the autonomy of unions.[18]

2. *Paternalism*

This form of state control represents the structural connection of *laissez-faire* as far as external conditions of control are concerned together with the internal regulation of the role of unions deriving from, to varying degrees, corporate forms of political representation which exclude rather than incorporate working class interests and struggles. Examples of this would be the Combination Acts of 1799 and 1800, and the Taff Vale and Osbourne judgements, two highly significant judicial decisions taken in the early twentieth century in Britain which for a time confounded the liberalistic control of industrial relations by allowing for the regulation of unions by employers without direct, sustained and systematised state intervention of the kind identifiable with interventionism.

3. *Pluralism*

This represents the structural connection of, externally, state interventionism together with the internally autonomous role of trade unions deriving from, to varying degrees, pluralistic forms of political representation which institutionalise rather than exclude working class interests and struggles. As such, this form entails, for example, the development of means of intervention in industrial relations, like conciliation and arbitration services, such as were provided by the 1896 and 1919 Acts and the now defunct Ministry of Labour, which remain voluntary and which function to maintain the autonomy of trade unions from regulation by various means by the state or by capital units. This it can be argued characterises Conservative Reformism as well as Social Democracy and thus the relation of the state to British industrial relations, more or less, between the mid-1920s up to at least the mid-1960s.

4. *Corporatism*

This represents the external mode of control of industrial relations associated with state interventionism together with the regulation of the role of unions as the internal mode of controlling industrial relations, consistent with corporatist forms of political representation. This form of state control of industrial relations, it is suggested, has come increasingly to inform policies in Britain from the mid-1960s onwards aimed at the restructuring of industrial relations. It would entail if established in its pure form, which it can be argued has not yet been the case, at least not in any stable manner, the direct sanctioning and support of the internal control structure of trade unions and/or their incorporation by recognition procedures into collective bargaining structures together with external control effected by state apparatuses charged with the initiative and responsibility for the control of industrial relations.

These distinct conceptual categories are not intended to refer to empirically clear-cut distinctions but rather to act as the conceptual means of grasping and thereby empirically illustrating forms of capitalist state control of industrial relations, the class and political interests associated with and supporting the objectives embodied in each of these forms and thus conflicts over the role of the capitalist state in industrial relations. But before proceeding concretely to identify the class and political interests associated with these respective forms, the struggles grouped around the institution of corporatism, it is necessary to consider the problems that capital accumulation and the capitalist state in the British social formation were facing which provided the context for the articulation of conflicts over the form to be taken by state intervention in industrial relations and which raised corporatism as a possible form for such intervention.

Capital Accumulation, Class Struggle and State Intervention

The problems that confronted capital accumulation in the British social formation in the period under consideration, roughly from the late 1950s onwards, are sufficiently familiar as not to require an extensive recapitulation here. In essence, they concerned a decline in accumulation, registered both in terms of declining profitability and a lack of investment, particularly in manufacturing industy or productive capital, and a general failure to increase markedly the productivity and competitiveness of British industry in the face of international competition. Ultimately connected with this has been the changing balance of power in the class struggle with the increasing assertion of working-class pressure and strike militancy by certain groups of workers, at the level of production in the shape of opposition to schemes to restructure capital, and at the level of distribution in conflicts over wages.

For the purposes of this paper it is the latter point which is of most significance but class struggles, needless to say, feed in directly to capital accumulation problems, given that it has been argued that capital accumulation is marked by class conflict and that identified above is one example of its concrete expression. Despite the controversy that has been stirred up over the extent of the decline of profitability[19] and investment,[20] it is still possible to argue on the basis of the existing literature that these trends have become problematic for the process of capital accumulation necessitating capital re-structuring involving the role of the state. And it is important to note that to a significant extent such problems have been exacerbated by the economic policies of governments.[21] However, especially via the medium of rising inflation,[22] these specific issues are bound up with our more central concern, the structural dimensions of accentuated class conflict in both production and distribution which gave rise to attempts by the state to reform industrial relations.

In summary form, it can be argued that the increasing specialisation and interdependence of and between production, realisation, exchange and distribution units that has come to characterise the structure of modern capitalism, together with the state's maintenance of 'full employment' as a result of the postwar 'welfare consensus' or 'compromise' constructed by the state with organised labour,[23] have generated for certain groups of workers, strategically situated within this structure, the capacity or conditions for the assertion of working-class power at the point of production, within the structure of production relations[24] and over the distribution of income between wages and profits. This 'socialisation of the forces of production' and maintenance of relatively low levels of unemployment increasing competition between capital units for labour as a consequence of tighter labour markets and thereby encouraging wage competition between these units, has provided the context for a change in the balance of power between classes in the area of industrial relations, namely the increase in 'shop floor power' for the role of shop steward and its work group constituency.[25] This has been manifest in the escalation of strikes, their frequency and their generally unofficial and unconstitutional nature rather than in terms of duration or numbers involved, although the large-scale official strike began to re-emerge around 1970;[26] and in increasing wage and earning rates, in particular the much noted phenomenon of wage drift which, together with the lack of marked increases in labour productivity, has served to increase labour costs[27] which are, as noted above, also influenced by wage competition between employers.

As a consequence, the assertion of militancy and its expression in the indices noted as above has, due to the systemic relationship between capital accumulation and the capitalist state, and its disruptive effect on the former, led to state intervention in the form of incomes policies and the reform of industrial relations. The conditions for the increase in shop floor power also entailed the devolution of bargaining power to the shop floor and to the shop steward thereby subverting the previously established structure of collective bargaining, negotiations at national and industry level between employers and/or employers' organisations and trade unions. Instead, it became more common for collective bargaining to be conducted by means of discrete, autonomous, localised and fragmented bargaining between management and shop stewards at factory, plant or company level which, at the same time, tended also to be associated with the erosion of what previously constituted managerial prerogatives, most especially the determination of work practices and arrangements (Hyman, 1973:p.110).

This complex of factors, unified by the concept of class struggle, constituted the problems confronting capital accumulation which thereby structured state intervention to organise the control of such problems, even though such intervention would as much overdetermine as resolve such contradictions. In terms of the concrete example being discussed, it can be suggested that the particular conditions generating state intervention resided in the structure of competition between capital units. As the evidence cited in the next section illustrates, the wage competition between capitals for labour and the acceptance by particular capitals of shop floor worker power meant that capital in Britain was not itself capable of organising, nor would particular capitals necessarily agree to, policies to deal with such problems as discussed above which were hindering the process of capital accumulation as a whole. This necessitated state intervention and provided the structural conditions for the autonomous operation of the role of the capitalist state in formulating incomes policies, the reform of industrial relations and the restructuring of state apparatuses (Altvater, 1975). The instability of capital accumulation, the competitive structure of capital (Rosdolsky, 1974) and the power of labour formed the conditions for the intervention of the state in industrial relations, engendered by the macro-structural or systemic relationship between the state and capital accumulation. But while state intervention as such has been necessarily generated, its nature has not been predetermined but has rather been the outcome of class and political interests and conflicts. Thus, the contention that state intervention derives in one respect from the essentially competitive structure of the relations between particular capitals, and that its actual form and content are organised by state apparatuses in the context of class and political interests and struggles requires that we now consider this factor.

State Intervention, Class Conflict and the Reform of Industrial Relations

In analysing the determination of state intervention in industrial relations, the nature of such intervention and the interests and struggles that inhere in such a process, it is essential to take account of the logic of interests or objectives of capital and labour and their representative organisations — as well as groups differentiated within such classes — as well as political organisations and state apparatuses. To assess this use will be made of the typology developed regarding the role of the capitalist state in industrial relations in order to conceptualise, clarify, and provide a logic for some of the available empirical evidence on class and political interests in, and conflicts over, the forms of state control of industrial relations. This will illustrate the role of the state *vis-à-vis* class conflicts and will identify the structure of the conflicts surrounding the institution of the interventionist state and corporatist political representation in Britain.

Capital and the Reform of Industrial Relations

This task requires a consideration of the interests of capital, labour, their respective organisations, political organisations and the state in the reform of industrial relations. If we take capital first, the structure and differentiation characterising its interests can be set out as follows, so identifying the positions occupied by different sections of capital in terms of the dimensions of state control of industrial relations.

Figure 6.3, while not intended as a static picture but rather as a means of indicating the reality of the adoption of changing positions in response to capital accumulation problems, more or less accurately summarises the argument of this section. But in order to establish such claims and the evidence being used we shall briefly consider, in turn, the contentions advanced in respect of the interests of the 'fractions' of capital outlined above.[28]

1. *International Industrial Monopoly Capital*[29] With the notable exception of the motor industry, this form of industrial or productive

Figure 6.3: Capital, the Capitalist State and Industrial Relations: Competing Structures and Strategies in Britain

		Internal Control of Industrial Relations: The Role of Labour Collectivities	
		Autonomous	Heteronomous
External control of industrial relations: the role of the state	Laissez-faire	**Liberalism** International monopoly capital; majority of multinationals;	**Paternalism** Petit-bourgeois capital; money capital
	Interventionism	**Pluralism**	**Corporatism** National monopoly capital; international monopoly capital (minority of multinationals, especially in the motor industry)

capital tended to be the leading capital in the British social formation in terms of innovations in industrial relations such as productivity bargaining, company fixed term agreements, and financial incentives to observe procedure agreements, as well as in terms of wage rates. It tended to favour company-level bargaining autonomous from membership of the relevant employer organisation and thus from industry-wide collective bargaining and agreements. While being no more or no less affected by increasing industrial conflict and to a lesser extent but nonetheless still prone to the profitability crisis this group of employers, their industries being capital intensive, tended not to regulate or incorporate trade unions save by means of financial incentives. Either one or a number or all of these features were heavily criticised and opposed by other capitals, especially in view of the fact that foreign capital contributed to the acceleration of wage rates and the decentralisation of collective bargaining, structural processes leading to but, needless to say, not directly determining the institution of incomes policies and the re-structuring by the state of industrial relations. There are also notable examples of foreign capitals opposing union recognition (Gennard, 1972; Kodak and ACTT evidence to Donovan). However, overall the bias of the logic of interests was not in favour of state supported regulation but rather towards liberalism. Its objectives entailed employer and managerial autonomy and initiative; a preparedness to countenance strike action, plus and more especially financial rewards to blunt such action and buy industrial peace given that the highly capital intensive nature of the industries in which this capital was concentrated were generally more capable of generating high wages than facing disruption by frequent strikes; internally generated re-structurings of capital and reforms of industrial relations structure coupled with little direct support for state intervention, especially of a legally coercive kind;[30] and the retrenchment of autonomous company or plant-level bargaining, that is, collective bargaining resting upon the autonomy of employers and the representative organisations of labour.

As already indicated, the major exception to the general orientation of this fraction of capital was to be found amongst British and American companies in the motor industry[31] which was more acutely confronted with industrial conflict. This group came much closer to corporatism in expressing their interests in the shape of demands for state controls on unofficial and unconstitutional strikes mainly by direct fines on strikers under a system of industry-wide legally enforceable procedure agreements. While these objectives will be discussed more fully below, it may be noted here that they entail direct state intervention in industrial relations together with state regulation of trade unions by means of state support for union control of rank and file memberships.

2. *Money-Capital* This section is concerned with the logic of interests associated with those financial institutions within the British social formation, sometimes included together under the rubric 'The City', involved in banking, insurance, credit houses, etc., and generally concerned with capital as money.[32] Also, the very global role of the City in international finance makes this capital in Britain essentially international such that the national/international distinction loses some of the significance it has for industrial or productive capital.[33] But here what must be emphasised is the commitment in the identifiable objectives of this fraction of capital to a liberalised as opposed to directly interventionist role for the state in the economy and industrial relations[34] and to the paternalistic regulation within financial enterprises of organisations representing employees, the labour power of this capital.

It has been noted that government economic policy in Britain, because of its commitment to the maintenance of the international role of sterling and thus due to generally deflationary monetary and fiscal policies has tended to favour the City's interests at the expense of building up Britain's productive, industrial base: that is, reproduction of capital accumulation in Britain has entailed the reproduction of money rather than productive capital (Thompson, G., 1977; Longstreth, this volume; Brittan, 1971). As a consequence, sections of industrial capital have petitioned for the institution of more stable, long-term corporatist planning mechanisms aimed at reinvigorating productive capital's conditions of existence (Brittan, 1971; Blank, 1973). Be that as it may, what this argument does imply is that the interests of money capital are more clearly tied to the more 'liberal', allocative economic functions of the state than are those of industrial capital; although both share the general interest of capital in the maintenance of capital accumulation, differences and conflicts arise over the content of such a process. It might be equally if not more correct to argue that the hegemonic position of money capital in Britain and the hegemony of this capital amongst money capitals internationally tends to make it somewhat indifferent to, rather than positively interested in, *laissez-faire* state intervention; but it would more certainly be opposed, nonetheless, to the economic controls involved in the economic nationalism of corporatism such as autarchic constraints on international transactions. As such, this sort of opposition to corporatist economic policy must extend to the corporatisation of industrial relations in view of the centrality of incomes policies[35] for economic policy and thereby the difficulty in structurally differentiating economic policy from industrial relations (Longstreth, this volume; Corina, 1975). This is a crucial implication of the conceptual distinction between *laissez-faire* and interventionist forms of the role of the state.

Furthermore, the relative opposition to corporatism of money capital, including the City, in the British social formation rests upon its profitability and the international basis of its operations, which make it relatively independent of the fortunes of the domestic economy, therefore rendering it less demanding of the interventionist role of the state. It can, however, be argued that at least incomes policies designed to combat the effects of inflation on currency stability on which the business of the City depends (more so in fact than on the stability of sterling *per se*) may be consistent with the logic of interests of money capital (Panitch, 1976:p.2-3). But the structural connections between incomes policies, the corporatist mode of political representation and interventionist direction by the state of economic activity mitigate this consistency and exemplify the contradictions marking such interests. This contradiction, it may be noted at this point, can be found to characterise most of the interests of the different fractions of capital discussed, in that, in more general terms, opposition to state interventionism is aligned with an implied recognition of the need for such intervention, and this is so even if the latter takes an explicit form as is the case with sections of national monopoly capital. This constitutes a phenomenal expression of the system contradiction marking the role of the capitalist state.

As far as its internal industrial relations are concerned, money capital has developed employer-sponsored and internally confined staff organisations to represent labour. This has tended to ensure the internal containment of industrial conflict and the effective, paternalistic regulation by exclusion of trade unions, without reliance upon direct state intervention.[36] However, this form of control came to be challenged by demands among employees of the financial institutions for autonomous trade union organisation and recognition, disruptive of money capital's 'private corporatism', demands which tended to attract opposition both from staff associations and employers. Thus, in the light of the potential basis of its opposition to state interventionism and corporatism, and its commitment to the internal regulation of unionism, money capital's basic orientation to state control of industrial relations can be designated paternalism.

3. Petit-Bourgeois Capital[37] The conceptual designation of paternalism can be applied with even more conviction, given its less ambiguous ideological opposition to state intervention, to small-scale, non-monopoly or petit-bourgeois capital. More clearly than money capital this fraction is *laissez-faire* in its orientation towards the means of intervention employed by the state and paternalist in respect of the representation of trade unions. Its logic of interests has tended to favour the complex of factors associated with *laissez-faire*; and when provided with such minimal external conditions by the state for the control of industrial relations, as was the case with the Heath government's Industrial Relations Act of 1971 (although this also contained corporatist as well as liberalist elements), it was mainly small-scale employers who took up the option of using the sanctions provided by this legislation (Thomson and Engleman, 1975:p.149). However, it is interesting to note that in this respect as well as in terms of the internal regulation of trade unions, the national organisations representing this capital did tend to move much further towards the corporatist form of state control of industrial relations than its constituency would have allowed (evidence to Donovan of Society of Independent Manufacturers and National Association of British Manufacturers). But as a whole this interest implied the minimisation of direct state intervention in industrial relations, save for the use of coercive powers under the rule of law.

This is directly bound up with the petit-bourgeois, paternalistic, internal regulation of unions which has consisted of an outright opposition to collective labour organisations as such and/or the notion that due to the small-scale nature of the business, the close and informal industrial relations thereby made possible preclude the need for trade unions. As such, for example, apart from some multinational companies, the greatest opposition to the recognition of trade unions, both manual and non-manual, is typically to be found in Britain among small-scale, paternalistic employers (Gennard, 1972:p.25). It is also interesting to note that while this capital shares large-scale capital's criticisims of the devolution of the bargaining power of labour to the shop floor, it nonetheless was hostile towards what it saw as large-scale capital's tendency and greater capacity to comply with worker demands for higher pay, thus attracting labour away from small-scale industry. This is a particularly useful exemplification of the way in which, at the level of distribution and exchange, wage competition over labour supply compounds and the structure division between fractions of capital, a division which forms one of the conditions for the generation of state intervention. But to conclude this section, on the whole petit-bourgeois capital was unambiguously paternalistic both regarding the internal control of industrial relations as well as the *laissez-faire* role of the state, exhibiting little need to resort to the ideology of voluntarism.

4. *National Industrial Monopoly Capital*[38] Voluntarism was, by contrast, clearly marked in the orientation of this fraction of capital, which was characterised generally by an ideological appeal to liberalism while factually being drawn towards corporatism.[39] More than those of other fractions of capital, its interests entailed the corporatisation of trade unions coupled with state intervention to buttress and externally sanction such control.

To take this capital's commitment to state interventionism first, it involved an adherence to the autonomous regulation of collective bargaining purely by the parties concerned, namely, employers and unions, without direct state assistance apart from certain minimal conciliation and arbitration services. But in view of the fact that this system as it has been embodied in national or industry level bargaining between employers' associations and unions was breaking down, this capital's objectives could no longer be realised by means of such a system. Factually congenial if not ideologically congenial was a more direct and coercive role for the state in providing the external conditions and state apparatuses for effecting control over industrial conflict. This was conceived of as necessary in order to counter the effects of declining profitability, low productivity, inflationary wage settlements and increasing industrial conflict on capital accumulation. Hence, while expressing commitment to voluntarism, the claim was also advanced that the existing system of industrial relations and collective bargaining was ineffective as a means of control and required direct external state supported and state initiated conditions of control. This was expressed, for example, by demands for the establishment of a Registrar with powers to oversee the operations of unions together with state-initiated prosecution of unofficial strikers — the EEF moving further in this direction than the CBI. It is important to note the emphasis on state rather than employer initiative, because this has formed a central point of contention between sections of capital, on the one hand, and state apparatuses and political organisations, on the other, which have otherwise been implicated in the institution of corporatism (Thomson and Engleman, 1975:pp.31,32; 166-8). Thus conflicts over the appropriate means and the institutional responsibility for establishing corporatism are as significant as those over the validity of corporatism *per se.*

Clearly associated with this theme has been the objective of securing the corporatist regulation of trade unions. The hierarchy of control internal to official unionism has been viewed as the appropriate organisational mechanism for constraining rank and file industrial militancy. Trade unions become the agencies of social control required by corporatism. This entailed support for the state's sanctioning of the control structure of official unionism by, for example, determining the nature of union rules and constitutions, and by, in effect, making unions organisations legally constituted by the state. This, it has been thought, will control class conflict by allowing for the internal regulation of union memberships by union leaderships by means of the state's codification of the authority hierarchy of the official control structure of unions. Hence it can be argued that the logic of interests of this fraction of capital would appear to have come closest to favouring the corporatist form of state control over industrial relations, although it must be stressed here that a crucial role has been played by certain legal and political elites in cohering, systematising and actually constituting such a fraction and its interests as a political force at the level of political conflicts within the state: that is to say, as will be suggested below, such a class interest needed autonomous political organisation before it came to be properly framed as a political interest; and, as such, involves the restructuring of political as well as economic relations, as attempts to institute corporatism illustrate.

Capital, British Capitalism and State Intervention

This suggestion has also a more general relevance for the discussion of the division of interests between different fractions of capital. It is hopefully clear from the above that while there may exist a conception, however abstract and diffuse, of what the general interests of capital in relation to the process of capital accumulation may consist of among these different sections of capital, given such divisions, very little emerges as a directive, conditional or otherwise, for state action that could be considered tantamount to the general interest of capital. What does emerge is an expression of distinct interests which the state must take account of but which do not determine in any instrumental fashion the direction of state intervention. The bases of the differentiation of capital resides in factors (some of which have been noted, like varying the role of the state), which provide the context for but correspondingly to restructure production and distribution relations, and conceptions of the role of the state, provides the context for but correspondingly cannot directly generate the inception of state intervention structured more fundamentally by its relationship with capital accumulation. While particular capitals, in the case in which we are considering them, may articulate the problems of capital accumulation that require state mediation, they cannot directly resolve them by changing the overall conditions of existence of accumulation, although localised and particularised responses can be realised. This situation provides for a specific role for the state, the historically variable economic and political re-structuring of capitalism, and it is in the determination of the nature of this that the interests of particular sections of capital as part of wider conflicts over the role of the state can have their effects and influence, especially if constituted as coherent political forces.

This last point is of special significance, for the general point we are making here is that the relationship between the state and economy under capitalism is, in the first instance, a system relationship which leads to the elaboration of the role of the state in the economy

(Offe, 1972a). But, in the light of this, it is also being asserted that the determination of the nature of the form and content of state intervention derives from the outcome of the structure of class, political and state interests and conflicts — conflicts within and between classes, political organisations and state apparatuses — in the context of the system relation between state and economy organised around capital accumulation. And the political constitution of interests acquires significance in that and insofar as it occurs within the confines of the state and the polity which is where the mediatory institutional links such as the construction of state apparatuses between the economy and state intervention are organised: for it is the relation of the state to capital accumulation and to the control and organisation of class and political conflicts which engenders the autonomy of the state.

Labour, State Intervention and the Reform of Industrial Relations[40]

The central structural features of labour in contemporary British capitalism — the escalation of shop floor power and industrial conflict attendant upon the division between official leaderships and rank and files in certain unions and industries and the breakdown of centralised collective bargaining — have already been discussed. But the orientation of the interests of particular sections of labour towards the role of the state in industrial relations do not conform in any simple sense to this division within organised labour. Nor is it possible to argue that the labour movement has generally been opposed on principle to the introduction of law into industrial relations. Corporatism and state interventionism in effect imply, by the incorporation and sanctioning of the authority of official union leaderships, an accentuation of the division between leaders and led. It can be suggested that one of the most important (but not the only) sources of opposition to corporatism is the localised militancy of powerful rank and file work groups at the point of production. And in fact one of the most notable divisions within labour hinges upon differing conceptions of the role of the state in industrial relations as such, which cannot be traced back so directly, as is the case with capital, to underlying structural characteristics — that is, apart from the division between official leaderships and rank and files; even this is not unambiguously expressed, especially given the increased tendency for some leaderships to support and follow rather than control their mass memberships. This is illustrated in Figure 6.4.

It is thus possible to identify four distinct logics of interests within the ranks of labour and these will now be considered in turn.

Figure 6.4: Labour, The Capitalist State and Industrial Relations:
Competing Structures and Strategies in Britain

		Internal Control of Industrial Relations[41] The Role of Labour Collectivities	
		Autonomous	**Heteronomous**
		Liberalism	**Paternalism**
External control of industrial relations: the role of the state	Laissez-faire	Shop stewards movement and militant rank and file work groups	Staff associations
		Pluralism	**Corporatism**
	Interventionism	Official union leaderships *(TUC)	

*The brackets indicate the ambiguous position occupied between two alternative paradigms.

1. *Liberalism*[42] Informed by a commitment to voluntarism or socialism, this orientation has entailed opposition to the introduction by the state of legal machinery into industrial relations and hierarchically organised structures for the management of industrial relations. It therefore rejects controls on the autonomy of unions and a role for the state in industrial relations. A good example of this is the ideology of free collective bargaining and labour opposition to the corporatist elements of the Heath government's Industrial Relations Act.

2. *Paternalism*[43] Obviously limited in the extent of its appeal, this orientation involved either the rejection of a role for the state in industrial relations coupled with employee acceptance of internal employer generated and guaranteed modes of labour representation or demands for minimal state support for union recognition as a way of securing harmonious industrial relations. Rare though this objective is, the orientation of staff associations in financial institutions provides an illustrative exemplification of its expression.

3. *Pluralism*[44] This entailed a positive acceptance of the need for and the extension of the direct but 'external' buttressing by the state of

trade union organisation and activities to enable them more adequately to fulfil their functions as autonomous representatives of workers' interests such as the establishment of state mechanisms for securing, enforcing and scrutinising the legal enforcement of trade union recognition. It therefore implied the state's certification of unions and their functions phrased often in terms of redressing the balance of advantages accruing to employers in industrial relations and thus conceived of as a constraint on the power of capital. This was coupled with an emphasis on the autonomy of unions, if this was guaranteed by the state, to pursue their members' interests and to control their own affairs and organisation, even, in some cases to the extent of ensuring their independent control of their rank and file memberships. It stands in a somewhat ambiguous relationship to voluntarism, denoting the contradiction in the interests of sections of labour towards the role to be played by the state in industrial relations, and can be regarded as still the most common orientation of unionism in Britain.

4. *Corporatism*[45] What this involved for the orientation of certain, albeit few, unions in Britain in the 1960s was the acceptance of state-provided legal controls for the authoritative containment of their rank and file and an explicit commitment to pursue and accede to such state supported control. This includes the acceptance and pursuance of externally provided sanctions made available by the state, such as those for unofficial strikers. It has been conceived of as being in accord with the extension of the external conditions provided by the state for the sanctioning of trade unions and their organisation and functions, such as legal support for the closed shop and union recognition. As such, while like pluralism supporting the external guarantees the state could provide for unionism, it conceived of this as being consistent not with the securement of union autonomy but with union heteronomy, with the state's sanctioning of the control structures of unions.

The Role of the Capitalist State in the Re-structuring of Industrial Relations

State Apparatuses and Political Organisations

It is now necessary in respect of the reform of industrial relations in the contemporary British social formation to consider developments at the level of the state and politics. In considering the processes leading to the re-structuring of industrial relations as political processes, we must take particular note of the political forces and state apparatuses serving to constitute, organise and systematise particular class interests within the state. Although we shall not be able to discuss all the organisations mentioned as examples below we can still use the already developed schema to identify the nature of the political conflicts over forms of state control of industrial relations, as shown in Figure 6.5.

Figure 6.5:
State Apparatuses, Political Organisations, the Capitalist State and Industrial Relations: Competing Structures and Strategies in Britain

		Internal Control of Industrial Relations: The Role of Labour Collectivities	
		Autonomous	Heteronomous
		Liberalism	**Paternalism**
External control of industrial relations: the role of the state	Laissez-faire	Monetarism	Judiciary & courts; 'Petit-bourgeois' section of Conservative Party
	Interventionism	**Pluralism** Keynesianism; social democracy; conservative reformism	**Corporatism** Politico-legal elites

*(NBPI);
*(CIR———ACAS);
*(Labour and Conservative
Governments from 1964 onwards)

*The brackets indicate the ambiguous position occupied between two alternative paradigms.

Apropos the role of political organisations in the development of the legal framework for corporatism an important function was performed, in the case under consideration, by what have been termed politico-legal elites. In terms of the formulation, for example, of the Industrial Relations Act, a crucial part was played by such elites in organising, clarifying, codifying and giving plausible shape to what otherwise remained somewhat partial and inarticulate class interests, in particular those of national, monopoly capital. While a number of doctrinal, precious juridical emphases separated one elite group from another, they collectively provided a coherent framework for the articulation and politicisation of inchoate class interests. These elites, political and legal in nature though not part of the state itself, constructed legal normative structures for the purpose of implementing a corporatist form of state control of industrial relations, establishing the basis both for the legal intervention of the state and for the legal codification and regulation of unions by the state's authoritative sanctioning of their control structures. And, while having their echoes in the interests of the CBI and EEF, these formulations went far beyond the claims advanced by the latter, representing the political construction of the interests of these class fractions.[46] It is therefore suggested that in this instance class interests, far from directly determining political processes, received much of their formulation and constitution at the level of the political by collectivities like political organisations and state apparatuses.

However, to continue with the example of the Industrial Relations Act, this influence was by no means unambiguously reflected in legislation and state action. Together with the corporatist elements, it is also possible to discern paternalistic components in the Act (Wedderburn, 1972). And this has been more characteristic of the orientation of certain state apparatuses, in particular the judiciary, which although having the same objective of controlling industrial conflict began to evolve different means for achieving this. By a series of decisions in cases involving trade unions, the courts from the early 1960s onwards began to reverse precedents and statutes which had defined trade unions and trade disputes, accepted the autonomy of unions, their right to organise, engage in collective bargaining, strike in furtherance of industrial disputes and picket peacefully, thereby under-mining previous juridical acceptance of such actions and hence of the legal immunities granted to unions (Wedderburn, 1971:pp.324-84; Clegg, 1972:p.475; Griffith, 1977; O'Higgins and Partington, 1969). This escalation in the legal coercion and control of trade unionism has been more comparable to a similar phase of judicial opposition to trade unions in the late nineteenth and early twentieth centuries rather than corporatism, given its tendency to stress the rule of law, the allocation rather than production of legal machinery for controlling industrial relations, opposition to collectivism and state interventionism, and the reliance implicitly placed upon employer initiatives in bringing cases to court. As such, the control exercised by judicial state apparatuses over unions and industrial relations has been more consist-ent with *laissez-faire* than with interventionist forms of state mediation, especially given the contradictions posed for the judiciary by the trend towards the centralisation of power in the executive or government that corporatism and state interventionism have as their consequences for the structure of the state.

What is being pointed to in this example is a conflict, albeit often un-recognised, between legal-political organisations and a legal state apparatus over the role to be played by the state in controlling industrial relations and the manner in which this relates back, without directly expressing but rather politically organising, certain class interests: the aim being to describe by way of this example, the structure of political conflicts *vis-a-vis* the role of the state. It has however, in contrast, been argued that the attitudes and decisions of the courts have formed merely one part of a general employers' offensive against labour (Hyman, 1973). We have already begun to question this kind of over-simplification by way of the argument we have begun to deploy. But both in contention and for illustrative purposes, a number of points need to be stressed. Firstly, the history of the relationship between the state and labour in Britain has been characterised, at various times, by a contradiction within the state itself between judiciary and parliament, the former tending, save for the period 1920 to 1960, towards coercion, the latter, given the political institutionalisation of class conflict, towards the incorporation of organised labour (Wedderburn, 1971; 1972; Milne-Bailey, 1924). The status of parliament as the forum for working-class and popular-democratic struggles makes it structurally more conducive to the incorporation rather than the coercion of labour, being the legitimate arena for the free play of democratised class conflict. The judiciary by contrast is relatively insulated from such legitimated pressure and has greater autonomy to control labour by means of the institutionalisation of the norms of judicial discretion and judicial interpretation of statute and precedent inscribed in the judiciary's role. Hence, corporatism represents not only a way of insulating state decision making processes from parliament but also a way of overcoming a particular conflict between state apparatuses and the indeterminacy that arises from the judiciary's relative autonomy from other state structures for the systematic and long-term planning that corporatism requires. Moves towards the construction of executive sponsored and executive controlled systems of courts for dealing with industrial relations cases outside the ambit of the established courts constitute an attempt to re-structure the state apparatuses so as to by-pass the conflict between parliament and judiciary, to curtail the courts' power, and to surmount the incalculability and unpredictability deriving from the role of the judiciary. This last point rests upon the

somewhat unique quality of the judiciary in that it is less susceptible
than other, though not all, state apparatuses to central direction within
the state as a whole.[47]

Viewed objectively the re-emergence of the coercive orientation of
the judiciary towards organised labour cannot therefore, in any simple
sense, be seen as serving the interests of capital. Rather, the judiciary's
role, as it has already been argued in respect of the politico-legal elites,
has been consistent with and constitutive of petit-bourgeois political
interests and forms an important obstacle to the development of
corporatism. In particular, this has been manifest in two main implications of the control of industrial conflict by means of the existing
courts and the rule of law; the commitment of the judiciary to classical
liberalism and hence its opposition to both collectivism and the extension of state interventionism (Dicey, 1905); and the maintenance of
the initiative for instituting legal action against unions with employers,
that is with private rather than state agencies consistent with liberal
opposition to state interventionism. One crucial consequence of this
has been a trend towards the construction of para-state apparatuses, that
is, apparatuses ideologically represented as being 'independent of
government', and organised increasingly outside the purview of parliament and the courts, for the control of industrial relations. Given
however that this consequence is embedded in the structure of conflicts
we have been discussing, the insulation of such agencies from external
surveillance has by no means yet been continuously or adequately
organised.

Associated and aligned with this has been the construction of
'executive' state apparatuses, apparatuses constructed by the executive
to organise and buttress its means of intervention, and which have
corporatist implications for political representation. It is such
apparatuses which are charged with and act as a token of the institution
of corporatism, as means of mediating the state-economy relationship
and reorganising economic and political relations. It is not intended to
be part of this argument to suggest that such institutions once established are effective and continuous since their operation can and has
been conflictual and unstable. But it is important to note the way in
which they conform to 'interventionist' forms of the role of the state
noted earlier, being increasingly aligned to capital re-structuring and
productive state functions, as well as to corporatist modes of political
representation, incorporating the leaderships of hierarchically
structured organisations representing capital and labour into state
administration and co-operation with the state to facilitate their

control over their memberships. As such, one may cite the following as examples, however prototypical, of such state apparatuses institutionally linking economic and political processes and establishing corporatist modes of political representation and interventionist mechanisms for the role of the state in the economy and industrial relations: the National Economic Development Office, the National Board for Prices and Incomes, the Industrial Reorganisation Corporation, the National Enterprise Board, the Commission on Industrial Relations (CIR) and the Advisory, Conciliation and Arbitration Service (ACAS).[48] In view of our specific concern with industrial relations in this paper, we shall extend our illustration of this process with a consideration of the latter two apparatuses in the context of the actual nature of the re-structuring of industrial relations undertaken in Britain from the mid 1960s onwards.

Re-structuring the State Apparatuses and Industrial Relations

We can conveniently divide this discussion into three analytically if not substantively separate sections: (a) Incomes policies; (b) Reform of the structure of collective bargaining; (c) Restructuring the state apparatuses.

(a) *Incomes Policies* Without going into the details of the successive incomes policies pursued by governments in Britain (Panitch, 1976; Crouch, 1977), it can still be argued that they have certain specific structural effects. Incomes policies have been central to corporatist developments given their implications for the need to secure union co-operation and their consequence of centralising wage bargaining and thus endeavouring to counteract the devolution of wage bargaining power to the shop floor (Panitch, 1977). They provide one means of meeting the problems facing capital accumulation by controlling the content of economic or industrial class conflicts, containing the effects of distribution relations on accumulation, and they are necessitated by the inability of capital to contain such relations as a consequence of wage competition between capital units. Thus incomes policies have operated within a structure which is marked by the disruption posed to its aims both by this competition between capitals and by powerful groups of rank-and-file workers. They have therefore also entailed in connection with this the incorporation of union leaderships, in particular the TUC, into economic policy making and the surveillance of the application of incomes policy criteria. This sanctions as a consequence the control hierarchy of unions though this form of union heteronomy does not unambiguously secure control of rank-and-file militancy. The Labour government's efforts in the late 1960s to secure TUC scrutiny of wage bargaining, the Heath government's experiments with tripartism together with an elaborate incomes policy, and the 'Social Contract', all bear witness to this process, identifiable as the corporatist structuration of politics.

(b) *The Reform of the Structure of Collective Bargaining* Incomes policies, though widely publicised and now being extensively treated in the academic literature, have a limited scope and success; their un-intended consequences in sharpening awareness of and politicising income divisions, sources and justifications have been contradictory to their initial intentions (Blackburn 1972; Watson, 1975; Richter, 1973; Habermas, 1976; Poulantzas, 1975; Offe, 1973). In this sense, attempts by the state to re-structure the form of industrial relations takes on as much if not more significance than incomes policy (although centralis-ing effects of the latter are crucial in this respect) and attests to the importance of the Industrial Relations Act and, though very different, the legislation passed by the post-1974 Labour government to reform the framework within which wage bargaining and the re-structuring of labour takes place.

The extensive and profound nature of this mode of re-structuring industrial relations can be gauged by a consideration of the objectives of the Conservative government's Industrial Relations Act of 1971, which in terms of our typology of forms of state control of industrial relations conforms most closely, though by no means unambiguously so, with what has been termed corporatism. While insisting on the general principles of free and orderly collective bargaining and free association, the Act was based on the following pillars:[49] the statutory right to belong or not to belong to a union; the right of trade union recognition; registration of trade unions and employers' associations; legal enforce-ability of contracts; limitation of the legal immunities previously granted to trade unions; emergency provisions, secret ballots and cooling off periods for strikes of national and economic importance; selective enforcement of procedure agreements; the regulation of bargaining structures; rights against unfair dismissal, and the redefinition of picketing. It also, and importantly, entailed the establishment of a National Industrial Relations Court, a Registrar to supervise union rules and the Commission on Industrial Relations charged with the function of improving industrial relations.

Now this Act was quite clearly aimed at redressing the changing balance of power in class relations and so to reverse the decentralisation of the structure of collective bargaining. It was thus not an exercise in 'union bashing' but an attempt to strengthen and centralise trade union organisation in order to enhance its efficacy as an agency of social control, thereby subverting the local power base of militant rank-and-file sections of the labour movement. The corporatist implications of the Act are apparent in this state codification and sanctioning of union organisation, together with the establishment of externally guaranteed sanctions and means of intervention for the control of strikes (Panitch, 1977:p.85; Nichols and Beynon, 1977:pp.162-7).

But the Act itself was not unambiguously corporatist in content and intent. Wedderburn has pointed out how the Act contained a contradictory admixture consisting of an organisational or collectivist and an individualist or liberalistic ideology (Wedderburn, 1972:pp.281-90). And this contradiction may be seen as corresponding to the distinction we have already drawn between corporatism and paternalism and their expressions within different branches of the state and polity. It represents a deep seated equivocation rooted in the role of the state in this particular conjuncture over the role it had to play in controlling industrial relations, as well as within the Conservative party (Harris, 1972), and between sections of capital located within the British social formation. What it therefore provides us with is an illustrative example of the specificity of the structure of political forces and conflicts over the role of the state, together with the structural connections between the latter and the process of capital accumulation and class interests and struggles.

(c) *Re-structuring State Apparatuses* The reorganisation of the structure of industrial relations also entails the re-organisation of political structures. The construction of state apparatuses appropriate for the corporatist form of state control of industrial relations has obvious links with the above discussion, most particularly in that such restructuring exemplifies the state's management of the relationship between accumulation and class struggles and political conflicts on the one hand, and the formulation and implementation of state intervention on the other. The nature of the re-structuring and construction of state apparatuses likewise has important implications for the relationship between capital and the state. Taking the conflicts over the Industrial Relations Act to illustrate this point, central to the interests of significant sections of capital, in particular the CBI, was the transference of the responsibility for activating the legal machinery and sanctions provided by the Act for controlling indus

provided by the Act for controlling industrial conflict from employers
to the state, especially since it was felt by some employers that if this
was not done their use of the machinery of the Act would do more to
harm rather than harmonise their own industrial relations. This conflict
over the institutional responsibility for the elaboration of corporatism
was resolved, in this case, by the state's rejection of the demands of
capital (CBI evidence to Donovan; Thomson and Engleman, 1975:
pp.31,32, 166-8; Barnett, p.13-19; *The Director,* December 1972),
due, no doubt in part, to the Conservative government's need to
organise and balance such demands with the contrasting objectives of
petit-bourgeois interests which also made their presence felt in the
formation of the Act, as well as its own liberalistic reluctance to become
too deeply implicated in 'interventionism'.

The industrial and political struggles against the Act mounted by the
labour movement served to defeat statutory, legalised attempts to
establish corporatist means of ensuring state control over industrial
relations. But it has only served to shift the structural basis for furthering
its development to other state apparatuses and has led to the rejection
of fully legal means. It is in this sense that para-state apparatuses like
the CIR and its successor, ACAS, constructed by the state as organisational forms for managing industrial relations and constituted ideologically as agencies independent of government, take on central importance
for they signify alternative and more covert mechanisms (Winkler, J.T.
1976b and 1977) for the establishment of state interventionism and
corporatist political representation. And, moreoever, they have significance in so far as they become increasingly insulated from parliamentary
scrutiny and more directly political and organised class and popular-
democratic struggles.

Let us briefly consider this example in the light of these contentions.
The CIR[50] was established as a state-sponsored organisation to prevent
industrial disputes and promote improvements in industrial relations, in
particular, orderly collective bargaining. It gave notable emphasis to the
value of strongly organised trade unions in facilitating the task of
management by fostering harmonious industrial relations, giving
emphatic support to trade union recognition. It thus expressed an
orientation close to the corporatist notion of internal control of
industrial relations by means of union heteronomy. While, like the
Ministry of Labour's conciliation and arbitration agencies before, it
stressed the ideology of voluntarism — the state as the 'third party'
desisting from intervention as far as possible, complementing rather
than organising employers and unions — it clearly went beyond the

latter in the direction of state interventionism by becoming embedded in the machinery of the Industrial Relations Act.

The lack of co-operation on the part of the TUC with the Industrial Relations Act and the generalised opposition of the labour movement, and the consequent lack of consensus considerably hindered the control functions of the CIR. The Industrial Relations Act, through the establishment of powers of reference for the Secretary of State for Employment and the potential for the referral of disputes to the NIRC as well as to the CIR, subverted to some extent the voluntaristic ethos previously adhering to the CIR's role by locking it into a more directly interventionist and corporatist set of state institutions. But it retained some of this ethos, and the legitimation of its being independent of government survived into and discovered more conducive ground for its control functions in the subsequent tripartism developed by the Heath government.

At the stage at which it was wound up, the CIR, as a consequence of its own operations, stressed the need for any future organisation taking its place to incorporate more fully into its structure employer and union representatives, and to be more unambiguously dissociated from, and independent of, government and other state agencies. This it was thought would better equip such an institution to control industrial relations and create a more adequately based consensus upon co-operation between capital, labour and the state by means of such an independent agency. These strategic emphases have now been built into the role of ACAS, the establishment of which represents a further stage in the process of restructuring state apparatuses by constructing quasi-governmental channels for the implementation of government legislation on industrial relations, such as the Employment Protection Act. The ideological emphasis placed upon such a state apparatus's independence from the executive serves to illustrate its corporatist character insofar as this represents a trend towards the removal of such apparatuses from parliamentary scrutiny and politically organised working-class opposition. Thus, this example has been cited in order to illustrate the development of one of the most likely organisational forms of state apparatus to effect state control of industrial relations and to mediate state and economy relations, so providing conditions for the maintenance of capital accumulation,[51] if corporatism and state interventionism are to be characteristic of the role of the state in late twentieth century capitalism. But this is still to a large extent indeterminant, being dependent upon on-going class struggles and political conflicts, although these will serve to overdetermine, within the structure of British capitalism, the system contradiction indicated that marks the intervention of the capitalist state in industrial relations (Habermas, 1976).

Notes

1. Earlier versions of this paper were read to a conference held by the British Sociological Association's 'State and Economy' study group at the London School of Economics in February 1978 and to a staff seminar in the Department of Sociology, University of Leicester, in May 1978, and I wish to thank those present on each occasion for their comments. I would also like to thank in particular the following for their valuable advice and criticisms: Colin Crouch, Chris Dandeker, Bob Jessop, Roger Penn, John Scott and Angus Stewart. Responsibility for the contents of the article is entirely mine.

2. What follows has been heavily influenced by, in particular, the following: Offe, 1972a, 1973, 1974, 1975a, 1975b, 1976; Offe and Ronge, 1976; Jessop, 1976, 1977a, 1977b, 1977c; Altvater, 1975.

3. For specification of the concepts of social and system integration as they are used here, see Lockwood, 1964; Mouzelis, 1974; Godelier, 1972; Strinati, 1977.

4. The above is not meant to imply that the nineteenth-century *laissez-faire* state conformed to capitalist ideology whereas the twentieth-century interventionist state does not: both forms of state intervene in the economy and industrial relations.

5. The theorisation provided is somewhat assertive in character and to be adequately argued would require more space than is available here. But see footnotes 2 and 3 above.

6. The alternative to this, it can be argued, is a fully fledged 'functionalism' treating what ought to be metatheoretical guidelines as explanations. This is what, I would argue, characterises Poulantzas's work. See Poulantzas, 1973, and Strinati, 1977.

7. The brief argument outlined above emphasising the autonomy of politics needless to say owes much to the work of Max Weber, although it has also emerged in Marxist theoretical writings – like Poulantzas's stress on the specificity of the political – and has also been broached in some Marxist empirical work such as O'Connor, 1973. However, although I can only assert it here, their analyses, in terms of the actual problem, do not approach the sophistication that marks Weber's. See, e.g., Beetham, 1974; Giddens, 1972. Weber's work, however, tends to beg the question of the nature of the relationship between the economy and the polity and between class interests and the state. Compare also G.D.H. Cole, 1934: pp. 31-2.

8. For a cogent and illuminating extension of this argument and approach see Crouch, 1977, especially chapter 1. See also Braverman, 1974.

9. The tentative and exploratory nature of the diagram and what follows must be stressed. However, I think that a move in this direction is necessary, that is, towards specifying the possible relations between the state and economy historically and in a non-reductionist way. This is so for a number of reasons but especially because so many ventures in this area either begin by asking the wrong questions or by presupposing answers to more important questions: so, for example, Weberian sociology tends to ask 'What are the interests specific to politics and the state?' while much Marxist writing tends to come round to the question, 'How are economic interests expressed politically?' Both of these questions rest upon the assumption that the structural relationship between state and economy is known

whereas it is only when this has been dealt with that the above questions can be asked. On what follows see Habermas, 1976.

10. This is, however, fraught with contradictions. See Offe, 1975a; Habermas, 1976.

11. For discussions of *laissez-faire* and state intervention in nineteenth-century Britain, see Taylor, 1972; Brebner, 1962; Roberts, 1969; and especially Polanyi, 1945.

12. For some indications of the changes involved in the rise of the interventionist state, particularly with respect to the economic functions taken on by the state, see Hannah, 1976: ch. 2 and pp. 168-77, 196-9; Feis, 1961: pp. 83-117; Dobb, 1963; Mattick, 1971; Mandel, 1975: ch. 15.

13. Notable exceptions in this respect are Panitch, 1977; Jessop, 1978. But the latter's treatment is preferable to the former's especially since it is not predicated solely upon the question of class interests. See also Crouch, 1977.

14. That is, with productive state functions, administrative re-commodification, the re-structuring of capital, etc.

15. For a detailed analysis of incomes policies in Britain in terms of attempts to establish such a structure, see Panitch, 1976; Beer, 1965; Shonfield, 1965; Crouch, 1977; Harris, 1972. Panitch's definition is close to that of Schmitter, 1974:pp.93,94.

16. This is often seen as being more important for labour organisations but it is equally crucial for capital organisations. Also, the overall process ought not to be seen as arguing for the reduction of politics to the economy. A good example to establish these points is the formation of the Confederation of British Industry out of three previously distinct organisations as a consequence of the British state's establishment of tripartite institutions, like the National Economic Development Council which required only one organisation representing British industry. This is not, of course, to say that the CBI did or does effectively represent the whole of capital in Britain (Blank, 1973).

17. Part of the motivation behind this is to prevent the long-term planning and rationalisation that corporatist economic policies entail from being disrupted by such struggles. As such, it also entails the exclusion of the constitution of the interests of certain sections of capital at the level of politics (Habermas, 1976).

18. For details on this and the following examples cited, see Wedderburn, 1971; Webb, 1920; Pelling, 1971; Phelps Brown, 1959; Citrine, 1967; Hedges and Winterbottom, 1930; Thompson, E.P., 1968; Lewis, 1976; Allen, 1960; Milne-Bailey, 1924.

19. See Glyn and Sutcliffe, 1972; Maddison, 1964; p. 53; Hughes, 1974; NEDO, 1975; Winkler, 1976a; Yaffe, 1973; Panic and Close, 1973; Burgess and Webb, 1974; King, 1975.

20. See Kennedy, 1972:p.34; Glyn and Sutcliffe, 1972:pp.120-6; Pollard, 1969:p.442. Associated with this is, firstly, Britain's growth rate, for which see Gamble and Walton, 1976:p.6; Livingstone, 1974:p.168; Denison, 1968:p.232; Dow, 1968: pp. 368 and 393; Pollard, 1969: pp. 408, 409, 434-40; and secondly the balance of payments deficit, for which see: Central Statistical Office, 1976: Dow, 1968:p.386. For some indications of the effect of industrial conflict on the UK's international economic competitive position see Ministry of Labour, 1965.

21. See Gamble and Walton, 1976; Pollard, 1969:pp.442-7; Dow, 1968: ch. 15, esp.pp.369-73 and 391, 392; Mattick, 1971; Yaffe, 1973.

22. See Kennedy, 1972:p.36; Dow, 1968:pp.343-50; Gamble and Walton, 1976:pp. 6, 7, 13; Gough, 1975:pp.80-92; Jackson *et al.*, 1975.

23. See Warren, 1972; Gough, 1975; Crouch, 1977; Kalecki, 1971; Department of Employment, 1971:pp.216; 1975:p.201.

24. This has entailed in the main opposition to capital re-structuring, e.g. what are termed 'restrictive practices' and the abrogation of managerial prerogatives.

These were and remain issues of grave concern for capital in Britain as the evidence used in the next section on its attitude to the role of the state and the reform of industrial relations shows.

25. On this widely noted phenomenon of the increase in shop-floor power and militancy, see: Panitch, 1976; Crouch, 1977; Royal Commission on Trade Unions . . . , 1968; McCarthy, 1966; McCarthy and Parker, 1968; McCarthy and Ellis, 1973; Turner, 1969; Hyman, 1973; Phelps Brown, 1973; Ingham, 1974; Fox, 1971; Flanders and Fox, 1969; Dobb, 1963:pp.23, 24; Kuhn, 1961; Sayles, 1958.

26. See Department of Employment, 1971: Tables 197-9; 1969: Tables 158-61; 1973: Tables 141-4; Hyman, 1972,1973; Ingham, 1974; Turner, 1969; McCarthy, 1966, 1970; and especially Silver, 1973.

27. See Department of Employment, 1971: Tables 15, 85 and 203; 1969: Tables 3, 34, 36, 37; 1973: Tables, 3, 40, 41, 43, 44, 151; Glyn and Sutcliffe, 1972:pp.108-10; Jackson *et al.*, 1975.

28. It should be pointed out here that in what follows much use has been made of the evidence submitted by various representative bodies to the Royal Commission on Trade Unions and Employers' Associations, chaired by Lord Donovan, between 1965 and 1968. In order to curtail extensive quoting of this source below the following abbreviations will be adopted in respect of the evidence submitted by any particular group to the Royal Commission: RC will refer to evidence submitted to the Royal Commission; ME followed by a number will refer to the Minutes of Evidence of a particular group which usually includes both its written evidence and oral evidence to the Commission but occasionally the former is omitted – these Minutes of Evidence have been published by HMSO; WE followed by a number will refer to the written evidence only of a particular group which has not been published.

29. This concerns primarily, though not exclusively, American multinational corporations in manufacturing industries. The evidence used in support of this section is as follows: Gennard, 1972; Dunning, 1970; Hymer and Rowthorn, 1970; Steuer and Gennard, 1971; *Massey-Ferguson*, RC/ME/25/1966; *Phillips Industries*, RC/ME/28/1966; *Esso*, RC/ME/39/1966; *Mobil Oil*, RC/ME/49/1966; *Kodak*, RC/ME/67/1967; *Dunlop Rubber Company*, RC/WE/281/Vol.8, n.d.; *Henry Wiggins and Co.Ltd.*, RC/WE/390/Vol.9/1967.

30. Thus even where representatives of this trend, like Massey-Ferguson, argued for the legal enforceability of collective agreements and sanctions on unconstitutional strikes, they saw the initiative and control resting with the employer.

31. See *Motor Industry Employers*, RC/ME/23/1966. And Panitch, 1976: pp.165 and 169. Among such companies, Ford was particularly aggressive in pursuing legal restrictions on strikes (Panitch, 1976: pp. 179-80). See also *H. Wiggins and Co. Ltd.* In fact, the latter and Ford (both foreign multinational companies) took the initiative in attempting to secure by existing legal means sanctions on unconstitutional strikes.

32. I cannot enter here into the theoretical nature of the distinction between industrial and banking or finance capital nor its particular manifestation in British capitalism, and, in this context, its relation to economic policy – this being, it has been argued, much more in the interest of money than industrial capital. For an excellent analysis of both of these points see Thompson, 1977. On the latter point see Aaronvitch, 1961; Glyn and Sutcliffe, 1972: pp. 41-3 and 47; Barratt-Brown, 1972: pp. 17, 61, 62; Prais, ch. 5, 1976; Blank, 1973: especially pp. 197-207; Brittan, 1971; and the paper by Longstreth in the present volume. On the City itself see Spiegelberg, 1973.

33. On the international role of the City, including its relation to sterling, see: Strange, 1971; Hirsch, F., 1969:pp.205-10; Clarke, 1967; Brittan, 1971: pp. 444-8; Cohen, 1971. It may be appropriate to point out here that money capital has not

234 *Capitalism, the State and Industrial Relations*

been nearly as much affected by the profitability crisis as industrial, manufacturing capital. On this see: NEDO, 1975:pp. 1, 6-8, 17, 18; Glyn and Sutcliffe, 1972:pp.122-6, 170, 171; Pollard, 1969:p.449; Central Statistical Office, 1976: p.48, 1971:pp.62, 63.

34. It may ostenisibly appear surprising to argue that internationalised forms of capital are more compatible with *laissez-faire* as opposed to interventionist forms of the state: but it must be remembered that the very possibility of capital being internationalised is dependent upon liberalising conditions provided by national capitalist states, for example, by liberalising world trade (Warren, 1971). This raises the question of whether such capitals, as well as militant rank-and-file elements within the labour movement, may not be equally inimical to the national economic autarchy and control that corporatism must, as Winkler, J.T. (1976a) argues, entail, and thus also contribute to its instability. I am indebted to discussions with Clive Ashworth for clarifications of this point, both here and in the main text.

35. Clarke (1967:p.251) argues that whether it realises it or not the City has a vested interest in a successful incomes policy and sustained economic growth.

36. This comes close to what Crouch (1977:pp. 35, 36, 44) has termed private corporatism. On the above see Bain, 1966; *Lloyds Bank Staff Association,* RC/WE/131/Vol.4/1965; *Guild of Insurance Officials,* RC/WE/132/Vol.4/1965; *National Federation of Professional Workers,* RC/ME/27/1966; *National Union of Bank Employees,* RC/WE/118/Vol.4/1965; *Federation of Insurance Staff Associations,* RC/WE/232/1966; *National Provincial Bank Staff Association,* RC/WE/87/1965; *Midland Bank Staff Association,* RC/WE/179/1965; *Lloyds Bank Ltd.,* RC/WE/85/1965; *National Provincial Bank,* RC/WE/44/1965. Money capital would appear to have shared with other capitals an opposition to the unionisation of white-collar workers. See, for example, the letters sent to their members by the British Employers' Confederation in 1964 and the CBI in 1965, in, amongst much of the union evidence given to the Donovan Commission, that of the *Association of Supervisory Staffs, Executives and Technicians* (ASSET), RC/ME/53/1966, paragraph 90, pp.2253-4.

37. For what follows see especially *Society of Independent Manufacturers* (SIM), RC/ME/32/1966. And *National Association of British Manufacturers,* RC/WE/1/Vol.1/1964. This, when the CBI was formed, was composed mainly of small firms and tended to merge into the CBI and SIM. See also *British Federation of Master Printers,* RC/WE/185/Vol.6/1966; *Joinery and Woodwork Employers' Federation,* RC/WE/25/Vol.1/1965; *National Federation of Master Painters and Decorators,* RC/WE/37/Vol.2/1965; *British Spinners' and Doublers' Association,* RC/WE/58/Vol.2/1965; *Hull Fishing Industry Association,* RC/WE/123/Vol.4/1965; *National Federation of Meat Trades Associations,* RC/WE/201/Vol.6/1966; *Pianoforte Manufacturers' Association,* RC/WE/147/Vol.4/1965. My endeavour to determine the size of the capitals which particular employer associations represent has been greatly assisted by Munns and McCarthy, 1967.

38. For what follows I have, somewhat controversially, relied on, among others, the evidence given by the CBI and the Engineering Employers' Federation (EEF). I feel however that there is sufficient indirect evidence at least to suggest that it is reasonably valid to regard such organisations as being particularly representative of large-scale industrial capital in Britain. This contention regarding the CBI is supported by the opposition of small companies within the CBI to its efficacy in pursuing their interests, as well as the breakaway of such companies from CBI membership. See, for example, Harland, 1977. On the EEF and its development of adequate and strategic representation for large companies after 1957 see Wigham, 1973. On the formation and early history of the CBI see Blank, 1973. Thus for what follows see mainly the CBI's written evidence in the Royal Commission on Trade Unions and Employers' Associations,

Selected Written Evidence (in one Volume), HMSO, 1968; the *CBI*, RC/ME/6 and 9/1965, RC/ME/22/1966; EEF's written evidence in *Selected Written Evidence*, op.cit.; the EEF, RC/ME/20/1966; the EEF, *The Donovan Report: An Assessment*, London, 1969. But see also, National Federation of Building Trades Employers' written evidence in *Selected Written Evidence*, op. cit. and RC/ME/16/1966; 6/ *Newspaper Proprietors' Association*, RC/WE/216/Vol.6/1965; cf. the stance tance taken by the *Shipbuilding Employers' Federation*, RC/ME/48/1966.

39. The basis of this dilemma, indicative of the concept of system contradiction developed above, is in a more general sense graphically summarised in a key statement in a recent CBI document 'Road to Recovery': economic 'planning and government action arising from it should try to assist, not to supplant the market economy' (quoted in *The Times*, 9 November 1977). On the CBI and its relationship to planning in Britain as well as on state intervention in the economy as a whole see Smith, 1974; also Blank, 1973.

40. Less attention will be paid to this here, not only because the terms used have been established above, but also because of its fuller treatment in the existing literature. See especially Panitch, 1976. Paradoxically, the recent Marxist theorisation of the bases of differentiation of capital has paid far less attention to the structural differentiation of labour, that is, to the problem of 'particular labours'.

41. Quite obviously not all unions and sections of labour regard these strategies in terms of control similarly to the way capital regards them. Rather they may be seen as the means by which the rights of labour are secured. Nonetheless, it is intrinsic to the argument that commitment to the paradigms of paternalism and corporatism factually entails a commitment to control.

42. On this see: Panitch, 1976; Crouch, 1977; *Watermen, Lightermen, Tugmen and Bargemen's Union*, RC/WE/269/1966; *Joint Shop Stewards' Committee of Garringtons Ltd*, RC/WE/293/1966; *Transport and Salaried Staffs Association* (TASS), RC/WE/192/1966; *National Union of Railwaymen* (NUR), RC/ME/17/ 1966; *Transport and General Workers' Union* (TGWU), RC/ME/30/1966.

43. See the evidence of the staff associations cited above, and *Draughtsmen's and Allied Technicians' Association*, RC/ME/36/1966.

44. See, e.g., *National Union of General and Municipal Workers Union*, RC/ME/42/1966; *National Association of Local Government Officers*, RC/ME/ 26/1966, and its written evidence in *Selected Written Evidence*, op.cit.; *Trades Union Congress* in ibid, and RC/ME/61 and 65/1966 and 1967. It can be suggested that during phases of the 1964 to 1970 Labour government's incomes policy (Panitch, 1976), the Tory government of 1970-74 with its experiment with tripartitism and the present Labour government, the TUC leadership has shifted to a more corporatist position, as is illustrated in Figure 6.4. See also, *Association of Supervisory Staffs, Executives and Technicians*. RC/ME/53/1966.

45. See *Union of Shop, Distributive and Allied Workers* (USDAW); RC/ME/29/ 1966; *Amalgamated Engineering Union* (AEU), RC/ME/24/1966. Needless to say, the latter shifted its position somewhat with the establishment of H. Scanlon as its leader (Scanlon, 1967). At times *ASSET*, op. cit., was somewhat ambiguous in respect of the distinction between pluralism and corporatism.

46. On the above see Inns of Court Conservative and Unionist Society, 1958; *idem*, RC/ME/35/1966; *Law Society*, in *Selected Written Evidence*, op.cit. and RC/ME/52/1966; *Bar Council*, RC/ME/43/1966; *Bar Association for Commerce, Finance and Industry*, RC/WE/271/Vol.7, n.d.; the Conservative Party, 1968. One important point which emerges from this evidence is the way in which external controls such as the statutory registration of unions and their rules which, as a consequence, buttress their internal control structure are seen as a more effective way of controlling industrial conflict than the more publicised measure

of merely removing legal immunities in tort from unions for unofficial strike action (*Law Society,* op.cit. Q's 8329-8342, pp.2222-4).

47. For a particularly clear statement of the problems posed by 'the vagaries of judge-made law' for corporatist institutions, see Shonfield, 1977; see also J. Winkler, 1977.

48. On the above, see Panitch, 1976, 1977; Crouch, 1974, 1977; Winkler, 1977; Fels, 1972; Mitchell, 1972; NBPI, RC/ME/51/1966; Department of Economic Affairs, RC/ME/18/1966; Ministry of Labour, RC/ME/2 and 3/1965; *idem,* 1965; Jessop, 1977c.

49. For this and what follows, see Industrial Relations Act, Eliz II, 1971, ch. 72; Thomson and Engleman, 1975: pp. 22-5; Wedderburn, 1971, 1972; Barnett, 1973.

50. On what follows, see Commission for Industrial Relations, 1970, 1971, 1973, 1974; Thomson and Engleman, 1975; ACAS, 1975, 1976; Ministry of Labour, 1965; James, 1977.

51. It can also be considered to be a way of resolving the conflict between capital and the state over the institutional responsibility for activating state control of industrial relations.

NOTES ON CONTRIBUTORS

Colin Crouch is lecturer in sociology at the London School of Economics and Political Science. He is the author of *The Student Revolt* (Bodley Head, 1970) and *Class Conflict and the Industrial Relations Crisis* (Heinemann, 1977); and editor of (with L. Lindberg and others) *Stress and Contradiction in Modern Capitalism* (D.C. Heath, 1975), *British Political Sociology Yearbook,* Volume 3, *Participation in Politics* (Croom Helm, 1977), and (with A. Pizzorno) *The Resurgence of Class Conflict in Western Europe since 1968* (two volumes) (Macmillan, 1978). He is currently engaged in research on relations between the state and trade unions in western Europe.

Michael Harloe is a senior researcher at the Centre for Environmental Studies, London. He is the author of a number of books and articles and edited a recent collection of papers entitled *Captive Cities: Studies in the Political Economy of Cities and Regions* (Wiley, 1977). He is a member of the Board of the International Sociological Association's Research Committee on Urban and Regional Development. He is also Editor of the *International Journal of Urban and Regional Research.*

Frank Longstreth is a lecturer in sociology at the University of Birmingham. Having studied at Harvard, Frankfurt and the London School of Economics and Political Science, he is currently engaged on research into the politics of economic planning and policy.

Andrew Martin a research associate at the Center for European Studies, Harvard University. Taught at Columbia University, University of Massachusetts and Boston University. Publications include articles on the comparative politics of economic policy, of which the most recent is 'Political constraints on economic strategies in advanced industrial societies', *Comparative Political Studies,* 10 (3), 1977. Current research is on capital formation policy; trade unions and economic policy; development of Swedish political economy.

Robert Skidelsky is professor of international studies at the University of Warwick. He previously taught in the department of history and philosophy at the Polytechnic of North London. His works include *Politicians and the Slump* (Macmillan, 1967) and a biography of Oswald Mosely. He is the editor (with V. Bogdanor) of *The Age of Affluence,* and of *The End of the Keynesian Era* (Macmillan, 1977). He is now working on a biography of Lord Keynes.

Dominic Strinati is a lecturer in sociology at the University of Leicester. He studied Sociology at Leicester University and as a Ph.D. research student at the London School of Economics. He is working on a study of the structure of state intervention in industrial relations in Britain in the context of the changing relationship between the state, economy and class conflict.

BIBLIOGRAPHY

Aaronovitch, S. *The Ruling Class* (Lawrence and Wishart, London, 1961)

ACAS *Annual Reports* (HMSO, London, annually)

Alford, R. 'Paradigms of Relations between State and Society', in L.N. Lindberg *et al.* (eds) *Stress and Contradiction in Modern Capitalism* (D.H. Heath, Lexington, 1975)

Allen, V.L. *Trade Unions and the Government* (Longmans, London, 1960)

Althusser, L. *For Marx,* English ed (Vintage, New York, 1970)

Althusser, L. and Balibar, E. *Reading Capital,* English ed (New Left Books, London, 1970)

Altvater, E. 'Notes on Some Problems of State Interventionism', *Kapitalistate,* 1 and 2 (1973)

Anderson, C.W. 'Political Design and the Representation of Interests', in Schmitter, P.C. (ed.) *Comparative Political Studies,* 10, 1 (1977)

Anderson, J. *The Political Economy of Urbanism: an Introduction and Bibliography* (Architectural Association, London, 1975)

Ardagh, J. *The New France* (Penguin, Harmondsworth, 1977)

Arndt, H.W. *The Economic Lessons of the Nineteen-Thirties* (Oxford University Press, London, 1944)

Bachrach, P. and Baretz, M. *Power and Poverty* (Oxford University Press, New York, 1970)

Bain, G.S. *Trade Union Growth and Recognition.* Donovan Commission Research Paper No. 6 (HMSO, London, 1966)

Baran, P. and Sweezey, P. *Monopoly Capital* (Penguin, Harmondsworth, 1966)

Barnett, A. 'Class Struggle and the Heath Government', *New Left Review,* no. 77 (1973)

Barratt-Brown, M. *From Labourism to Socialism* (Spokesman Books, Nottingham, 1972)

Beckerman, W. (ed.) *The Labour Government's Economic Record 1964-70* (Duckworth, London, 1972)

Beer, S.H. *Modern British Politics* (Faber and Faber, London, 1965)

Beetham, D. *Max Weber and the Theory of Modern Politics* (Allen and Unwin, London, 1974)

Bell, D. *The Coming of Post Industrial Society* (Heinemann, London, 1974)

Bell, D. *The Cultural Contradictions of Capitalism* (Heinemann, London, 1976)

Benn, A. *The New Politics: a Socialist Reconnaissance,* Fabian Tract 402 (Fabian Society, London, 1970)

Bergström, V. 'Industriell utveckling, industrins kapitalbildning och finanspolitiken', in E. Lundberg, *et al. Svensk Finanspolitik i Teori och Praktik* (Aldus Bonniers, Stockholm, 1971)

Bergström, V. *et al. Dags för Tilvöxt?*(Studieforbundet Näringsliu och Samhälle, Stockholm, 1975)

Berman, S. 'The Impact of Economic Theory on the Policy and Ideology of the Swedish Social Democratic Party between the Wars' (mimeo, 1974)

Bird, R.M. 'Wagner's "Law" of Expanding State Activities', *Public Finance/Finances Publiques.* vol. xxvi (1971)

Blackburn, R. 'The New Capitalism', in R. Blackburn (ed.) *Ideology and Social Science* (Fontana, London, 1972)

Blank, S. *Government and Industry in Britain* (Saxon House, Farnborough, 1973)

Blank, S. 'Britain: the Politics of Foreign Economic Policy, the Domestic Economy and the Problem of Pluralist Stagnation', *International Organisation,* vol. 31, no. 4 (1977)

Bourdieu, P. *Outline of a Theory of Pratice,* English edn (Cambridge, Cambridge University Press, Cambridge, 1977)

Braverman, H. *Labour and Monopoly Capital* (Monthly Review Press, New York, 1974)

Brebner, J.B. 'Laissez-faire and State Intervention in Nineteenth Century Britain' in E.M. Carus-Wilson (ed.) *Essays in Economic History,* vol. III (Arnold, London, 1962)

Brenner, M.J. 'Functional Representation and Interest Group Theory', *Comparative Politics,* 2, 1 (1969)

British Market Research Bureau Ltd. *BMRB Survey* (HMSO, London, 1977)

Brittan, S. *Steering the Economy* (Penguin, Harmondsworth, 1971)

Brittan, S. 'The Economic Consequences of Democracy', *British Journal of Political Science,* 5 (1975)

Brittan, S. 'Can Democracy Manage an Economy?' in R. Skidelsky (ed.) *The End of the Keynesian Era* (Macmillan, London, 1977)

Brittan, S. 'Inflation and Democracy', in F. Hirsch and J.H. Goldthorpe (eds) *The Political Economy of Inflation* (Martin Robertson, London, 1978)

Brown, G. *In My Way* (Penguin, Harmondsworth, 1972)

Brown, W.A. 'The Conflict of Opinion and Economic Interest in

England', in S. Pollard (ed.) *The Development of the British Economy, 1914-67* (Edward Arnold, London, 1970)

Buchanan, J.M. and Wagner, R.E. *Democracy in Deficit: The Political Legacy of Lord Keynes* (Academic Press, New York, 1977)

Bullock, P. and Yaffe, D. 'Inflation, the Crisis and the Post-war Boom', *Revolutionary Communist,* 3/4 (1975)

Burgess, F. and Webb, A. 'Rates of Return and Profit Shares in the United Kingdom', *Lloyds Bank Review* (April 1974)

Butler, D. and Stokes, D. *Political Change in Britain* (London, 1971)

Calleo, D.P. *et al. Money and the Coming World Order* (Columbia University Press, New York, 1976)

Calmfors, L. 'Inflation in Sweden', in L.B. Krause and W.S. Salent (eds) *Worldwide Inflation* (The Brookings Institution, Washington, 1977)

Castells, M. *Luttes Urbaines* (Maspero, Paris, 1973)

Castells, M. (ed.) *Estructura de Clases y Politica Urbana en America Latina,* vol. 1 (SIAP, Buenos Aires, 1974)

Castells, M. *Collective Consumption and Urban Contradictions in Advanced Capitalism,* in L.N. Lindberg, *et al.* (eds) *Stress and Contradiction in Modern Capitalism* (D.H. Heath, Lexington, 1975)

Castells, M. *La Crise Economique et la Société Américaine* (PUF, Paris, 1976a)

Castells, M. 'Crise de l'Etat, Consommation Collective et Contradictions Urbaines', in N. Poulantzas (ed.) *La Crise de l'Etat* (PUF, Paris, 1976b)

Castells, M. *The Urban Question,* revised English edn (Arnold, London, 1977)

Castells, M. 'Urban Social Movements and the Struggle for Democracy: the Citizens Movement in Madrid', *International Journal of Urban and Regional Research,* vol. 2, no. 1 (1978)

Castells, M., Cherki, E., Godard, F. and Mehl, D. *Sociologie des Mouvements Sociaux Urbains,* vol. I (Mouton, Paris, 1977)

Castells, M. and Godard, F. *Monopolville* (Mouton, Paris, 1974)

CDP Collective *Profits against Houses: an Alternative Guide to Housing Finance* (CDP Collective, London, 1976)

Cecco, M. de 'The Last of the Romans', in R. Skidelsky (ed.) *The End of the Keynesian Era* (Macmillan, London, 1977)

Central Statistical Office *United Kingdom Balance of Payments 1970* (HMSO, London, 1970)

Central Statistical Office *United Kingdom Balance of Payments 1965-1975* (HMSO, London, 1976)

Cherky, E., Mehl, D. and Metaillé, A.M. 'Urban Protest in Western
Europe', in C.J. Crouch and A. Pizzorno (eds) *The Resurgence of
Class Conflict in Western Europe since 1968: Volume 2:
Comparative Analyses* (Macmillan, London, 1978)

Christoph, J.B. 'The Birth of Neddy', in J.B. Christoph (ed.) *Cases in
Contemporary Politics* (Little Brown, Boston, 1965)

Clarke, W.M. *The City in the World Economy* (Penguin, Harmondsworth, 1

Clay, Sir H. *Lord Norman* (Macmillan, London, 1957)

Citrine, N.A. *Trade Union Law,* third edn (Stevens, London, 1967)

Cockburn, C. *The Local State* (Pluto, London, 1977)

Cohen, B.J. *The Future of Sterling as an International Currency*
(Macmillan, London, 1971)

Cohn-Bendit, D. and G. *Obsolete Communism: the Left Wing
Alternative* (Seuil, Paris, 1968)

Cole, G.D.H. *What Marx Really Meant* (Gollancz, London, 1934)

Commission on Industrial Relations (annually) *Annual Report*
(HMSO, London)

Congdon, T. 'Are we Really Keynesians Now?' *Encounter* (April 1975)

Conservative Centre for Policy Studies *Why Britain Needs a Social
Market Economy* (The Centre, London, 1975)

Conservative Political Centre *Fair Deal at Work* (The Centre, London, 1968

Corina, J. 'Planning and the British Labour Market: Incomes and
Manpower Policy, 1965-1970' in J. Hayward and M. Watson (eds)
Planning, Politics and Public Policy (Cambridge University Press,
Cambridge, 1975)

Crick, B. 'Fraternity: the Forgotten Value', in C.J. Crouch and F. Inglis,
(eds) *Morality and the Left*, special issue of *New Universities Quarterly*,
32, 2 (1978)

Crossman, R.H.S. *The Diaries of a Cabinet Minister, Vol. II* (Hamish
Hamilton and Jonathan Cape, London, 1976)

Crouch, C.J. 'The Ideology of a Managerial Elite: the National Board
for Prices and Incomes 1965-70', in I. Crewe (ed.) *British Political
Sociology Yearbook: Volume I: Elites in Western Democracy.*
(Croom Helm, London, 1974)

Crouch, C.J. *Class Conflict and the Industrial Relations Crisis*
(Heinemann, London, 1977a)

Crouch, C.J. 'The Place of Participation in the Study of Politics',
in C.J. Crouch (ed.) *British Political Sociology Yearbook: Volume
3: Participation in Politics* (Croom Helm, London, 1977b)

Crouch, C.J. 'The Changing Role of the State in Industrial Relations in
Western Europe', in C.J. Crouch and A. Pizzorno (eds) *The*

Resurgence of Class Conflict in Western Europe since 1968: Volume 2: Comparative Analyses (Macmillan, London, 1978)

Dahl, R.A. *Who Governs* (Yale University Press, New Haven, 1971)

Dahmén, E. 'Equilibrium and Development Problems in the Swedish Economy', *Skandinaviska Enskilda Banken Quarterly Review,* 1-2 (1977)

Dahrendorf, R. 'Recent Changes in the Class Structure of European Societies', *Daedalus (Winter 1964)*

d'Arcy, F. and Jobert, B. 'Urban Planning in France', in J. Hayward and M. Watson (eds) *Planning, Politics and Public Policy* (1975)

Denison, E.F. 'Economic Growth' in R. Caves (ed.) *Britain's Economic Prospects* (Brookings Institution, Washington DC, 1968)

Denton, G. *Planning for Growth,* PEP Broadsheets, vol. 31, no. 487 (PEP, London, 1964)

Denton, G., Forsyth, M. and Maclennan, M. *Economic Planning and Policies in Britain, France and Germany* (Allen and Unwin, London, 1968)

Department of Employment *British Labour Statistics Yearbook* (HMSO, London, annually)

Department of Employment *British Labour Statistics: Historical Abstract* (HMSO, London, 1971)

Dicey, A.V. *Law and Public Opinion in England during the Nineteenth Century* (Macmillan, London, 1905)

Dobb, M. *Studies in the Development of Capitalism* rev. edn (Routledge, London, 1963)

Dow, J.C.R. *The Management of the British Economy 1945-1960* (Cambridge University Press, Cambridge, 1968)

Dunleavy, P. 'Methodological Sentorianism in Urban Sociology', *International Journal of Urban and Regional Research,* vol. 1, no. 1 (1977a)

Dunleavy, P. 'Protest and Quiescence in Urban Politics: a Critique of some Pluralist and Structuralist Myths', *International Journal of Urban and Regional Research,* vol. 1, no. 2 (1977b)

Dunning, J.H. 'Foreign Investment in the UK', in I.A. Litvak and C.S. Maule (eds) *Foreign Investment: the Experience of Host Countries* (Praeger, New York, 1970)

Edgren, G, Faxén, K.-O. and Odhner, C.-E. *Wage Formation and the Economy* (Allen and Unwin, London, 1973)

Eichner, A.S. and Cornwall, J. 'A Guide to the Post-Keynesians', *Challenge,* 21, 2 (1978)

Eliasson, G. *Investment Funds in Operation* (National Institute of
  Economic Research, Stockholm, 1965)
Engineering Employers Federation *The Donovan Report: an Assessment*
  (EEF, London, 1969)
Esping-Andersen, E., Friedland, R. and Olin Wright, E. 'Modes of Class
  Struggle and the Capitalist State', *Kapitalistate*, 4/5 (1976)
Eversley, D.E.C. *The Growth of Planning Research since the Early
  Sixties* (SSRC, London, 1975)

Feis, H. *Europe — the World's Banker 1870-1914* (Kelley, New York,
  1961)
Feiwel, G.R. *The Intellectual Capital of Michael Kalecki* (University of
  Tenessee Press, Knoxville, 1975)
Fels, A. *The British Prices and Incomes Board* (Cambridge University
  Press, Cambridge, 1972)
Flanders, A. and Fox, A. 'Collective Bargaining: From Donovan to
  Durkheim', *British Journal of Industrial Relations* (1969)
Fox, A. *A Sociology of Work in Industry* (Collier-Macmillan, London,
  1971)
Friedman, M. *Inflation and Unemployment* (Institute of Economic
  Affairs, London, 1977)
Fulcher, J. 'Class Conflict in Sweden', *Sociology*, 7, 1 (1973)

Galbraith, J.K. *The Age of Uncertainty* (BBC and André Deutsch, 1977)
Gamble, A. and Walton, P. *Capitalism in Crisis* (Macmillan, London,
  1976)
Gardner, R.N. *Sterling-Dollar Diplomacy,* second edn (Clarendon Press,
  Oxford, 1969)
Gates, R.A. 'German Socialism and the Crisis of 1929-33', *Central
  European History,* VII, 4 (1974)
Gennard, J. *Multinational Corporations and British Labour* (British-
  North American Committee, London, 1972)
Giddens, A. *Politics and Sociology in the Thought of Max Weber*
  (Macmillan, London, 1972)
Giddens, A. *The Class Structure of the Advanced Societies* (Hutchinson,
  London, 1973)
Gilpin, R. *US Power and the Multinational Corporation* (Basic Books,
  New York, 1975)
Glyn, A. and Sutcliffe, B. *British Capitalism, Workers and the Profits
  Squeeze* (Penguin, Harmondsworth, 1972)
Godelier, M. 'Structure and Contradiction in Capital', in R. Blackburn
  (ed.) *Ideology and Social Science* (1972)

Gough, I. 'State Expenditure in Advanced Capitalism', *New Left Review*, no. 92, 80-92 (1975)

Grant, W. 'Corporatism and Pressure Groups' in D. Kavanagh and R. Rose (eds) *New Trends in British Politics* (Sage, London, 1977)

Grant, W. and Marsh, D. *The CBI* (Hodder and Stoughton, London, 1977)

Griffith, J.A.G. *The Politics of the Judiciary* (Fontana, London, 1977)

Habermas, J. *Legitimation Crisis* (Heinemann, London, 1976)

Halsey, A.H. *Change in British Society since 1900* (Oxford University Press, Oxford, 1978)

Hancock, D. *Sweden: the Politics of Post-Industrial Change* (The Dryden Press, Hinsdale, Ill ., 1972)

Hannah, L. *The Rise of the Corporate Economy* (Methuen, London, 1972)

Harland, P. 'Small Companies Talk Big', *Sunday Times* (25 Sept. 1977)

Harloe, M. (ed.) *Captive Cities* (Wiley, London, 1977a)

Harloe, M. 'The Attack on Housing' and 'Dog's Dinner', *New Statesman*, (28 Jan./1 July 1977b)

Harloe, M. 'Will the Green Paper Mean Better Housing', *Roof*, vol. 2, no. 5 (1977c)

Harloe, M. (ed.) *Urban Change and Conflict* (Centre for Environmental Studies, London, 1978)

Harloe, M., Issacharoff, R. and Mins, R. *The Organisation of Housing: Public and Private Enterprise in London* (Heinemann, London, 1974)

Harris, N. *Competition and the Corporate Society* (Methuen, London, 1972)

Harrod, R. *The Life of John Maynard Keynes* (Macmillan, London, 1951)

Harvey, D. *Social Justice and the City* (Edward Arnold, London, 1973)

Harvey, D. 'The Urban Process under Capitalism: a Framework for Analysis', *International Journal of Urban and Regional Research*, vol. 2, no. 1 (1978)

Hayward, J. 'Planning and the French Labour Market', in J. Hayward and M. Watson (eds) *Planning, Politics and Public Policy* (Cambridge University Press, Cambridge, 1975)

Hedges, R.Y. and Winterbottom, A. *The Legal History of Trade Unionism* (Longmans, London, 1930)

Hibbs, D.A. Jr. 'Political Parties and Macroeconomic Policy', *American Political Science Review*, 71,4 (1977)

Himmelstrand, U. 'Socialism and Social Liberalism in the Context of Swedish Societal Change' (symposium on the Small Welfare State between Internal Pressures and International Dependency, University of Uppsala)

Hirsch, F. *The Pound Sterling: a Polemic* (Gollancz, London, 1965)

Hirsch, F. *Money International* (Penguin, Harmondsworth, 1969)

Hirsch, F. *Social Limits to Growth* (Routledge and Kegan Paul, London, 1977)

Hirsch, J. 'Scientific–Technical Progress and the Political System', *German Political Studies* (1973)

Hirsch, J. 'Remarques Théoriques sur l'Etat Bourgeois et sa Crise', in N. Poulantzas (ed.) (1976) *La Crise de l'Etat*

Hirschman, A.O. *Exit, Voice and Loyalty* (Harvard University Press, Cambridge, Mass., 1970)

HM Government *Housing Policy: A Consultative Document,* Cmnd. 6851 and technical volumes I-III (HMSO, London, 1977a)

HM Government *Policy for the Inner Cities* (HMSO, London, 1977b)

Holland, S. *The Socialist Challenge* (Quartet Books, London, 1975)

Holloway, J. and Picciotto, S. 'Capital, Crisis and the State, *Capital and Class,* 2(1977)

Holloway, J. and Picciotto, S. 'Towards a Materialist Theory of the State', in J. Holloway and S. Picciotto (eds) *State and Capital* (Edward Anrold, London, 1978)

Howson, S. *Domestic Monetary Management in Britain, 1919-38* (Cambridge University Press, Cambridge, 1975)

Hughes, J. *Profit Trends and Price Controls* (Spokesman Books, Nottingham, 1974)

Hume, J. 'The Gold Standard and Inflation', in S. Pollard (ed.) *The Development of the British Economy, 1914-67* (1969)

Hunt, A. (ed.) *Class and Class Structure* (Lawrence and Wishart, London, 1977)

Huntingdon, S.P. 'Post-industrial Politics: How Benign Will it Be?', *Comparative Politcs,* 6 (1975)

Hutchison, T.W. *Economics and Economic Policy in Britain 1946-1966* (Allen and Unwin, London, 1968)

Hutchison, T.W. *Keynes versus the 'Keynesians'?* (Institute of Economic Affairs, London, 1977)

Hyman, R. *Strikes* (Fontana, London, 1972)

Hyman, R. 'Industrial Conflict and the Political Economy', *Socialist Register* (1973)

Hymer, R. and Rowthorn, R. 'Multinational Corporations and International Oligopoly: the non-American Challenge', in C.P. Kindleberger (ed.) *The International Corporation* (Harvard University Press, Cambridge, Mass., 1970)

Industrial Council for Social and Economic Studies *On Incomes Policy* (The Council, Stockholm, 1969)

Ingham, G.K. *Strikes and Industrial Conflict* (Cambridge University Press, Cambridge, 1974)

Inns of Court Conservative and Unionist Society *A Giant's Strength* (The Society, London, 1958)

Institute of Economic Affairs *Inflation* (The Institute, London, 1975)

Inter-Bank Research Organisation *The Future of London as an International Finance Centre* (HMSO, London, 1973)

Jackson, D. Turner, H.A. and Wilkinson, F. *Do Trade Unions Cause Inflation?* 2nd edn (Cambridge University Press, Cambridge, 1975)

James, B. 'Third Party Intervention in Recognition Disputes: the Role of the Commission on Industrial Relations', *Industrial Relations*, 8, 2 (1977)

Jay, P. in *The Times Business News* (15 April 1976)

Jessop, R.D. 'The Relative Autonomy of the State' (mimeo, 1976)

Jessop, R.D. 'Corporatism: the Highest Form of Social Democracy' (mimeo, 1977a)

Jessop, R.D. 'Remarks on some recent Theories of the Capitalist State', *Cambridge Journal of Economics*, 1,4 (1977b)

Jessop, R.D. 'Theses on the Restructuring of State Apparatuses' (mimeo, 1977c)

Jessop, R.D. 'Capitalism and Democracy: the Best Possible Shell', in G. Littlejohn (ed.) *Power and the State* (Croom Helm, London, 1978)

Jewkes, J. *Delusions of Dominance* (Institute of Economic Affairs, London, 1977)

Johnson, T. 'What is to be Known — the Structural Determination of Social Class', *Economy and Society*, 6,2 (1977)

Kahn, Lord *On Re-reading Keynes* (British Academy, London, 1974)

Kaldor, N. in *The Times* (6 Sept. 1971)

Kalecki, M.L. 'Political Aspects of Full Employment', *The Political Quarterly*, xiv, 4 (1943)

Kavanagh, D.A. 'Crisis Management and Incremental Adaptation in British Politics', in G.A. Almond *et al.* (eds) *Crisis, Choice and Change* (Little, Brown, Boston, 1973)

Kennedy, M.C. 'The Economy as a Whole', in A.R. Prest and D.J.

248   *Bibliography*

Coppock (eds) *The UK Economy* 4th edn (Weidenfeld and Nicholson, London, 1972)

Keynes, J.M. *Economic Consequences of the Peace* (Macmillan, London, 1919)

Keynes, J.M. *Treatise on Money,* vol. II (Macmillan, London, 1930)

Keynes, J.M. *Essays in Persuasion* (Macmillan, London, 1931)

Keynes, J.M. *The General Theory of Employment, Interest and Money* (Macmillan, London, 1936)

Kindleberger, C.P. *The World in Depression 1929-39* (University of California Press, Berkeley, 1973)

Kindleberger, C.P. 'Systems of International Organisation', in D.P. Calleo *et al. Money and the Coming World Order* (1976)

King, M. 'The United Kingdom Profits Crisis: Myth or Reality?', *Economic Journal* (March 1975)

Kipping, Sir N. *Summing Up* (Hutchinson, London, 1972)

Kocka, J. 'Organisierter Kapitalismus oder Staatsmonopolistischer Kapitalismus? Begriffliche Vorbemerkungen', in H.A. Winkler (ed.) *Organisierter Kapitalismus* (1974)

Kornhauser, W. *The Politics of Mass Society* (Routledge, London, 1960)

Kuhn, J.W. *Bargaining in Grievance Settlement* (Columbia University Press, New York, 1961)

Lal, D. *Unemployment and Wage Inflation in Industrial Economies* (OECD, Paris, 1977)

Laski, H. *The State in Theory and Practice* (Allen and Unwin, London, 1935)

Leeds, A. and E. 'Accounting for Behavioural Differences', in J. Walton and L.H. Masotti (eds) *The City in Comparative Perspective* (Sage, London, 1976)

Lehmbruch, G. 'Liberal Corporatism and Party Government', in P.C. Schmitter (ed.) *Comparative Political Studies* (1977)

Lerues, J. *Planification et Politique en Grande Bretagne* (Armand-Colin, Paris, 1972)

Lewis, R. 'The Historical Development of Labour Law', *British Journal of Industrial Relations* 14 (1976)

Lindbeck, A. *Swedish Economic Policy* (University of California Press, Berkeley, 1973)

Lindberg, L.N., Alford, R., Crouch, C. and Offe, C. (eds) *Stress and Contradiction in Modern Capitalism* (D.H. Heath, Lexington, 1975)

Lindblom, C.E. *Politics and Markets* (Basic Books, New York, 1977)

Linder, M. and Sensat, J. *Anti-Samuelson* (Urizon Books, New York, 1977)

Littlejohn, G. *et al.* (eds) *Power and the State* (Croom Helm, London 1978)

Livingstone, J.M. *The British Economy in Theory and Practice,* (Macmillan, London, 1974)

LO *The Postwar Programme of Swedish Labour* (LO, Stockholm, 1948)

LO *Trade Unions and Full Employment* (LO, Stockholm, 1953)

Lockwood, D. 'Social Integration and System Integration', in G.K. Zollschan and W. Hirsch (eds) *Explorations in Social Change* (Routledge, London, 1964)

Lojkine, J. *Le Marxisme, l'Etat et la Question Urbaine* (PUF, Paris, 1977)

Lowi, T. 'Towards a Politics of Economics: the State of Permanent Receivership', in L. Lindberg, *et al.* (eds) *Stress and Contradiction in Modern Capitalism* (1975)

Lukes, S. *Power: a Radical View* (Macmillan, London, 1974)

Lundberg, E. *Business Cycles and Economic Policy* (Harvard University Press, Cambridge, Mass., 1957)

Lybeck, J.A. 'The Effects of the Riksbank's Credit Policy on Consumption, Investment and Foreign Capital Imports', *Skandinaviska Enskilda Banken Quarterly Review,* 1-2 (1977)

McCarthy, W.E.J. *The Role of Shop Stewards in British Industrial Relations,* Donovan Commission Research Paper No. 1 (HMSO, London, 1966)

McCarthy, W.E.J. 'The Nature of Britain's Strike Problem', *British Journal of Industrial Relations,* vol. 8 (1970)

McCarthy, W.E.J. and Ellis, N.D. *Management by Agreement* (Hutchinson, London, 1973)

McCarthy, W.E.J. and Parker, S.R. *Shop Stewards and Workshop Relations,* Donovan Commission Research Papers No. 10 (HMSO, London, 1968)

McCracken, P. *et al. Towards Full Employment and Stability* (OECD, Paris, 1977)

McEachern, N. 'Government Action and the Power of Private Capital' (unpublished PhD thesis, University of Leeds)

MacRae, C. Duncan 'A Political Model of the Business Cycle', *Journal of Political Economy,* 85 (1977)

Maddison, A. *Economic Growth in the West* (Twentieth Century Fund, New York, 1964)

Maier, C.S. 'Strukturen Kapitalistischer Stabilität in der Zwanziger Jahren: Errungschaften und Defekte', in H.A. Winkler (ed.) *Organisierter Kapitalismus* (1974)

Mandel, E. *Late Capitalism* (New Left Books, London, 1974)

Martin, A. 'The Politics of Economic Policy in the United States: a Tentative View from a Comparative Perspective', *Sage Professional Papers in Comparative Politics,* 4 (1973)

Martin, A. 'Is Democratic Control of Capital Economies Possible?' in L. Lindberg, *et al.* (eds) *Stress and Contradiction in Modern Capitalism* (1975)

Martin, A. 'Sweden: Industrial Democracy and Social Democratic Strategy', in D. Garson (ed.) *Worker Self-Management in Industry* (Praeger, New York, 1977)

Marx, K. *Grundrisse* (Penguin, Harmondsworth, 1973)

Marx, K. *Capital* vol. 1 (Lawrence and Wishart, London, 1974)

Marx, K. and Engels, F. *Selected Works,* vol. 1 (Moscow, 1962)

Mattick, P. *Marx and Keynes* (Merlin Press, London, 1971)

Meidner, R. *Employee Investment Funds* (Allen and Unwin, London, 1978)

Mellor, J. *Urban Sociology in an Urbanised Society* (Routledge, London, 1977)

Miliband, R. *Parliamentary Socialism,* second edn (Merlin Press, London, 1972)

Miliband, R. *Marxism and Politics* (Oxford University Press, Oxford, 1977)

Milne-Bailey, W. *Trade Unions and the State* (Allen and Unwin, London, 1924)

Mingione, E. 'Pahl and Lojkine on the State: a Comment', *International Journal of Urban and Regional Research,* vol. 1, no. 1 (1977)

Ministry of Labour *Written Evidence for the Royal Commission on Trade Unions and Employers' Associations* (HMSO, London, 1965)

Mishan, E.J. 'The New Inflation', *Encounter* (May, 1974)

Mitchell, J. *The National Board for Prices and Incomes* (Secker and Warburg, London, 1972)

Moggridge, D.E. (ed.) *Keynes: Aspects of the Man and his Work* (Cambridge University Press, Cambridge, 1974)

Moran, M. *The Politics of Industrial Relations* (Macmillan, London, 1977)

Mouzelis, N. 'Social and System Integration' *British Journal of Sociology,* vol. 25 (1974)

Müller, W. and Neusüss, C. 'The Welfare-State Illusion', in Holloway and Picciotto (eds) *State and Capital* (1978)

Munns, V.G. and McCarthy, W.E.J. *Employers' Associations,* Donovan Commission Research Paper No. 7 (HMSO, London, 1967)

Nedelmann, B. and Meier, K.G. 'Theories of Contemporary Corporatism: Static or Dynamic' in P.C. Schmitter (ed.) *Comparative Political Studies* (1977)

NEDO *Financial Performance and Inflation* (HMSO, London, 1975)

Nichols, T. and Beynon, H. *Living with Capitalism* (Fontana, London, 1977)

Nordhaus, W.D. 'The Political Business Cycle', *Review of Economic Studies* 42 (1975)

O'Connor, J. *The Fiscal Crisis of the State* (St Martin's Press, New York, 1973)

OECD *Economic Surveys: Sweden* (OECD, Paris, 1977)

Offe, C. *Strukturprobleme des Kapitalistischen Staates* (Frankfurt am Main, 1972a)

Offe, C. 'Advanced Capitalism and the Welfare State', *Politics and Society,* vol. 2 (1972b)

Offe, C. 'The Abolition of Market Control and the Problem of Legitimacy', *Kapitalistate,* 1 and 2 (1973)

Offe, C. 'Class Rule and the Political System', *German Political Studies,* vol. 1 (1974)

Offe, C. 'The Theory of the Capitalist State and the Problem of Policy Formation', in L.N. Lindberg *et al.* (eds) *Stress and Contradiction in Modern Capitalism* (1975a)

Offe, C. 'Further Comments on Müller and Neusüss', *Telos,* 25 (1975b)

Offe, C. 'Political Authority and Class Structure', in P. Conneton (ed.) *Critical Sociology* (Penguin, Harmondsworth, 1976)

Offe, C. *Industry and Inequality* (Edward Arnold, London, 1977)

Offe, C. and Ronge, V. 'Thesen zur Begrundung des Konzepts des "Kapitalistischen Staates" und zur materialistischen Politikforschung', in C. Pozzoli (ed.) *Rahmbedingungen und Schranken staatlichen Handelns: zehn Thesen* (Suhrkamp Verlag, Frankfurt am Main, 1976)

O'Higgins, R. and Partington M. 'Industrial Conflict: Judicial Attitudes', *Modern Law Review,* 32, 1 (1969)

Otter, C. von 'Sweden: Labour Reformism Reshapes the System' in S. Barkin (ed.) *Worker Militancy and its Consequences, 1965-1975* (Praeger, New York, 1975)

Pahl, R.E. 'Patterns of Urban Life in the Next Fifteen Years' *New Universities Quarterly* (1976)

Pahl, R.E. 'Castells and Collective Consumption: a Critical Note' *Sociology* 12, 2 (1978)

Pahl, R.E. and Winkler, J.T. 'The Coming Corporatism', *New Society* (10 October 1974)

Panić, M. and Close, R. 'The Profitability of British Manufacturing Industry', *Lloyd's Bank Review* (April 1973)

Panitch, L. *Social Democracy and Industrial Military*, (Cambridge University Press, Cambridge, 1976)

Panitch, L. 'The Development of Corporatism in Liberal Democracies', in P.C. Schmitter (ed.) special issue of *Comparative Political Studies* (19

Parkin, F. 'System Contradiction and Political Transformation' *European Journal of Sociology* 13 (1972)

Parkin, M. 'The Politics of Inflation', *Government and Opposition*, 10 (1975)

Payer, C. *The Debt Trap* (Penguin, Harmondsworth, 1974)

Pelling, H. *A History of British Trade Unionism* (Penguin, Harmondsworth, 1971)

Petersson, O. and Särlvik, B. 'Valet 1973', *Allmanna Valen 1973*, Del 3 (Statistiska Centralbyran, Stockholm, 1975)

Phelps Brown, E.H. *The Growth of British Industrial Relations* (Macmillan, London, 1959)

Phelps Brown, E.H. 'New Wine in Old Bottles', *British Journal of Industrial Relations*, vol. 11 (1973)

Pickvance, C.G. (ed.) *Urban Sociology: Critical Essays* (Methuen, London, 1976)

Pickvance, C.G. 'Marxist Approaches to the Study of Urban Politics', *International Journal of Urban and Regional Research*, vol. 1, no. 2 (1977)

Pinto-Duschinsky, M. 'Bread and Circuses', in V. Bogdanor and R. Skidelsky (eds) *The Age of Affluence* (1970)

Poggi, G. 'The Constitutional State of the Nineteenth Century', *Sociology,* vol. 11, no. 2 (1977)

Polanyi, K. *The Great Transformation* (Gollancz, London, 1945)

Pollard, S. *The Development of the British Economy, 1914-67* (Edward Arnold, London, 1969

Pollard, S. (ed.) *The Gold Standard and Employment Policies between the Wars* (Methuen, London, 1970)

Polsby, N.W. *Community Power and Political Theory* (Yale University Press, New Haven, 1963)

Poulantzas, N. *Political Power and Social Classes* (New Left Books, London, 1973)

Poulantzas, N. *Classes in Contemporary Capitalism* (New Left Books, London, 1975)

Poulantzas, N. 'The Capitalist State: a Reply to Miliband and Laclau', in *New Left Review,* 95 (1976a)

Poulantzas, N. (ed.) *La Crise de l'Etat* (PUF, Paris, 1976b)

Prais, S.J. *The Evolution of Giant Firms in Britain* (Cambridge University Press, Cambridge, 1976)

Preteceille, E., Pincon, M. and Rendu, P. *Equipements Collectifs, Structures Urbaines et Consommation Sociale* Centre de Sociologie Urbaine, Paris, 1975)

Preteceille, E. 'Equipements Collectifs et Consommation Sociale', *International Journal of Urban and Regional Research,* vol. 1, no. 1(1977)

Rawls, J. *A Theory of Justice* (Clarendon Press, Oxford, 1971)

Richter, I. *Political Purpose in Trade Unions* (Allen and Unwin, London, 1973)

Roberts, D. *Victorian Origins of the British Welfare State* (Yale University Press, New Haven, 1969)

Robinson, J. in *Challenge,* 20, 5 (1977)

Rosdolsky, R. 'Comments on the Methods of Marx's Capital', *New German Critique,* no. 3 (1974)

Rose, R. and Peters, G. 'The Political Consequences of Economic Overload' (University of Strathclyde, Centre for the Study of Public Policy, 1977)

Ross, G. 'The New Popular Front in France', in R. Miliband and J. Saville, (eds) *The Socialist Register 1977* (Merlin Press, London, 1977)

Royal Commission on Trades Unions and Employers' Associations *Report,* Cmnd 3623 (HMSO, London 1968)

Runciman, W.G. *Relative Deprivation and Social Justice* (Routledge, London, 1966)

Rustow, D.A. *The Politics of Compromise* (Princeton University Press, Princteon, 1955)

Sayer, R.S. *The Bank of England, 1891-1944, Vol. 1* (Cambridge University Press, Cambridge, 1976)

Sayles, L.R. *The Behaviour of Industrial Work Groups* (Wiley, New York, 1958)

Scanlon, H. 'Interview – the Role of Militancy', *New Left Review,* no. 46 (1967)

Scase, R. *Social Democracy in Capitalist Society* (Croom Helm, London, 1977)

Schmitter, P.C. 'Still the Century of Corporatism?', *Review of Politics*, 36, 1 (1974)

Schmitter, P.C. 'Modes of Interest Intermediation and Models of Societal Change in Western Europe', in P.C. Schmitter, (ed.) *Corporatism and Policy-Making in Contemporary Western Europe*, special issue of *Comparative Political Studies*, 10, 1 (1977)

Schumpeter, J.A. *Capitalism, Socialism and Democracy* (Allen and Unwin, London, 1942)

Select Committee on Nationalised Industries *First Report: Bank of England* Session 1969-70, House of Commons 258 (HMSO, London, 1970)

Semmel, B. *Imperialism and Social Reform* (Allen and Unwin, London, 1960)

Shonfield, A. *Modern Capitalism* (Oxford University Press, London, 1965)

Shonfield, A. 'Making the Unions Work to the Public's Rule Book', *The Times* (19 October 1977)

Silver, M. 'Recent British Strike Trends: a Factual Analysis', *British Journal of Industrial Relations*, vol. I (1973)

Skidelsky, R. *Politicians and the Slump* (Macmillan, London, 1967)

Skidelsky, R. (ed.) *The End of the Keynesian Era* (Macmillan, London, 1977)

Smith, T. 'The United Kingdom', in R. Vernon (ed.) *Big Business and the State* (Macmillan, London, 1974)

Smith, T. 'Trends and Tendencies in Re-ordering the Representation of Interests in Britain' (annual conference of Political Studies Association, Nottingham, 1976)

Söderstrom, H.T. and Viotti, S. 'Money Wage Disturbances and Stabilisation Policy in the Small Open Economy', seminar paper no. 70 (Institute for International Economic Studies, Stockholm, 1977)

Spiegelberg, R. *The City* (Blond and Briggs, London, 1973)

Steuer, M. and Gerrard, J. 'Industrial Relations, Labour Disputes and Labour Utilisation in Foreign-owned Firms in the UK', in J.H. Dunning (ed.) *The Multi-National Enterprise* (Allen and Unwin, London, 1971)

Strange, S. *Sterling and British Policy* (Oxford University Press, London, 1971)

Strinati, D. 'Capitalism and the State' (mimeo, 1977)

Sveriges Industriförbund och Svenska Arbetsgivareföreningen *Företagsvinster Kapitalförsörjning Läntagarfonder* (Näringslivets Förlagsdistribution, Stockholm, 1976)

Swedish Government *The Swedish Economy 1971-1975 and the General Outlook up to 1990* (Allmänna Förlaget, Stockholm, 1971)

Swedish Government *Kapitalmarknaden i Svensk Ekonomi* (SOU, Stockholm, 1978)

Taylor, A.J. *Laissez-faire and State Intervention in Nineteenth-century Britain* (Macmillan, London, 1972)

Thompson, E.P. *The Making of the English Working Class* (Penguin, Harmondsworth, 1968)

Thompson, G. 'The Relationship between the Financial and Industrial Sector in the United Kingdom Economy', *Economy and Society*, 6, 3 (1977)

Thomson, A.W.J. and Engleman, S.R. *The Industrial Relations Act* (Martin Robertson, London, 1975)

Tristram, R. 'Ontology and Theory', *Sociological Review*, 23, 4 (1975)

Turner, H.A. *Is Britain Really Strike-prone?* (Cambridge University Press, Cambridge, 1969)

Turvey, R. (ed.) *Wages Policy under Full Employment* (William Hodge, London, 1952)

Uutma, T. and Lydahl, R. 'Company Reports for 1976 — Comparison with Earlier Years', *Scandinaviska Enskilda Banken Quarterly Review*, 3-4 (1977)

Wagner, R.E. 'Economic Manipulation for Political Profit', *Kyklos*, 30 (1977)

Warner, S.B. *The Urban Wilderness* (Harper and Row, New York, 1972)

Warren, B. 'The Internationalisation of Capital and the Nation State: a Comment', *New Left Review*, no. 68 (1971)

Warren, B. 'Capitalist Planning and the State', *New Left Review*, no. 72 (1973)

Watson, M. 'A Comparative Evaluation of Planning Practice in the Liberal Democratic State', in J. Hayward and M. Watson (eds) *Planning, Politics and Public Policy* (1975)

Webb, B. *Our Partnership* (Longmans, London, 1948)

Webb, S. and B. *The History of Trade Unionism* (Longmans, London, 1920)

Weber, M. *Economy and Society* (Bedminster Press, New York, 1968)

Wedderburn, K.W. *The Worker and the Law*, 2nd edn (Penguin, Harmondsworth, 1971)

Wedderburn, K.W. 'Labour Law and Labour Relations in Britian', *British Journal of Industrial Relations*, vol. 10 (1972)

Wigham, E.L. *The Power to Manage: a History of the Engineering Employers' Federation* (Macmillan, London, 1973)

Winkler, H.A. (ed.) *Organisierter Kapitalismus* (Vandenhoeck und Ruprecht, Göttingen, 1974)

Winkler, J.T. 'Corporatism', *European Journal of Sociology*, 17, 1 (1976a)

Winkler, J.T. 'Law, State and Economy: the Industry Act 1975 in Context', *British Journal of Law and Society*, 2, 2 (1976b)

Winkler, J.T. 'The Corporate Economy: Theory and Administration', in R. Scase (ed.) *Industrial Society: Class, Cleavage and Control* (Allen and Unwin, London, 1977)

Winkler, J.T. 'The Coming Corporatism', in R. Skidelsky (ed.) *The End of the Keynesian Era* (1977)

Woytinsky, W.S. *Stormy Passage* (Vanguard, New York, 1961)

Yaffe, D. 'The Crisis of Profitability', *New Left Review,* no. 80 (1973a)

Yaffe, D. 'The Marxian Theory of Crisis, Capital and the State', *Economy and Society,* vol. 2 (1973b)

Young K. and Kramer, J. *Strategy and Conflict in Metropolitan Housing* (Heinemann, London, 1978)

SUBJECT INDEX

accumulation, *see under* capital
Advisory, Conciliation and Arbitration
  Service 204, 226, 229, 230
Agrarian Party (Sweden) 98, 106, 107
Argentina 19
Aristocracy 64
Authoritarianism 23, 24, 54n, 58, 59

Baader-Meinhoff group 36
Bank of England 64, 161, 164-75
  passim, 185-9
banks, *see* capital, finance
bargaining, collective: wage 108, 210,
  212, 216, 217, 223, 226-8
Belgium 86n
Birmingham 162
bourgeoisie 64, 137
Bretton Woods 63, 74, 75, 161, 189
Brigate Rosse 36
Britain: United Kingdom 17, 18, 23,
  27, 28, 71-4, 83, 96-9, 103, 121n,
  134, 140, 144-53 *passim*, 154n,
  159, 160, 174-6, 180, 184, 187,
  189, 208-14, 221, 222
business 37, 38, 59, 76, 107

Cambridge 63
Canada 86n, 135
Capital: capitalism 13-54, 55, 58,
  61-4, 69, 77-80, 86n, 88, 92, 108,
  110, 128-30, 133, 134, 137,
  138, 146-8, 156n, 157-62, 165-9,
  188, 191-236 *passim*; accumulation
  of 146, 159, 191, 199-203, 208-11,
  214, 218; finance: banks: money
  160, 164, 165, 168-72, 175, 187,
  213-5; fractions of 25, 27; monopoly 78, 141, 142, 202, 203,
  211-13, 216-18; organised 21, 43;
  state monopoly 123, 124, 137,
  138, 141
capital-logic 26, 34, 157, 184
Catholicism, Roman 17, 22, 51
Centre Party (Sweden) 111
change, social 31, 32
Chile 135, 154n
class 19, 22, 54n, 77, 133, 136, 137;
  interests 33, 35-7, 40-4, 134, 148,
  159, 194, 195, 224; struggle
  conflict 77-9, 123, 137, 157, 158,
  180, 192, 196, 208-21, 224, 226,

230; working 18, 22, 29-35, 42,
  59, 61, 69, 70, 98, 137, 163, 180,
  188, 204, 207, 230
Combination Acts 1799, 1800 207
Commissariat du Plan 178, 179
Commission for Industrial Relations
  204, 226-30
Communism: Communist Parties 21,
  32; France 36, 123, 124, 137,
  139, 141, 144; Germany 34;
  Sweden 101
community 50, 51
Community Development Project
  156n
Confederation of British Industry
  187, 189, 223, 228, 232-5n
Conservatism 22
Conservative Party 83, 175, 180, 181,
  228, 229, 235n
consumption, collective 131, 132,
  135, 138, 139
corporatism: corporate state 16-24,
  45-8, 51, 83, 180, 188, 190, 200-8,
  214-30 *passim*, 235n
Cunliffe Committee 63, 164
Czechoslovakia 110

democracy (liberal) 13-54 *passim*,
  59-64, 77, 78, 81, 85, 203;
  industrial 111
Denmark 82
Department of Economic Affairs 181,
  182
Department of the Environment 152
Depression, the great 59-61, 88, 92,
  97, 99

economy 15, 192-5, 200, 232n
elites 41, 43, 62, 63, 218, 222-5
Empire, British 74, 177
employment 112; full 55-7, 62, 89-
  101 *passim*, 104-9, 120, 121n
Employment Protection Act 230
Engineering Employers Federation
  223, 234n
expenditure, public 14, 30, 33, 66,
  150, 151

fascism 18, 22, 172
Federation of British Industry 167,
  178, 179, 187

257

NAME INDEX